GW00857369

Corrupting the Image challenges t
traditional opinion, as it delves deep
with the fundamental purpose of pro
we *may* know of Satanic influence pa
thrilling read for the detective-at-hear .

— WILLIAM C. HARVEY, M.S.
Author, Barrons Educational Series, Inc.

Absolutely astonishing! *Corrupting the Image* provides a biblical, scientific, and enlightening way of looking at the "big picture" of the end times that is so logical it will blow your mind.

— DR. SCOTT A. COLLIE D.C.
CSN, BodyPro Wellness

One of the most important books of our time! It will help you understand Satan's goal to alter the DNA of mankind so that a false government leader plus a false religious leader can be produced to join Satan as an unholy trinity. The Bible is the Word of God, and Doug's book is based on the Bible. We need to understand these major truths that are already beginning to impact life on earth.

— DON SECRIST
Founder, www.bibleeasylearn.org

Douglas Hamp's latest lesson, applying his well-honed skills with biblical Hebrew and Greek as well as Aramaic, addresses mysteries and controversies that span the times from antediluvian Genesis, to post-flood, the present day, and on toward eschatological expectations of end times. This entire study elucidates a thread of continuity that bears consideration as it chronicles Satan's continuing and unrelenting attack on God's image, which includes us, as we have been created in His image, and ultimately portends to the ancestry and *modus operandi* of the Antichrist, which some will someday be able to witness and verify.

— DR. STAN SHOLAR
Retired Aerospace Scientist

A thought-provoking must-read, this book examines of one of the most fascinating, yet often-neglected undercurrents of Scripture. As with his past work, Doug Hamp's command of the original languages gives teeth to this timely look at challenging questions of history, prophecy, and modern efforts in genetic manipulation. *Corrupting the Image* compels the reader to probe deeper into the Bible to discover the enemy's past and future attempts to pervert the creation of mankind as the very image of God.

- PAUL BERRY
Pastor, Mountainside Christian Fellowship

This is a page-turner! A fresh look at who the sons of God truly are in Genesis 6:4 and the return of the Nephilim.

- TIM HUNTER
Student

Riveting! This book brings together, perhaps for the first time ever, a comprehensive explanation of how the Antichrist will be a genetic counterfeit of the virgin birth. This book is at the cutting edge of research and is written so that the average person can grasp the sinister plan that is unfolding before our very eyes.

- DR. KENTON BESHORE
President of World Bible Society

Startling! This book takes what the Bible says and magnifies it so you can see clearly how genetics is vital to opening the door for the return of the Nephilim. No matter where you stand on biblical eschatology this book will affect you. Read it.

- DR. J. DAVID LEHMAN
Senior Bible Researcher and Lecturer World Bible Society

Corrupting the IMAGE

Angels, Aliens, and the Antichrist Revealed

Douglas Hamp

www.douglashamp.com
DEFENDER PUBLISHING LLC

Corrupting the Image
Angels, Aliens, and the Antichrist Revealed

Cover by Neil Godding

Unless otherwise indicated, all Scripture quotations are taken from the New King James Version, Thomas Nelson Publishers (1997). The Hebrew text is from the Biblia Hebraica Stugartensia. The Greek Old Testament Scriptures are from the Septuagint. New Testament Greek quotations are from the Greek New Testament according to the Byzantine Textform, edited by Maurice A. Robinson and William G. Pierpont, 2000 edition; this is the edition by Pierpont and Robinson of a Majority, or Byzantine, text of the NT. Quotations marked KJV are from the King James Version. Quotations marked ESV are from the English Standard Version. Quotations marked ISV are International Standard Version. Quotations marked JPS are from the Jewish Publication Society. Quotations marked NET are from the New English Translation. Quotations marked NASB are from the New American Standard Bible. Quotations marked RYLT are from the Revised Young's Literal Translation. Quotations marked ASV are from the American Standard Version. Quotations marked ERV are from the English Revised Version. Quotations marked WBT are from the Webster's Bible Translation. Quotations marked WEB are from the World English Bible. Quotations marked YLT are from the Young's Literal Translation. All Scripture quotations have been retrieved using theWord Bible Software www.theword.net. All emphases of Scripture verses are mine.

First printing, 2011

ISBN: 978-1-4921493-0-9

Printed in the United States of America.

To my little daughter Abigail,
who often woke up in the wee hours of the night and sat
with me and held my hand as I was writing this book.

Table of Contents

Table of Figures

Foreword

MOST PROPHECY EXPERTS today believe a man of superior intelligence, wit, charm, and diplomacy will soon emerge on the world scene as a savior. He will seemingly possess a transcendent wisdom that enables him to solve problems and offer solutions for many of today's most perplexing issues. His popularity will be widespread, and his fans will include young and old, religious and non-religious, male and female. Talk show hosts will interview his colleagues, news anchors will cover his movements, scholars will applaud his uncanny ability to resolve what has escaped the rest of us, and the poor will bow down at his table. He will, in all human respects, appeal to the best idea of society. But his profound comprehension and irresistible presence will be the result of an invisible network of thousands of years of collective knowledge. He will, quite literally, represent the incarnation of a very old, super-intelligent and super-deceptive spirit known as Satan. As Jesus Christ was the "Seed of the Woman" (Genesis 3:15), he will be the "seed of the Serpent." Moreover, though his arrival in the form of a man was foretold by numerous Scriptures, the broad masses will not immediately recognize him for what he actually is—paganism's ultimate incarnation; the "beast" of Revelation 13:1.

If you asked the average person today to explain how this could be possible—that evil will be so incarnated as a man—most would return blank expressions, having no capacity to fathom nor to believe it possible. Yet as far back as the beginning of time and within every major culture of the ancient world, the astonishingly consistent story is told of "gods" that once before descended from heaven and materialized in bodies of flesh. From Rome to Greece—and before that, to Egypt, Persia, Assyria, Babylonia, and Sumer—the earliest records of civilization tell of the era when powerful beings known to the Hebrews as *Watchers* and in the book of Genesis as the *benei ha-elohim* (sons of God) mingled themselves with humans, giving birth to part-celestial, part-terrestrial hybrids known as *Nephilim*. The Bible says this happened when men began to increase on earth and daughters were born to them. When the sons of God saw the women's beauty, they took wives from among them to sire their unusual offspring.

This story in the Old Testament book of Genesis is not fanciful myth. It is widely supported in other ancient texts, including the books of Enoch, Jubilees, Baruch, Genesis Apocryphon, Philo, Josephus, and many others, where it unfolds as fact that the giants of the Old Testament, such as Goliath, were the part-human, part-animal, part-angelic offspring of a supernatural interruption into the divine order and natural evolution of the species—a corruption of the images God had made. The Bible and the apocryphal books even give a name to the angels involved in this cosmic conspiracy, calling them "Watchers." We read:

> And I Enoch was blessing the Lord of majesty and the King of the ages, and lo! the Watchers called me—Enoch the scribe—and said to me: "Enoch, thou scribe of righteousness, go, declare to the Watchers of the heaven who have left the high heaven, the holy eternal place, and have defiled themselves with women, and have done as the children of earth do, and have taken unto themselves wives: Ye have wrought great destruction on the earth: And ye shall have no peace nor forgiveness of sin: and inasmuch as they delight themselves in their children [the Nephilim], The murder of their beloved ones shall they see, and over the destruction of their children shall they lament, and shall make supplication unto eternity, but mercy and peace shall ye not attain" (1 Enoch 10:3–8).

According to 1 Enoch, which is quoted by Peter and Jude in the New Testament, two hundred of these powerful angels departed "high heaven" and used women (among other things) to extend their progeny into mankind's plane of existence. The Interlinear

Hebrew Bible (IHN) offers an interesting interpretation of Genesis 6:2 in this regard. Where the King James Bible says, "The sons of God saw the daughters of men that they [were] fair," the IHN interprets this as, "The benei Elohim saw the daughters of Adam, that they were *fit extensions*" (emphasis added). The term "fit extensions" seems applicable when the whole of the ancient record is understood to mean that the Watchers wanted to leave their proper sphere of existence in order to enter earth's three-dimensional reality. They viewed women—or at least their genetic material—as part of the formula for accomplishing this task. Departing the proper habitation that God had assigned them was grievous to the Lord and led to divine penalization. Jude described it this way: The "angels which kept not their first estate, but left their own habitation, he hath reserved in everlasting chains under darkness unto the judgment of the great day" (Jude 6 KJV).

Besides apocryphal, pseudepigraphic, and Jewish traditions related to the legend of the Watchers and the "mighty men" born of their union with humans, mythologized accounts tell the stories of "gods" using humans to produce heroes or demigods (half-gods). When the ancient Greek version of the Hebrew Old Testament (the LXX or Septuagint) was made, the word "Nephilim"—referring to the part-human offspring of the Watchers—was translated *gegenes*, a word implying "earth born." This same terminology was used to describe the Greek Titans and other legendary heroes of partly celestial and partly terrestrial origin, such as Hercules (born of Zeus and the mortal Alcmena), Achilles (the Trojan hero son of Thetis and Peleus), and Gilgamesh (the two-thirds god and one-third human child of Lugalbanda and Ninsun). These demigods were likewise accompanied in texts and idol representation by half-animal and half-human creatures like centaurs (the part-human, part-horse offspring of Apollo's son, Centaurus), chimeras, furies, satyrs, gorgons, nymphs, Minotaurs, and other genetic aberrations, all of which indicates that the Watchers not only modified human

DNA during the construction of Nephilim, but animals as well, a point the Book of Enoch supports, saying in the seventh chapter that the fallen angels "sinned" against animals as well as humans. Other books such as *Jubilees* add that this interspecies mingling eventually resulted in mutations among normal humans and animals whose "flesh" (genetic makeup) was "corrupted" by the activity, presumably through crossbreeding (see 5:1–5; 7:21–25). Even the Old Testament book of 2 Samuel contains reference to the genetic mutations that developed among humans following this time frame, including "men" of unusual size, physical strength, six fingers, six toes, animal appetite for blood, and even lion-like features (21:20; 23:20).

In *Corrupting the Image: Angels, Aliens, and the Antichrist Revealed*, Douglas Hamp employs finely tested skills, magnificently interpreting the Hebrew Bible, Greek, and Semitic languages to vividly warn how this offspring of fallen angels and humans may not remain a thing of the past; that in fact a repeat of the activity was prophesied for the end of times, activity providing for modern versions of genetic aberrations and finally the personage of Antichrist.

Readers will be amazed how, along this analysis, Douglas asks all the right questions about emerging fields of human-transforming sciences—genetic engineering, synthetic biology, transhumanism, and even alien abduction phenomenon—to ultimately draw conclusions that fit the whole of the redemption story—from Satan's first attempt to corrupt the image of God to his last attempt and finally the judgment of Satan and the redemption of man.

- THOMAS HORN
Author, Forbidden Gates *and Founder of* Raidersnewsnetwork.com

Preface

GENESIS 3:15 TELLS US of two seeds that will come upon the world—one will be the Seed of the Woman, which is Jesus. However, the other seed spoken of is Satan's and that is where my research took off. I wanted to discover if the seed of Satan (Antichrist) would be an imitation of the virgin birth and if so, how that was possible genetically. What I uncovered was a war to destroy the image of God led by Satan since the earliest of times.

MY METHOD

Due to my language studies in Hebrew, Greek, and Aramaic at the Hebrew University of Jerusalem, Israel, I have been able to do my own linguistic research throughout this book. I primarily conducted my own investigation of words and phrases using theWord Bible Software and therefore, I may not always cite a lexicon for authority. TheWord allowed me to search words in Hebrew, Greek, and Aramaic and trace their usage throughout the entire Bible. I used primary sources wherever possible and drew my own conclusions from those. However, I did frequently turn to secondary literature to demonstrate that there are others that have come to similar conclusions—therefore when I state that a Hebrew, Greek, or Aramaic word means such and such, the conclusion is based on my investigation. If I cite another, then I state the source. I use extra-biblical material (e.g. the Book of Enoch and the Targumim) as I would a modern commentary—it is not sacred canon. However, unlike a modern commentary, those ancient works were often written by Jews who very likely had some insight that we do not. The method of discovery throughout this book will be to take the words as literally as possible and use the grammatical-historical approach of interpretation and we will find that doing so will make all of the pieces fit precisely.

ONE PIECE OF THE END-TIMES PUZZLE

The topic of the image and how it is corrupted is central to the end times but is only one piece of the end-times puzzle. The study of the end times is complex as there are numerous pieces of the puzzle that need to be accounted for. Consequently, I am not specifically looking at the prophecies concerning the nation of Israel nor the wars and rumors of wars, nor the environment, etc. in this book. Those issues are clearly part of the puzzle but will not be covered here. Rather, I believe that this topic of the image serves as a larger backdrop to those issues. I believe that I have properly identified the root cause of many of the events that are coming upon the world through the study of the image. Because the image is under attack and Satan wants to destroy humanity (those who hold God's image), certain things have happened in history and more is on the way.

PREMILLENNIAL

I hold to the premillennial position (the Lord will return bodily to set up His thousand-year reign on earth) and I believe it has ample proof and thus I will not attempt to prove it here, but will simply use it as my starting point. Given the many texts that I use to support my thesis, I believe the reader will see that a literal reading of the Bible warrants the premillennial approach.

READING PLAN

There are parts of this book that go into a lot of detail at times to prove beyond a doubt what has happened and what is coming. I have labored to write the book in a non-technical way and have put the non-essentials in the notes at the end of the book. Each chapter is the foundation for the next. Part one of the book discusses the Genesis 3:15 prophecy as it pertains to the Messiah and our future restoration. Parts two and three show the evidence of Satan's plan to raise up his own seed. For those only interested in the end times (without the explanation of why things are the way they are) read the narrative and then proceed to part two. However, to get the full picture of the makeup of the Antichrist please begin in part one. The image of God serves as a foundation for the rest of the book and in fact I believe a proper understanding of the image of God serves us well as we study the Bible in general. I hope that by understanding who God is and what He is like, you will have a greater appreciation of just how much God loves us and what exciting things He has in store for us! Please skip over the Hebrew and Greek language insertions if those are a distraction to you. They are included because I felt that it was important to thoroughly prove the points that I am making.

FUTURE BOOK

My intention is to write another book as a follow-up to this book describing in detail the events of the Messianic age (Millennium). We will examine biblically the conditions on the earth and the New Jerusalem and also how those that survive the tribulation will receive their new bodies.

TO CONTACT ME

Please visit my website to leave comments on the book or to reach me with a question or to request me to come and speak at your group. *www.douglashamp.com.*

Acknowledgments

Special thanks to my wife Anna, Dr. Stan Sholar, Robert Rico, Don Secrist, Dr. Bill Gallagher, Corina Morrison, Randall Stucky, Romy Godding, and John Shaffer for their help in reviewing, offering suggestions, and for editing this book.

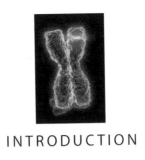

INTRODUCTION

The Genesis Prophecy and the Two Seeds

SOMETHING OMINOUS is coming upon the world: it is Satan's final effort in the battle to destroy the image that man was created in, which has been raging since the beginning of time. If Satan can destroy the image, then he can avert his own destruction.

God created man in His own image and likeness; when man sinned that image was marred, but not lost. However, as a result man cannot be with God in person since man's genetic code (and spiritual composition) has been compromised (or corrupted). God sent His Son to give His life to correct the genetic (and moral) problem through the cross; the correction will be ultimately fulfilled when we receive our new bodies. However, there has also been a move on the enemy's part to completely destroy what is left of the image.

The principle verse of this book is found in the declaration of Genesis 3:15: her seed brought forth the Savior; Satan's seed will bring the destroyer. In other words, the Serpent will one day mix his seed as a counterfeit of the incarnation (subsequent chapters will demonstrate this). Our aim therefore is to fully investigate the prophecy from the pages of the Bible, from a genetics perspective, from a historical perspective, and finally its end-times' impact.

WHEN THE IMAGE WAS CORRUPTED

The story begins in the garden of Eden and ends with the Lord's second coming. Immediately after the sin of Adam and Eve, God declared that there would be hatred between the Serpent and the woman.

> And I will put enmity between you and the woman, and between your seed [זַרְעֲךָ] and her seed [זַרְעָהּ]; He shall bruise [יְשׁוּפְךָ] your head, and you shall bruise [תְּשׁוּפֶנּוּ] His heel (Genesis 3:15).

This statement is often called the proto-Gospel in that it is the first declaration by God that He will make a way for man to be saved and for the devil to be destroyed. It not only speaks of good news for humans and bad news for Satan, but also tells us something about how that redemption will be played out and how Satan has and will try to subvert God's plans. God specifically declared that there would be hatred between Satan's seed and the Seed of the Woman and that "He," the offspring of her seed (Jesus), would strike the Serpent [on] the head and that Satan would strike His heel. "Her seed" became a reality through the Lord Jesus, and therefore, consistent Bible interpretation means that "your seed" (that is Satan's seed) will be fulfilled in like manner.

Ever since the fall in the garden and in a manner similar to the virgin birth of Jesus, Satan has been trying to find a way for "his seed" to become a reality. He almost succeeded in the days of Noah when the sons of God (fallen angels) came down and took women as wives and engendered a race called the Nephilim, which were genetic hybrids (Genesis 6). The Nephilim were on the earth again and had overrun the land of Canaan while the

THE GENESIS PROPHECY AND THE TWO SEEDS

children of Israel were in Egypt. Daniel spoke of a time when ten kings would mingle (hybridize) themselves with the seed of men (Daniel 2:43). Lastly Jesus said that the last days would be like the conditions before the flood (Matthew 24:37). According to the Genesis prophecy, Satan will one day mix his seed with humanity to bring forth the Antichrist as a counterfeit of the incarnation of Jesus.

THE PROMISED SEEDS

We can be confident that the "Seed of the Woman" is referring to the Messiah by the personal pronoun "he" (Hebrew: אוה). This is not just talking collectively about mankind versus Satan (the Serpent cf. Revelation 20:2) but rather is referring to what the Messiah would do to the work of Satan. This interpretation is testified to by many ancient Jewish and Christian commentators and modern scholars as well. Bible commentator Thomas Constable articulates well the importance of this most ancient of prophecies:

> This is a prophecy of the victory of the ultimate "Seed" of the woman (Messiah) over Satan (cf. Rev. 19:1-5; Gal. 3:16, 19; Heb. 2:14; 1 John 3:8). Most interpreters have recognized this verse as the first biblical promise of the provision of salvation (the *protoevangelium* or "first gospel"). The rest of the book, in fact the whole Old Testament, proceeds to point ahead to that seed [...] When that 'seed' is crushed, the head of the snake is crushed. Consequently more is at stake in this brief passage than the reader is at first aware of. **A program is set forth. A plot is established that will take the author far beyond this or that snake and his 'seed.' It is what the snake and His 'seed' represent that lies at the center of the author's focus.** With that 'one' lies the 'enmity' that must be crushed (Constable, Genesis 3:15, emphasis mine).[1]

The Targum of Pseudo Jonathan, what we might think of as an ancient Jewish commentary[2], says that this will take place in the days of Messiah: "and they shall make a remedy for the heel in

19

the days of the King Meshiha." The Targum of Onkelos, another ancient commentary of sorts, understood that both the Serpent (Satan) and the woman would each have a son of promise:

> And I will put enmity between thee and between the woman, and between **thy son** and **her son**. He will remember thee, what thou didst to him (at) from the beginning, and thou shalt be observant unto him at the end (Targum Onkelos, Genesis 3:15, emphasis mine).

From these two ancient sources we can understand that the remedy for the striking of the heel will center on the Messiah and also that her seed is referring to a son who is connected with Eve.[3] However, "thy son" is a reference to Satan's son who, according to hermeneutical consistency, must also be a genetic descendant.

Early Church Father Iranaeus, in his book *Against Heresies*, identified Jesus as the Seed of the Woman and Antichrist as the seed of the Serpent who would be trampled down by the Messiah:

> He, the sole of whose foot should be bitten, having power also to tread upon the enemy's head; but the other biting, killing, and impeding the steps of man, until the seed did come appointed to tread down his head,—which was born of Mary, of whom the prophet speaks: **"Thou shalt tread upon the asp and the basilisk; thou shalt trample down the lion and the dragon;"** (Psa 91:13)—indicating that sin, which was set up and spread out against man, and which rendered him subject to death, should be deprived of its power, along with death, which rules [over men]; **and that the lion, that is, antichrist, rampant against mankind in the latter days, should be trampled down by Him;** and that **He should bind "the dragon, that old Serpent"** (Rev 20:2) and subject him to the power of man, who had been conquered (Luke 10:19) so that all his might should be trodden down.[4] emphasis mine.

Note that Iranaeus identified the dragon of Psalm 91:13 (Hebrew *tannin*) as Satan in accord with Revelation 20:2 ("the dragon, that Serpent of old, who is the Devil and Satan"). However, he also identified the Antichrist who would come in the last days. Thus he sees in Genesis 3:15 both a reference to Satan's ultimate demise and to the ones who come in Satan's power. He later wrote concerning the incarnation of the Lord: "And the Lord summed up in Himself this enmity, when He was made man from a woman, and trod upon his [the Serpent's] head."[5]

The renowned commentators Keil and Delitzsch note that through Jesus' incarnation, which will be through the Seed of the Woman, Adam can be restored to his original state.

> This spiritual seed culminated in Christ, in whom the Adamic family terminated, henceforward to be renewed by Christ as the second Adam, and **restored by Him to its original exaltation and likeness to God**. In this sense Christ **is the Seed of the Woman**, [...] (*Keil and Delitzsch*, Genesis 3:15 emphasis mine).

Bible commentator Adam Clarke demonstrates his conviction that the Serpent was in fact actuated by Satan and that the Seed of the Woman was the Lord Jesus.

> **It is evident that Satan,** who actuated this creature, **is alone intended in this part of the prophetic declaration.** [...] the Seed of the Woman; the person is to come by the woman, and by her alone, without the concurrence of man. [...] **and it was in consequence of this purpose of God that Jesus Christ was born of a virgin;** this, and this alone, **is what is implied in the promise of the Seed of the Woman bruising the head of the Serpent** (Clarke, Genesis 3:15 emphasis mine).

THE BOTTOM LINE

We have seen that both Jewish and Christian interpreters are convinced that the reference to "her seed" found its culmination in the Messiah. We can write out the elements of Genesis 3:15 in the following way:

1. Enmity between Satan (Serpent) and Eve

2. Enmity between Satan's (your) seed and her seed (Christ)

3. Christ (He) will bruise Satan's head

4. Satan (you) would bruise Christ's (his) heel

We glean the following from the points above:

1. Enmity = antithetical, opposite, converse, contradictory

2. If "her seed" equals Christ, then "your seed" must be its antithesis, thus: antichrist

3. "Her seed" (Christ) is superior to "your seed" (Antichrist)

4. "Your seed" (Antichrist) is inferior to "her seed" (Christ)

Point number 2 is the most significant of the four; her seed did in fact result in the incarnation of the Lord Jesus. Before we can adequately understand what is meant by "your seed" we must first see that Scripture clearly states that Jesus' incarnation would be a union of the Seed of the Woman (Mary's seed) and that of the Holy Spirit.

UNRAVELING THE DECEPTION

In order to unravel the deception that is now unfolding in the world, we must go back to the beginning; we must first grasp what Adam was like when he was created, what he lost both spiritually and genetically, and how corruption through disobedience has caused us to be separated from God. From there we will be able to plumb the depths of the promise that the Seed of the Woman would bring redemption for man; and with that in mind, we will see how God will restore His perfect image in the believer via the new birth through the Seed of the Woman.

Once we have understood the implications of the Seed of the Woman then we will focus on how Satan has been attempting to destroy the image of God throughout history (as described in the Bible and confirmed by extra-biblical evidence) and how he plans on imitating and counterfeiting God's redemptive work in the ultimate hybrid of all time whom the Bible calls "the Beast" (Antichrist).

Satan's plan is already well underway and will be accomplished in part via transhumanism and the "alien" deception. These have both been made possible through the teaching of the theory of evolution which, at its core, denies there is a God. Satan has used this denial to pave the way philosophically for the acceptance of going to the next level of humanity and because man denies God, he believes he ought to continue evolving. The transhumanist movement boasts that man can direct his own destiny through the rewriting of his DNA code. Transhumanists seek to make man into gods by directing his own evolution. Rather than accepting that God originally created man in His image and man is now fallen, but (through Jesus) will be restored to that original and unfallen image, the transhumanist insists that man can do it himself. In fact, Transhumanist Richard Seed audaciously declared: "We are going to become Gods, period [...]"[6] Man is ready to forsake the image of the Creator who created him.

Satan will use man's desire to be his own god to deceive him into believing the ultimate lie—that his fallen messengers are both the Creators and saviors of man. He will not do this openly but will deceive mankind through demons which are masquerading as "aliens" who are spreading the message that the inhabitants of the earth can evolve to be like them and obtain transcendent powers. Finally, the seed of the Serpent will come; he will be a man who will be greater than his fellows, who will understand sinister schemes and shall rise up and become the Antichrist.

A NARRATIVE OF ADAM'S CREATION AND FALL

Author's Note: The following is the essence of part one in a narrative format. All of the theological points are proven in the rest of the book in great detail. If the details are not for you and you are are more concerned with what the enemy has been up to in the past then proceed directly to part two. A final narrative is found in the epilogue which continues where this one leaves off.

"Adam, where are you?" Adam could hear the voice of the One who not long ago created him and his wife Eve. Adam found himself out of breath and a strange sense of terror flooded his body at hearing that voice—the voice that once had only brought him tremendous delight.

Adam could remember well that first moment when he opened his eyes and beheld the very One who had taken the dust of the ground and with His own hands had formed him and then breathed His Spirit into him. The beauty of God's face was indescribable. The glorious light radiated off of His face onto the visage of the newly formed man. His eyes seemed to go on forever and spoke of the depth of love that God had for him. Even though Adam had just taken the first few breaths of his life, he understood the tender care that his Father had for him. Adam could see that God's eyes gleamed for him, his son.

That sixth day of creation—the day when God created Adam in His own image and His likeness; the day when Adam first gazed at his Creator—oh how sweet and wonderful it was! God had provided everything for him: trees, shade, delicious food, and a beautiful garden. God brought the animals to Adam, which He had created hours before making Adam, who then named them. However, there was none like him and then his Father did something most wonderful. He caused him to fall into a deep, deep sleep, removed one of his ribs, and then with the marrow of the bone took the building blocks, the base of who Adam was to the core, and formed one like Adam, but different—a complement to who Adam was. She was perfectly suited for Adam and Adam loved her.

His heart was racing and his hands were shaking as he tried to sew the vine through the leaves to make coverings for Eve and himself. With just a few more knots his new covering would be ready. The fig leaves were nothing like what they had had but they would at least provide something to cover them. The moment that they had eaten the fruit the light which had until then emitted out of their bodies was suddenly gone. The Serpent said they wouldn't die but that eating from the tree would simply make them like God. The words made sense at first. After all, God created everything and said that it was good. That tree was part of the creation which God had made. It was even in the middle of the garden. The knowledge of good and evil was clearly something that God desired man to have, yet if they ate from the tree God said they would surely die. The fruit had appeared so luscious and by eating it they would gain the knowledge of good and evil and be like God.

Adam hurriedly placed the makeshift coverings of fig leaves on himself and Eve. What had happened? Where was the light that once clothed them? What would God say once He saw them? How would he explain? Their eyes certainly were opened and now he realized that they had been deceived. The Serpent had promised them that they would become like God, but they already were! They had been clothed in light like God. They had been filled with the Spirit of God. Now those things were lost. Could they be regained? Adam now understood the point of the tree was simply a choice; to choose either to follow God, which was good, or to disobey and choose the evil. Either of those two options would make them like God more fully. He could have just resisted the tempting of the Serpent and become like God as well and have retained what God had given him: the light and His Spirit. Choosing to obey God would have opened his eyes as well and made him like God without the guilt because he would have made a choice, but for the good. Adam now understood what it was to choose the good and follow God's commandment—that was what had been required of him—but now it was too late—oh it was too late! He had made the wrong choice! He considered that he had indeed gained the knowledge of good and evil. Oh had he chosen to obey and been proven and remained alive forever. But now—death! He wiped the moisture away from his forehead. Already he could feel his body in ways that he had never felt before. Was this death?

God was walking his way as He did every day. Adam could see Him getting closer and would soon no longer be able to hide. In a frightened tone Adam called out in response to God's question: "I heard the sound of You in the garden, and I was afraid, because I was naked, and I hid myself." God's gentle voice became inquisitive as if He were probing. "Who told you that you were naked? Have you eaten of the tree of which I commanded you not to eat?" Adam thought quickly of what to say. What could he say to the One who loved him? How could Adam explain this betrayal, this unfaithfulness?

His eyes quickly glanced at the woman as she too stood motionless and pale. "The woman whom You gave to be with me," he said sensing that he was betraying her as well, "she gave me the fruit of the tree, and I ate." It worked, or so it seemed, for the Lord God, now standing in front of them, turned His face to the woman and asked with what sounded like a broken heart, "What is this that you have done?" Adam looked at his frightened wife, whom he had exposed, as she pointed her finger at the Serpent who was still in the garden and said, "The Serpent deceived me, and I ate."

Adam then noted a definitive change in God's countenance. In fact, he had never seen this side of God. Until today Adam had only known God to be loving and tender. But now with a voice of judgment, He declared to the Serpent, "Because you have done this, cursed are you above all livestock and above all beasts of the field; on your belly you shall go, and dust you shall eat all the days of your life. I will put enmity between you and the woman, and between your seed and her seed; he shall bruise your head, and you shall bruise his heel." God's words were good and brought a measure of comfort. There might be hope for Adam and his wife after all. Adam mused on the words even though he didn't fully understand all that they entailed.

Shortly after this time of judgment, God did something much unexpected. He took one of the animals, which Adam had named, and killed it! Oh, how immediate death was and dreadful. Why did that animal, which had done nothing wrong, need to die? After all, Adam thought, he was the one that had disobeyed God, not the animal. God then removed the skin from it, cleaned it of the blood, and then placed it on him and his wife Eve. The skin of the animal would be worn instead of the raiment of light which they lost. How pathetic it was in comparison to what they had! Adam longed for the day when the Promised One, the Seed of the Woman, would come and destroy the Serpent that had beguiled them and restore what they had lost, God's Spirit, and the glorious light that flowed from them. Adam sighed and thought of the day when this state called death, which now ensnared them, would be removed. How would the Promised One remove the corruption that touched every fiber of their being? How would He be from the woman's seed and yet have the power to restore them? To be free of that was his heart's desire. Oh for the day when the Promised One would come!

Upon hearing the sentence Satan began to plot his scheme to overcome the prophecy. Satan too would provide a savior for mankind but in his own image and not God's; perhaps if he could destroy the image of God, his own destruction would be averted.

PART ONE

THE IMAGE CORRUPTED
AND THE IMAGE RESTORED

CHAPTER ONE

The Master Image

IN ORDER TO SPOT THE DECEPTION we first need to understand the original. God is infinite and of course there are things that we will never understand about Him. However, all that the Bible does reveal we ought to firmly apply to our general concept of who He is and how He is. Something that is fundamental to understanding God is His image. God tells us that He made man in His image and in His likeness in Genesis 1:26 – but just what does that mean?

> Then God said, "Let Us make man in Our image, according to Our likeness; let them have dominion over the fish of the sea, over the birds of the air, and over the cattle, over all the earth and over every creeping thing that creeps on the earth" (Genesis 1:26).

How are we to understand image and likeness? Does image denote something physical in the way God "looks" or is it merely His divine character? Is the likeness simply talking about His attributes? Is it possible that it could be referring to what God looks like? Generally speaking commentators assume the word image refers only to God's attributes. Any time we have language in Scripture talking about God's hands, head, feet, or the like it is explained as anthropomorphic language (terms describing

God in ways that we mortals can understand). Nevertheless, the Scriptures demonstrate that where there is some prophetic vision or description of God we are catching a glimpse of His image (what God looks like).[7] Having a good grasp of the image of God will aid us in figuring out what is in the believer's future and also how the enemy has tried to destroy the image in us in the past and will deceive the world in the very near future.

According to Scripture, God is the eternal One and there is none like Him: "that the LORD Himself is God in heaven above and on the earth beneath; there is no other" (Deuteronomy 4:39). He is the One "Declaring the end from the beginning, and from ancient times things that are not yet done" (Isaiah 46:10). God states "I am the First and I am the Last; besides Me there is no God" (Isaiah 44:6). God also declares "I made the earth and created man on it; it was my hands that stretched out the heavens, and I commanded all their host" (Isaiah 45:12). God exists in and of Himself, was never created, and has no end. There is none like Him in heaven above, on the earth, or below the earth.

The first man (Adam) was created approximately six thousand years ago[8] and every last human being on the planet is a descendant of Adam, hence we are all created beings. We will never become gods in that we can never through our efforts attain godhood. We are not evolving to a higher order or existence. Man will never be a god nor equal to the Almighty! The Bible is clear that man fell from how he had been created. We were created in the image and likeness of God but at the fall, when sin and death entered into the world, the image of God in man was corrupted. The question before us, however, is just what exactly God meant when He said that He created us in His image and likeness.

There are several ways that we can ascertain the correct meaning of that phrase. First of all, we will examine the Hebrew words in every instance that they appear in the Bible to see how they are used in other contexts. In real estate the name of the game is location, location, location. In Bible studies it is context, context, context. A word's context determines what a word means. We can also use comparative linguistics to see how other Semitic languages understood the same root in their languages. We can turn to the early translations such as the Greek Septuagint and Aramaic Targumim to glean how those words were translated.

We will then turn our attention to what God reveals about Himself in portions of Scripture. The Bible says that God is spirit. Clearly God is not flesh and blood (dependent on oxygen, food, water – not a carbon-based life form) but does the fact that He is spirit mean that He does not have a body? Paul distinguishes amongst the different types of bodies in 1 Corinthians 15. We will also examine passages where a prophet, seer, or disciple "sees" a vision of God in heaven or the like. How should these be interpreted in light of Paul's discussion of heavenly bodies?

The next thing to look at is the seed of God. First John 3:9 says that we have the seed of God dwelling in us. The word, *sperm* [*sperma* σπερμα] is the same as is used to describe human and even animal seed which is used to propagate the race. Peter says that we have been redeemed with incorruptible seed. What does it mean that we have God's seed (incorruptible)? How does that differ from the corruptible seed that we currently have? Could it be that this is why Jesus so emphatically said that we had to be born again? Paul says that we are a new creation, the old has passed away. Does the imparting of the Holy Spirit have anything to do with the fact that God breathed into man in the garden? Was that lost when man sinned?

The biblical evidence will demonstrate that image and likeness of God refer **not only** to God's character and attributes but also to His form or shape, that is, what He generally "looks like" when perceived with the eye (or the mind's eye). Furthermore, God's seed, while not composed of proteins and amino acids in DNA strands, is what we receive in our new bodies. This was also the essence of what Adam was pre-fall. Adam was also clothed in light (as God is) before the fall—something that will be restored to us once in the heavenly/spiritual realm.

IN GOD'S IMAGE AND FORM

God states in Genesis 1:26-27 that He made Adam in his image. "Then God said, 'Let Us make man in Our image, according to Our likeness' [...] So God created man in His own image; in the image of God He created him; male and female He created them" (Genesis 1:26-27). This fact is reiterated: "Whoever sheds man's blood, by man his blood shall be shed; for in the image of God He made man" (Genesis 9:6). God is an infinite being and has many communicable and noncommunicable characteristics that are in view here. Certainly man is neither omnipotent nor omniscient like God. But he does share to a lesser extent God's creativity, vision, passion, ability to love, mercy, etc.— qualities that are part of His image and likeness. However, for our study, we will **not** focus on those aspects but specifically how both image and likeness are used in the Bible in relation to His form. Words and the combination of words are what make up the Bible and consequently, our theology is built upon the words that we find in Scripture. For this reason, tracing a word throughout Scripture is a very practical means of understanding its significance and just how we are to interpret it.

TSELEM צֶלֶם

The word image (Hebrew tselem צֶלֶם) is used 15 times[9] in the Hebrew Bible. The basic meaning of the root means a "shadow" cf. Gesenius' Hebrew Lexicon.[10] Based on its usage we can confidently deduce the following definition: 'a living or nonliving representation of something else.' In eleven of the fifteen verses image is used to refer to idols. Idols were the image (a physical representation) of a demon (or "men" in Ezekiel) as Paul tells us in 1 Corinthians. Paul states that idols were in fact demons: "that the things which the Gentiles sacrifice they sacrifice to **demons**[11] and not to God, and I do not want you to have fellowship with **demons**" (1 Corinthians 10:20).

The word *tselem* is used to describe these idols or images which were just representations of demons that were truly being worshiped. "Destroy all their engraved stones, destroy all their molded **images**, and demolish all their high places" (Numbers 33:52).[12] The verses from Ezekiel are especially telling since they demonstrate that the images were representations of men—a form we can certainly agree on: "As for the beauty of his ornaments, He set it in majesty; but they made from it the **images** of their abominations" (Ezekiel 7:20); "made for yourself male **images** and played the harlot with them" (Ezekiel 16:17). Ezekiel 23:14 shows that an image is accurate in its representation of the real thing: "She saw men portrayed on the wall, the **images** of the Chaldeans." Clearly an image is not the same as the real thing. An image can't walk or talk in these cases, but they do faithfully depict how the men looked – in the same way in that the modern photo of a person isn't the person but is an image of the person. Indeed, I have seen photos of people and know what they look like but perhaps knowing nothing about the person. Therefore, an image conveys only some information about a person and not all of the details.

The last verse which we need to discuss for our study to be complete is Genesis 5:3 which states that Seth was begotten to Adam in his image (*tsalmo* צַלְמוֹ).

> When Adam had lived 130 years, he fathered a son in his own likeness, after his **image**, and named him Seth (Genesis 5:3).

This verse is an amazing illustration of how we are in the image of God. Just as our children act like us (likeness) they also look like us. When I see my children I see in their faces and bodies a combination of my wife and me. They very much look like us—they are in our image. My little son reminds me of when I was a child in that he acts like me—he is in my likeness! When

God made man He fashioned Adam to both act like God and to look like God. Even though my children look like me and act like me, they are obviously separate and distinct beings. So too, God made Adam to act and look like God but Adam was not the same as God. Some people might argue that this lowers the majesty of God. I would argue that it rather demonstrates the level from which man has fallen. Furthermore, this does not make God in man's image; it was man who was made in God's image.

T`MUNAH

The word *t'munah* [תְּמוּנָה] means shape, image, or form and is very much analogous to the word *tselem* which we have already examined. According to God Himself, Moses saw the Lord's form (*t'munat* YHWH תְּמֻנַת יְהוָה).

> I speak with him face to face [*pe el pe* פֶּה אֶל־פֶּה], even plainly, and not in dark sayings; and he sees the **form** of the LORD [*t'munat YHWH* תְּמֻנַת יְהוָה]. Why then were you not afraid to speak against My servant Moses?" (Numbers 12:8).

Previously the Israelites were instructed to **not** make any *t'munah* of things in heaven or in earth:

> You shall not make for yourself a carved image [*pesel* פֶּסֶל]— any likeness [t'munah תְּמוּנָה] of anything that is in heaven above, or that is in the earth beneath, or that is in the water under the earth (Exodus 20:4).

The same word *t'munah* is used for what Moses **did** see and also to describe what the children of Israel did **not** see. They were not able to look upon the actual form of God as Moses had been able. Yet, this same word is used to describe "images" and likenesses of things—that is to say, what they looked like. Moses recounts to the people the fact that they did not see God's form—even though he had. Therefore they should not make an image of God.

> And the LORD spoke to you out of the midst of the fire. You heard the sound of the words, but saw no form [*t'munah* תְּמוּנָה]; you only heard a voice. Take careful heed to yourselves, for you

saw no form [*t'munah* תְּמוּנָה] when the LORD spoke to you at Horeb out of the midst of the fire, lest you act corruptly and make for yourselves a carved image [*pesel* פֶּסֶל] in the form [*t'munah* תְּמוּנָה] of any figure: the likeness of male or female, […] take heed to yourselves, lest you forget the covenant of the LORD your God which He made with you, and make for yourselves a carved image [*pesel* פֶּסֶל] in the form [*t'munah* תְּמוּנָה] of anything which the LORD your God has forbidden you. When you beget children and grandchildren and have grown old in the land, and act corruptly and make a carved image in the form of anything, and do evil in the sight of the LORD your God to provoke Him to anger (Deuteronomy 4:12, 15-16, 23, 25).

As testimony of what we have in store for us, the psalmist tells us that we will be in God's *t'munah* (form) when we awake or when we are resurrected. "As for me, I will see Your face in righteousness; I shall be satisfied when I awake in Your likeness, [*t'munatkha* תְּמוּנָתֶךָ]" (Psalm 17:15). Thus Moses saw God's form and we shall awake in His likeness (form); *t'munah* (תְּמוּנָה) is a shape/form of any figure.

EZEKIEL'S VISION OF GOD

The prophet Ezekiel tells of a vision he had in Chapter one of his book. He describes the visual aspects of a series of creatures which he saw that went wherever the Spirit went.

Now it came to […] that the heavens were opened and I saw visions of God. Then I looked, and behold, a whirlwind was coming out of the north, a great cloud with raging fire engulfing itself; and brightness was all around it and radiating out of its midst like the color of amber, out of the midst of the fire. Also from within it came the likeness [*d'mut* דְּמוּת] of four living creatures. And this was their appearance [*mareihen* מַרְאֵיהֶן]: they had the likeness [*d'mut* דְּמוּת] of a man [*adam* אָדָם]. As for the likeness of the living creatures, their appearance was like burning coals of fire, like the appearance of torches going back and forth among the living creatures. The fire was bright, and out of the fire went lightning. And the living creatures ran back and forth, in appearance like a flash of lightning (Ezekiel 1:1, 4-5, 10-14).

He then describes what he saw above the creatures: "The likeness [*d'mut* דְּמוּת] of the firmament above the heads of the living creatures was like the color of an awesome crystal, stretched out over their heads" (Ezekiel 1:22). Having described in great detail the appearance or likeness of the creatures Ezekiel then shares that he saw YHWH above the expanse:

> And above the firmament over their heads was the likeness of a throne, in appearance like a sapphire stone; on the likeness of the throne was a likeness [*k'mareh* כְּמַרְאֵה] with the appearance of a **man** [*adam* אָדָם] high above it. Also from the appearance of His waist and upward I saw, as it were, the color of amber with the appearance of fire all around within it; and from the appearance of His waist and downward I saw, as it were, the appearance of fire with brightness all around. Like the appearance of a rainbow in a cloud on a rainy day, so was the appearance of the brightness all around it. This was **the appearance of the likeness of the glory of the LORD**. So when I saw it, I fell on my face, and I heard a voice of One speaking (Ezekiel 1:26-28).

Verse 26 shows us that the one on the throne (whom we know clearly to be God or the Lord from verse 28) has the appearance of a human. The Hebrew text says "as the likeness of Adam" (*k'mareh adam* כְּמַרְאֵה אָדָם). In other words, God, the one sitting on the throne, looks like Adam. Ezekiel is not making God in man's image; if we recall Genesis 1:26-27, it is man who was made in God's image. Thus, Ezekiel tells us that God has the appearance like Adam which is really to say that man (Adam) has the appearance or image of God.

Ezekiel has another encounter with this person of fire:

> Then I looked, and there was a likeness, like the appearance of fire [Septuagint reads "man"[13]]—from the appearance of His

waist and downward, fire; and from His waist and upward, like the appearance of brightness, like the color of amber (Ezekiel 8:2).

We know that this also is God due to the fact that in the following verses "He" speaks in the first person and declares the He is the One who is being provoked and will also judge.

And He said to me, "Have you seen this, O son of man? [...] then they have returned to provoke Me to anger. [...] Therefore I also will act in fury. My eye will not spare nor will I have pity; and though they cry in My ears with a loud voice, I will not hear them" (Ezekiel 8:17-18).

ONE LIKE THE SON OF MAN

This "man" of fire is the same as the One that we see revealed in the book of Revelation as the One who says that He "lives, and was dead, and behold, I am alive forevermore." He is also described as the "Son of Man," which is the Hebrew way to say "human."

Then I turned to see the voice that spoke with me. And having turned I saw seven golden lampstands, and in the midst of the seven lampstands One like the Son of Man, clothed with a garment down to the feet and girded about the chest with a golden band. His head and hair were white like wool [like Daniel 7:9], as white as snow, and His eyes like a flame of fire; His feet were like fine brass, as if refined in a furnace, and His voice as the sound of many waters; He had in His right hand seven stars, out of His mouth went a sharp two-edged sword, and His countenance was like the sun shining in its strength. And when I saw Him, I fell at His feet as dead. But He laid His right hand on me, saying to me, "Do not be afraid; I am the First and the Last. I am He who lives, and was dead, and behold, I am alive forevermore. Amen. And I have the keys of Hades and of Death" (Revelation 1:12-18).

All of the evidence points out that man looks like God. Certainly God is infinitely far above His creation, but nevertheless, He has made us to look like Him. One day we will be like Him (Psalm 17:15, 1 John 3:2, etc.) in that we too will glow and have the fiery aspect as well.

A SPIRITUAL BODY

Nevertheless, how can this be when we are told so clearly in John 4 that God is spirit? How can God have a shape or form? We need to turn to 1 Corinthians 15 where Paul makes it clear that in the world to come we will not be bodiless but we will have a new kind of body. This body here, which Adam was originally made of, was made of dirt. That is to say, he was a carbon-based life form and literally had an earthly body. However, the heavenly body will be of a different nature and not limited like the carbon-based or dirt-based earthly one we have here and now. Paul responds to the question that was raised "How are the dead raised? With what kind of body do they come?" (1 Corinthians 15:35) by giving an in depth exposé of the various types of bodies (humans, animals, birds, fish, and natural and spiritual) and what our new bodies will be like.

> What you sow does not come to life unless it dies. And what you sow is not the body that is to be, but a bare kernel, perhaps of wheat or of some other grain. **But God gives it a body as he has chosen, and to each kind of <u>seed</u> its own body.** For not all flesh is the same, but there is one kind for humans, another for animals, another for birds, and another for fish. **There are heavenly bodies and earthly bodies,** but the glory of the heavenly is of one kind, and the glory of the earthly is of another. There is one glory of the sun, and another glory of the moon, and another glory of the stars; for star differs from star in glory (1 Corinthians 15:36-41 ESV).

Paul makes a series of important revelations concerning how Jesus is and how we will be upon resurrection. He starts by saying that there are first of all different kinds of flesh; animal, fish, human, and then he divides between heavenly and earthly.

> So is it with the resurrection of the dead. What is sown is perishable; what is raised is imperishable. It is sown in dishonor; it is raised in glory. It is sown in weakness; it is raised in power. **It is sown a natural body; it is raised a spiritual body. If there is a natural body, there is also a spiritual body** (1 Corinthians 15:42-44 ESV).

Paul is showing the parallels between the earthly body and the spiritual body. Just because our future body will not be made of dirt does not mean that it is not tangible. On the contrary, our future body will be tangible, touchable, and permanent.

> Thus it is written, "The first man Adam became a living being"; the last Adam became a life-giving spirit. But it is not the spiritual that is first but the natural, and then the spiritual. The first man was from the earth, a man of dust; the second man is from heaven. As was the man of dust, so also are those who are of the dust, and as is the man of heaven, so also are those who are of heaven. **Just as we have borne the image of the man of dust, we shall also bear the image of the man of heaven** (1 Corinthians 15:45-49 ESV).

Here we learn that just as we were in Adam's likeness (bodily) so too will we bear the image of Jesus (bodily).

> I tell you this, brothers: flesh and blood cannot inherit the kingdom of God, nor does the perishable inherit the imperishable. Behold! I tell you a mystery. We shall not all sleep, but we shall all be changed, in a moment, in the twinkling of an eye, at the last trumpet. For the trumpet will sound, and the dead will be raised imperishable, and we shall be changed. For this perishable body must put on the imperishable, and this mortal body must put on immortality. When the perishable puts on the imperishable, and the mortal puts on immortality, then shall come to pass the saying that is written: "Death is swallowed up in victory" (1 Corinthians 15:42-54 ESV).[14]

Paul's bottom line is that spiritual doesn't mean nebulous or bodiless. It simply means having a body but in the spiritual dimension (see Chapter six). The resurrected body of Jesus seems to be the paradigm for what ours will be like. His resurrected body is a body that is not subject to sin, corruption, decomposition, decay, or death. It can walk through walls and exist in the spiritual realm and yet enter into this one and eat and drink at will. If Jesus is the paradigm, then that means we will have a similar if not exactly parallel body. Paul states that our new self is in God's likeness: "and that you put on the **new man** which was created **according to God**, in true righteousness and holiness" (Ephesians 4:24).

CONFORMED TO HIS BODY

Paul is even more specific in the book of Philippians where he states that our bodies will be conformed to His body. Our existence in the world to come will not be a soul without a body, but we will have a body that is even more real and tangible than our current body. It just won't be made of the dirt that we are made of now. We will be made of "spirit" and that will be like the Lord Jesus Himself!

> Who will transform our lowly body that it may be conformed to **His glorious body**, according to the working by which He is able even to subdue all things to Himself (Philippians 3:21).

John corroborates this in his first epistle when he states: "when He is revealed, **we shall be like Him**, for we shall see Him as He is" (1 John 3:2). What we learn is God is spirit and of course He is not earthly—He is not composed of dirt; His essence is spirit (and uncreated). However, that is not to say that he is bodiless; He has a spiritual body and made man after Himself. Our body is a reflection or shadow of what His is. The heavenly realm according to Scripture is the original and things here on this earth are more or less a copy. We read in Hebrews 8:5 concerning the priests:

Who serve the **copy and shadow of the heavenly things**, as Moses was divinely instructed when he was about to make the tabernacle. For He said, "See that you make all things according to the pattern shown you on the mountain" (Hebrews 8:5).

In fact, every place where God is seen in a vision in the Bible He has traits that we would associate with a body. In addition to the revealing text from Ezekiel 1, there are several other texts in which something of the form or shape of God is described.

Then Moses went up, also Aaron, Nadab, and Abihu, and seventy of the elders of Israel, and they **saw the God of Israel**. And there was **under His feet** as it were a **paved work of sapphire stone**, and it was like the very heavens in its clarity. But on the nobles of the children of Israel He did not lay His hand. So they saw God, and they ate and drank (Exodus 24:9-11).

Here we have the same reference to the sapphire stone as we saw in Ezekiel 1:26. Here it appears that only His feet are visible, but that is significant. If we interpret this text straightforwardly, we must conclude that Moses and the elders actually saw God including His feet. Could it be that the text means just what it says? The prophet Micaiah in 2 Chronicles 18:18 describes what he saw "Therefore hear the word of the LORD: I saw the LORD sitting on His throne, and all the hosts of heaven standing on His right hand and His left." From this we learn that God sits. While we can surmise that God doesn't need to sit due to fatigue like human kings, His body is seen in a sitting position upon His throne. This is also seen by both Isaiah and Daniel:

- I saw the Lord **sitting** on a throne, high and lifted up, and the train of His robe filled the temple (Isaiah 6:1).

- I watched till thrones were put in place, and the Ancient of Days was **seated**; His garment was white as snow, and the **hair** of His **head** was like pure wool. His throne was a fiery flame, its wheels a burning fire (Daniel 7:9).

Daniel sees even more than Isaiah. He notes that the Ancient of Days was seated and also that His garments were white as snow and the **hair** of His **head** was like pure wool. Not only is God sitting but He has hair upon His head. Often scholars have sought to explain these descriptions away by interpreting them figuratively or by claiming that the biblical authors are using anthropomorphic language (see for example John Gill; Daniel 7:9). However, this interpretation breaks down under closer inspection. After all, we have seen that Ezekiel says that he saw the appearance like "Adam" seated on the throne. Certainly, God is far greater than we can understand, but His basic form or silhouette does not seem to be truly in question. He exists as a spiritual body.

Can we completely understand that? No. But the general idea is simple enough to grasp. Apparently scholars are zealous to guard God's character; they perhaps fear that if the language of God's hands, feet, head, and hair were taken too literally it might lead people to reduce God into man's image. But as we have already explored, just the opposite is true; God has created Adam and humanity in His image and likeness (see appendix one concerning the triune nature of God and how He could be seen). We were created perfectly in God's image and likeness (what He looks like and how He acts) but the fall of sin corrupted that image. When Adam and Eve listened to the cunning words of the Serpent they died immediately and yet it took Adam 930 years to finally succumb to death—how can both be true? The answer lies in the role of the Holy Spirit in Adam (see appendix two for a complete discussion) and in the light that he lost, which we will examine in our next chapter.

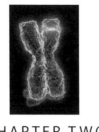

CHAPTER TWO

Adam's Biophotons and Future Bodies of Light

THE NEW AGE AND "ALIEN" CHANNELERS often speak of bodies of light that the supposed other-worldly beings possess. The truth is, however, that bodies of light were first spoken of in the Bible. In this chapter we will examine the many places that Scripture speaks of bodies of light and discuss how our DNA emits light. Understanding the truth will again help us to spot the demonic deception that is coming in these last days.

We have seen that Adam was created in God's image and likeness, which includes the appearance (form) of God. We can deduce more of how Adam was before the fall and also how we shall be upon resurrection from the teaching of the Lord Jesus. We first note that while up by Caesarea Philippi Jesus took His disciples, Peter, James, and John, to the top of Mount Hermon.[15] "And He was transfigured before them. His face shone like the sun, and His clothes became as white as the light [*phos* φως]" (Matthew 17:2). Jesus' clothes were not only white, but they were literally white as light, which is the Greek word φως *phos* from which we get the word photo or photon. In other words, the light of Jesus, who is the source of that light, **emanated through His clothing**. When the end of the tribulation draws to a close the Lord Jesus will return to earth on a horse and those who have trusted in Him will return with Him. Speaking of the called out ones (believers in Jesus) John notes in Revelation: "And to her it was granted to be arrayed in fine linen, clean and **bright** [*lampron* λαμπρον*], for the fine linen is the righteous acts of the saints" (Revelation 19:8).

We see from this verse that the covering will be bright or luminous. The Greek word λαμπρον *lampron* signifies bright or shining. The Liddell, Scott, and Jones Classical Greek Lexicon defines it as "bright, radiant, of the sun and stars." Thus, when we occupy our heavenly or celestial bodies we will also be enveloped in or clothed in garments of light. Jesus confirmed this reality when He said concerning the righteous in the world to come: "Then the righteous will **shine forth** [*eklampo* ἐκλάμπω] as the sun in the kingdom of their Father" (Matthew 13:43). The same was revealed to Daniel concerning the resurrection of the righteous. The Septuagint (LXX) version uses the same word as is found in Matthew 13 above, which is also related to the garments in Revelation 19:8.

> Those who are wise shall **shine** [LXX: *eklampo* ἐκλάμπω, Heb. וְיַזְהִרוּ] like the **brightness** [LXX: *lamprotes* λαμπρότης] of the firmament, and those who turn many to righteousness like the stars forever and ever (Daniel 12:3).

This truth was revealed as far back as the time of Judges when Deborah, Barak, and Abinoam sang: "Thus let all Your enemies perish, O LORD! But let those who love Him be like the sun when it comes out in full strength" (Judges 5:31). This is further evidenced in the book of Proverbs: "But the path of the just is like the shining sun, that shines ever brighter unto the perfect day" (Proverbs 4:18). If we recall that Jesus said that in the resurrection we will be like the angels, then taking a look at them and how they are radiant beings shows us that we too shall be like that. This is also the conclusion of Bible commentator Arthur Pink when he states in his book *The Doctrine of Revelation:*

So far from regarding his soul as a mysterious, nebulous and indefinable thing, the believer looks upon it as a living, intelligent, sentient being—his real self. We should view a disembodied soul as one which has cast off its earthly **clothing** and is now **appareled in a garment of light**, or, to use the language of Scripture, "**clothed in white raiment**" (Revelation 3:5; 4:4). At death the soul of the saint **is freed from all the limitations which sin had imposed upon it**, and its faculties are then not only purified, but elevated and enlarged.[16]

There are many verses that reference the angels' glorious appearance. We of course recall that the angels shone in the night sky at the announcement of the birth of the awaited Messiah in Luke 2:9. The root word in that passage is *perilampo* (περιλάμπω), meaning "to shine around," which is simply a derivative of *lampo*, "to shine." In Luke 24:4 we read that there were two men (or angels) who stood by the tomb in "shining garments" (*astrapto* ἀστράπτω, like what a star does). This same word for shining is used to describe lightning as it shines from one part of heaven to the other according to Luke 17:24.

Perhaps the most telling examples of what angels look like and how we will look are found in Daniel and Revelation. In Daniel Chapter ten, Daniel tells us of a vision in which he saw an angel (who was detained by the prince of Persia and thus could not be Jesus) and how he had a shining appearance.

> I lifted my eyes and looked, and behold, a certain man clothed in linen, whose waist was girded with gold of Uphaz! His body was like beryl, his face like the **appearance of lightning**, his eyes like **torches of fire**, his arms and feet like **burnished bronze** in color, and the sound of his words like the voice of a multitude (Daniel 10:5-6).

John also saw shining angels in the book of Revelation. The angels were clothed in linen that was shining (*lampron* λαμπρον). "And out of the temple came the seven angels having the seven plagues, clothed in pure bright [*lampron* λαμπρον] linen, and having their chests girded with golden bands" (Revelation 15:6). We can therefore conclude that our future "clothing" is in the likeness of how God is clothed in light according to Psalm 104:1-2 and because Adam was created in His image then Adam must have lost the light at the fall. "You are clothed with splendor and majesty, covering yourself with **light** as with a garment, stretching out the heavens like a tent" (Psalm 104:1-2).

SUPPORTED BY ANCIENT JEWISH INTERPRETATION

What is fascinating is that Jewish interpretation held that Adam and Eve were at first clothed in garments of light and then later clothed in garments of skin. The Midrash Rabbah (Rabbinic literature from the first or second century AD) of Genesis 3:21 reads:

AND THE LORD GOD MADE FOR ADAM AND HIS WIFE GARMENTS OF SKIN [or עוֹר], AND CLOTHED THEM (III, 21). In R. Meir's Torah it was found written, 'Garments of light (or)' this refers to Adam's garments, which were like a torch, broad at the bottom and narrow at the top.

The Soncino Zohar of Bereshith, though a medieval (Jewish) writing, describes in even greater detail how the rabbis interpreted the original garments of Adam and Eve:

AND THE EYES OF BOTH OF THEM WERE OPENED. R. Hiya says, their eyes were opened to the evil of the world, which they had not known hitherto. **Then they knew that they were naked, since they had lost the celestial lustre which had formerly enveloped them, and of which they were now divested**. AND THEY SEWED FIG LEAVES. They strove to cover themselves with the (delusive) images from the tree of which they had eaten, the so-called "leaves of the tree." AND THEY MADE THEMSELVES GIRDLES. [...] Afterward God clothed Adam and Eve in garments soothing to the skin, as it is written, HE MADE THEM COATS OF SKIN [or עוֹר]. At **first they had had coats of light [or אוֹר]**, which procured them the service of the highest of the high, for the celestial angels used to come to enjoy that light; so it is written, "For thou hast made him but little lower than the angels, and crownest him with glory and honour" (Ps. VIII, 6). Now after their sins they had only coats of skin [or עוֹר], good for the body but not for the soul (emphasis mine).[17]

The (Soncino) Zohar, chapter Shemoth (Exodus) further comments on how Adam was originally clothed with light [or אוֹר] so that he could be in the garden; if he had not had that, the text suggests that he could **not** have been in God's presence.

> Adam in the Garden of Eden was attired in **supernal raiment**, of **celestial radiancy**. As soon as he was driven from the Garden of Eden and had need of forms suited to this world, "the Lord God," Scripture says, "made for Adam and for his wife garments of skin [or עוֹר] and clothed them" (Gen. III, 21). Formerly they were **garments of light** [or אוֹר], to wit, of the **celestial light** in which Adam ministered in the Garden of Eden. For, inasmuch as it is the resplendency of the celestial light that ministers in the Garden of Eden, when first man entered into the Garden, the Holy One, blessed be He, clothed him first in the raiment of that light. Otherwise he could not have entered there. When driven out, however, he had need of other garments; hence "garments of skin" (emphasis mine).[18]

The Jewish apocryphal work of the Life of Adam and Eve, written sometime between the third and fifth century AD records the belief many held concerning the original state of Adam and Eve before their fall.

> But as they [Adam and Eve] were going in the way, and before they reached that place, Satan, the wicked one, had heard the Word of God communing with Adam respecting his covering. [...] Then came the Word of God to Adam and Eve, and said to them, "This is he who was hidden in the Serpent, and who deceived you, and **stripped you of the garment of light and glory in which you were.** This is he who promised you majesty and divinity. Where, then, is the beauty that was

on him? Where is his divinity? Where is his light? Where is the glory that rested on him? Now his figure is hideous; he is become abominable among angels; and he has come to be called Satan.[19] emphasis mine.

CONFIRMED BY ANCIENT CHRISTIAN INTERPRETATION

The understanding that Adam and Eve were once clothed in light before their fall is not only confirmed by the ancient Jews but also hinted at by the ancient Christians in what they have to say concerning the celestial bodies that are awaiting the believer. Church Father Arnobius, in his work *Against Heathens,* writes in the notes the following about what believers have to look forward to:

> But let us not reason from things *terrestrial* as regards things *celestial*: our coarse **material fabrics are "shadows of the true."** The **robes of light are realities**, and are conformed to spiritual bodies, as even here a mist may envelop a tree.[20] emphasis mine.

Methodius, another church father says the following concerning the light that we shall be clothed with. He derives his comments from Isaiah 60 which speaks of the future messianic kingdom in which Israel will be in the center. He envisions what a body completely free from sin and corruption will be like. He writes:

> Arise, shine; for thy light is come, and the glory of the Lord is risen upon thee. [...] It is the Church whose children shall come to her with all speed after the resurrection, running to her from all quarters. She rejoices receiving the light which never goes down, and clothed with the **brightness of the Word** as with a robe. For with what other more precious or honourable ornament was it becoming that the queen should be adorned, to be led as a Bride to the Lord, when she had received **a garment of light**, and therefore was called by the Father? Come, then, let us go forward in our discourse, and look upon this marvelous woman as upon virgins prepared for a marriage, pure and undefiled, perfect **and radiating a**

permanent beauty, wanting nothing of the brightness of light; and instead of a dress, clothed with light itself; and instead of precious stones, her head adorned with shining stars. For instead of the clothing which we have, she had light; and for gold and brilliant stones, she had stars; but stars not such as those which are set in the invisible heaven, but better and more resplendent, so that those may rather be considered as their images and likenesses (emphasis mine).[21]

The second century Christian document, the Revelation of Peter, written after 135 AD, affords us a wonderful commentary as to what undoubtedly many Christians believed had happened and would come to pass. Again, we do not look at such texts as inspired of God, but as early Christian commentary on the Scriptures. Concerning the resurrected believers, the text states:

There appeared two men standing before the Lord [...] upon whom we were not able to look. For there issued from their countenance a **ray as of the sun**, and their **raiment was shining** so as the eye of man never saw the like: for no mouth is able to declare nor heart to conceive the glory wherewith they were clad and the beauty of their countenance. Whom when we saw we were astonished, for their bodies were whiter than any snow and redder than any rose. And the redness of them was mingled with the whiteness, and, in a word, I am not able to declare their beauty. [...]These are your **(our) righteous brethren** whose appearance ye did desire to see. [...] the dwellers in that place were **clad** with the **raiment of shining angels**, and their raiment was like unto their land (emphasis mine).[22]

Note that the writer of this document believed that the resurrected saints would literally emit light from their bodies just as we have seen from numerous Scriptures. The writer identifies the two saints as Moses and Elias (Elijah). He also sees the shining analogous to the colors of a rainbow just like the colors that surround God in Ezekiel 1:28.

'The Son at his coming will raise the dead . . . and will make my righteous **ones shine seven times more than the sun**, and will make their crowns **shine** like crystal and like the rainbow in the time of rain (crowns) which are perfumed with nard and cannot be contemplated (adorned) with rubies, with the colour of emeralds shining brightly, with topazes, gems, and yellow pearls that shine like the stars of heaven, and like the rays of the sun, sparkling which cannot be gazed upon.' Again, of the angels: 'Their faces shine more than the sun; their crowns are as the rainbow in the time of rain. [...] Their eyes shine like the morning star. [...] Their raiment is not woven, but white as that of the fuller, according as I saw on the mountain where Moses and Elias were'.[23] emphasis mine.

There seems to be little doubt that the early church interpreted the resurrected bodies of the believers to be such that they would emit light and shine like the sun. Given that Jesus came as the second Adam and that we are in the corrupted image of the first Adam, we can infer that when God made the first Adam (in an uncorrupted state), Adam's earth-based body must have radiated light in a manner similar to our resurrection bodies.

WEREN'T THEY NAKED?

The fact that the English translation says in Genesis 2:25 "And the man and his wife were both **naked** [*arummim* עֲרוּמִּים] and were not ashamed" would seem to destroy the notion that they were "clothed" with light. However, a detail that we also must grapple with is that just one verse later we read (Genesis 3:1), "Now the Serpent was more **cunning** (עָרוּם) than any beast of the field which the LORD God had made." We see what looks like the same word for naked in Genesis 2:25 is used of the Serpent's character.[24] Nevertheless, there appears to be a pun or word play occurring in the Hebrew to indicate that Adam and Eve were not merely naked (*arom* עָרֹם) but possessed the quality of being "prudent," "wise," or "crafty."

According to the *Theological Wordbook of the Old Testament*, the word *arum* (עָרוּם) means to be "shrewd," "crafty," "prudent," "sensible" and so on. The connotation of the word can be either positive or negative depending on the context. For example in Proverbs 12:16 we read "A fool's wrath is known at once, but a prudent [*arum* עָרוּם] man covers shame." [25]

Some ancient Jews noted this word play in the Aramaic translation called the Targumim. While we do not consider anything but the Bible to be the authoritative Word of God, ancient sources can shed light on how a passage was being understood by ancient Jews and Christians. In the Aramaic Targum Jonathan (an ancient Aramaic translation of the Old Testament)[26] we read:

> And both of them were wise [חכימין], Adam and his wife; but they were not faithful (or truthful) [אמתינן] in their glory [ביקרהון] (Targum Jonathan Genesis 2:25).

To be fair we must note that this is the only ancient source that has caught this word play and therefore we cannot be dogmatic about the interpretation. However this reading would seem to be proven by the fact that after their eyes were opened to the fact that they were naked, another word of the same root (*eirom* עירֹם with the letter *yod* inserted) is used, in the Hebrew text, which means "naked"[27] and is never translated as "prudent."

> Then the eyes of both were opened, and they knew that they were **naked** [*eirummim* עֵירֻמַּם]. And they sewed fig leaves together and made themselves loincloths (Genesis 3:7).

The fact that after the first couple fell they realized they were "*eirom* (עֵירֹם)" attests that there may have been a slightly different meaning to *arummim* (עֲרוּמִּים)/*arom* (עָרֹם) in Genesis 2:25. Targum Jonathan notes the difference of the words by translating *eirummim* (עֵירֻמַּם) as "naked" in Genesis 3:7 (once again consistent with the rest of the occurrences in Scripture) and elaborates as to why they became naked:

> And the eyes of both were enlightened, and they knew that they were naked, **divested of the purple robe in which they**

had been created. And they saw the sight of their shame, and sewed to themselves the leaves of figs, and made to them cinctures (Targum Jonathan Genesis 3:7, emphasis mine).

In Genesis 3:21 Targum Jonathan explains that God made coverings for Adam and Eve in place of what they had before:

And the Lord God made to Adam and to his wife **vestures of honour** from the skin of the Serpent, which he had cast from him, upon the skin of their flesh, instead **of that adornment** which had been cast away; and He clothed them (Targum Jonathan Genesis 3:21, emphasis mine).

The message is that before their fall they were **wise** but through disobedience to God's command they were unfaithful which led to them seeing their nakedness—itself the result of losing their robes. We might also nuance this word play by consulting the Gesenius Hebrew Lexicon on the word *arom* (עָרֹם). For this root he has noted the various uses of the word, the most basic of which is nakedness—that is to be without clothing. However, several other definitions help to round out the ways that we might understand it; here is that it means to be only lightly dressed, for example only in a tunic.[28]

Gesenius notes that the Greek word for naked, as used in the Septuagint (the Greek translation of the Hebrew Bible) is *gumnos* γυμνός which is how Peter was before he swam to shore to meet the Lord after the resurrection in John 21:7.

Therefore that disciple whom Jesus loved said to Peter, "It is the Lord!" Now when Simon Peter heard that it was the Lord, he put on his outer garment (for he had removed [gumnos γυμνος[29]] it), and plunged into the sea.

Peter was not absolutely naked—that is to say without even one piece of clothing; he was wearing a little something. He had only taken off the outer garment but the word for naked *gumnos* is employed and is the same word that is used in the Greek Septuagint of Genesis 2:25. Thus we see that naked, from the Bible's point of view, does not **necessarily** mean naked in the **absolute sense**, but could mean poorly clothed, ill clad or without a proper covering.

PROPOSED READING

Therefore Adam and Eve were not wearing clothes like we do today but were covered with something—which we have discovered was light. The word play of *arom/arum* demonstrates that they were unashamed because of the covering that they had (and not simply because they were unaware of their lack of clothing). From the text and the linguistic nuances we see that they were not naked in the absolute sense before their fall. The different word for naked that is employed in Genesis 3:7 brings with it idea that after their fall they did become truly naked and therefore needed to be clothed with skins because they lost the coverings of light.

Therefore we propose the following reading with all of the linguistic nuances plus the ancient sources included:

> Now the two of them were naked [clothed with a basic garment]/prudent/wise [*arummim* עֲרוּמִּים] and they were not ashamed. Now, the Serpent was the most prudent/craftiest [*arum* עָרוּם] of all the creatures which the Lord God had made (Genesis 2:25; 3:1 translation mine).

This translation keeps the word play of *arum* and takes into consideration the ancient witnesses of the Targum. In other words before their fall they were wise, but through disobedience to God's command they were unfaithful which led to them seeing their nakedness—itself the result of losing their (light) robes.

Furthermore, this provides a plausible reason why the spelling of [*arummim* עֲרוּמִּים] changes in 3:7 to *eirummim* (עֵירֻמִּם). It would seem that the author (presumably Adam) was making mention of the fact that things radically did change. They became naked in the absolute sense. Knowing that when we receive the fullness of our salvation we shall be clothed in light (Revelation 19:8) and how Jesus became transfigured, we ought to conclude that Adam and Eve were clothed in light.

We know that God did in fact clothe them later after they had sinned. God in His mercy "made tunics of skin, and clothed them" (Genesis 3:21). We have seen that God clothes Himself with light as with a garment (Psalm 104:1-2) plus Ezekiel describes Him as being of amber, fire, and having (like a rainbow) brightness all around Himself. Jesus transfigured and His clothes became as white as light [*phos* φως] (Matthew 17:2). According to Revelation 19:8 the saints returning with the Lord will be in shining [*lampron* λαμπρον] garments. Coverings of light were almost certainly in our past and are absolutely in our future. See appendix three concerning the reason God put the tree in the garden which caused Adam and Eve to lose their light. Next we will consider just how it was possible that Adam and Eve could emit light out of their bodies.

BIOPHOTONS

Remembering that man is in the image of God will serve as a clue to answer our question as to the origin of the light and with a bit of logic we will see that the light must come from God's essence. Returning to Ezekiel 1 we recall that the prophet saw: "a whirlwind was coming out of the north, a great cloud with raging fire engulfing itself; and brightness was all around it and radiating out of its midst like the color of amber [*khashmal* חַשְׁמַל], out of the midst of the fire" (Ezekiel 1:4).

We learn in verse 28 that this was the entourage of the Lord Himself, a man of fire, as it were and thus, the light must radiate out from the Lord Himself (and not from His robes, per se). In fact, we are told that specifically "The city had no need of the sun or of the moon to shine in it, for the glory of God illuminated it. The Lamb is its light" (Revelation 21:23). Isaiah describes the light coming from God as well:

The sun shall no longer be your light by day, nor for brightness shall the moon give light to you; but the LORD will be to you an everlasting light, and your God your glory. Your sun shall no longer go down, nor shall your moon withdraw itself; for the LORD will be your everlasting light, and the days of your mourning shall be ended (Isaiah 60:19-20).

Paul affords us this insight into what we shall become: "to put on the new man who has been created in God's **image**—in righteousness and holiness that comes from truth" (Ephesians 4:24 NET).

Our new man has been created in God's image—imagine that! We as new creations are in the image of the One who made us! Paul states that Jesus is the image of God: "He is the **image** [*eicon* εικον (icon)] of the invisible God, the firstborn over all creation" (Colossians 1:15 NET). Then he states that we are in that image using the same Greek word *eicon* (εικον) "and have been clothed with the new man that is being renewed in knowledge according to the **image** [*eicon* εικον] of the one who created it" (Colossians 3:10 NET). We must not forget, however, that Adam was originally created in the image of God. Thus if in our new man we will be like God (not *be* God in all of his glory, but *like* Him!), then we must conclude that when God made Adam in His image (the Septuagint translates the Hebrew *tselem* צֶלֶם as *eicon* voκιε) and likeness, Adam emitted light in a way similar to God. Since we will have bodies of light once our image is fully restored, so too Adam must have had that covering of light before his fall into corruption. There appears to be no difference between Adam in his pre-fall state and us in our heavenly state as far as the light emitting from our bodies is concerned. Nevertheless, there will be one enormous difference: Adam could have refrained from sinning and so have enjoyed the bliss of the Lord's presence. However, he never would have known the depths to which God was willing to humble Himself to buy back His creation. As redeemed sons of God, we and Adam will now enjoy the bliss of heaven and know full well that we are there because of the mighty sacrifice of our Lord Jesus.

The ultimate deception that Satan so cleverly concocted for the first couple was to entice them to eat the fruit of the tree of the knowledge of good and evil in order to become like God when they already were! They looked like God (Exodus 24:9-10; Daniel 7:9, Isaiah 6:1-6, Ezekiel 1:26-28, Revelation 4), they had the Spirit of God, and they emanated light like God. Lastly, they were *already* wise (or prudent) and were not ashamed. Thus, they were perfectly suited to have fellowship with God. When Satan deceived them he suggested things that they already had—the real deception was that they already were like God.

We have seen that Adam being "clothed" with light is a very likely biblical possibility. Now let's consider just how Adam might have radiated light.

DNA EMIT LIGHT

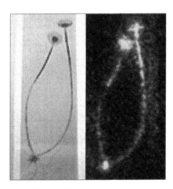

Around 1923 Ukrainian Biologist Alexander Gurwitsh discovered that living things such as onions and yeast produced an ultra weak photon emission according to the Fritz-Albert Popp Institute. This discovery was then confirmed independently by Russian scientists around 1950 when they discovered an "ultraweak photon emission" from living organisms. Again, the discovery of photon emission was confirmed independently of the previous finding by Italian nuclear physicists L. Colli, U. Facchini, G. Guidotti, and R. Dugnani-Lonati, M. Orsenigo in 1955 who "by chance discovered a 'bioluminescence' of seedlings" They published their finding in an article *Further Measurements on the Bioluminescence of the*

Figure 1 Living Systems emit biophotons (two algae Acetabularia acetabulum emit photons in darkness)

Seedlings[31] even though they did not believe it to be of great consequence.

The fact that DNA emits light is now a well-established fact, even if it is relatively unknown to the general public. The Fritz-Albert Popp Institut discusses the work going on in the field around the world.

> Independently from each other and driven by different motivations scientific groups in Australia (Quickenden), Germany (Fritz-Albert Popp), Japan (Inaba), and Poland (Slawinski) showed evidence of ultraweak photon emission from biological systems by use of modern single-photon counting systems.[32]

Just what is a biophoton? A biophoton is the emission of light from DNA. Dr. Popp and the Marburg group discovered that the "essential source of non-equilibrium biophoton emission is the DNA."[33] They define biophotons in the following way:

> Biophotons are single quanta being permanently and continuously emitted by all living systems. They are a subject of quantum physics and they display a universal phenomenon attributed to all living systems.[34]

Researchers from the School of Medicine at Kanazawa University, in Kanazawa, Japan confirm the universality of DNA emitting light. They add that light is not only emitted but also absorbed by living things.

> All organic life absorbs, emits and processes light. Biophoton emission or spontaneous ultraweak light emission has been observed from almost all living organisms, with intensities ranging from 10^{-19} to 10^{-16} W/cm^2.[35]

A recent article published by researcher Daniel Fels discusses the possibility that light appears to be the mode of communication with cells. Fels states the following:

> Cells can influence each other without using a molecular signal for the purpose: this means that not all cellular processes are

necessarily based on a molecule-receptor recognition. **The nonmolecular signals are most probably photons.** If so, cells use more than one frequency for information transfer and mutual influence. The effects are manifold, acting positively or negatively on cell growth, correlated growth and energy uptake […] **it might be that many cell processes are triggered by photons.**[36]

ADAM`S BIOPHOTONS

Could biophotons have anything to do with the covering that Adam once had? The answer is arguably yes. From all that we have seen, Adam was covered with light as with a garment, similar to his Creator. We also have seen that the Holy Spirit was indwelling Adam when he was created (see appendix two). Given all of the evidence so far, we can create a picture of what life was like before and after the fall. What life was like before the fall is especially exciting as we will be going back to those Edenic conditions in the age to come. A summary of the points will help us create the composite image of just what Adam was like back then.

- God is light and in Him is no darkness at all (1 John 1:5; Revelation 21:23).

- Jesus transfigured and emitted light (Matthew 17:2).

- Angels emit light (Daniel 10).

- Angels look very similar to God (Daniel 7, 10, Ezekiel 1, Matthew 28:3; Revelation 10:1, 22) and can be mistaken for God.

- We will be like the angels in the world to come (Matthew 22:30, Luke 20:36).

- Our bodies will be like God's (1 John 3:2, Psalm 17:15, Ephesians 4:24, Philippians 3:21, Colossians 3:4, 10; 2 Peter 1:4).

- Sons of God have the Holy Spirit (Romans 8:14).

- Adam was a Son of God (who fell) (Luke 3:38).

- We will be given shining garments (Revelation 9:8).

Thus God created Adam in His image and likeness concerning his general shape (head, shoulders, hands, and feet) plus Adam was emitting light in a manner similar to God and he was also inbreathed with the Spirit of God. We have learned that our DNA not only emits light, but absorbs light as well. It would seem that our DNA is **like** an electric capacitor which can store tiny amounts of electricity and then discharge it (capacitors do not produce their own energy like a battery). In a similar way,

Figure 2 Capacitors

we can speculate that the light that was coming from Adam was not being produced from his own self, but was first absorbed from God and then reemitted, very much **like** how things glow in the dark.

> "Glow-in-the-dark objects need to be exposed to light, or charged, in order to glow. The light energizes the phosphors and excites their electrons. As the electrons lose this extra energy, they release it as a light of their own."[37]

When Adam sinned the Holy Spirit left him and the direct connection to the light source was broken. Thus, the light that is now emitted from living things is not coming from the ultimate light source which is God himself but presumably from the sun. Before his fall, Adam therefore must have emitted large quantities of light, very similar to the angels who have access to God's light and energy. Thus we are left with the picture that as this light came out of Adam's very DNA, it would have covered his body in a way similar to the shining of the angels and he was therefore covered with a garment of light.

MOSES` SHINING FACE

We have apparent evidence of God energizing our DNA with His light when Moses was on the mountain with God for forty days. The Bible says:

> Now it was so, when Moses came down from Mount Sinai [...] that Moses did not know that the **skin of his face shone** [קָרַן עוֹר פָּנָיו] while he talked with Him. So when Aaron and all the children of Israel saw Moses, behold, the **skin of his face shone**, and they were afraid to come near him. And when Moses had finished speaking with them, he put a veil on his face. But whenever Moses went in before the LORD to speak with Him, he would take the veil off until he came out; and he would come out and speak to the children of Israel whatever he had been commanded. And whenever the children of Israel saw the face of Moses, that the **skin of Moses' face shone**, then Moses would put the veil on his face again, until he went in to speak with Him (Exodus 34:29-30, 33-35).

Moses didn't realize it, but in his talking with God he had received the light from God. In a manner similar to material that glows after being exposed to a light source, so too did Moses glow after being exposed to the light of God. As we have seen, God is a "man of fire" if you will. Tremendous energy and electricity[38] are radiating out of His being. Light is coming out of the Lord and as Moses spoke face to face with God, that light was absorbed by Moses and then reemitted, causing Moses to shine. Moses was apparently in very close proximity to the Lord as the Scriptures say: "So the LORD spoke to Moses face to face, as a man speaks to his friend (Exodus 33:11). However, Numbers 12:8 adds another level of closeness between the LORD and Moses. While the English translation reads "face to face," the Hebrew actually says "mouth to mouth": I speak with him face to face [pe el pe פֶּה אֶל־פֶּה], even plainly, and not in dark sayings; and he sees the form of the LORD [t'munat YHWH וּתְמֻנַת יְהוָה] (Numbers 12:8).

Just how close they were we do not truly know, but the description is sufficient to give us the picture that Moses was in fairly close proximity to God's face. Nevertheless, God must certainly have remained somewhat veiled, since God Himself said that no one could see His face and live. He must have indicated a complete unveiling of His glory was impossible, but a partial unveiling was possible.

We conclude, therefore, that Adam must have emitted large amounts of light or photons from his DNA. When he sinned, the light that he received from God, the source of the light, was presumably extinguished and the small traces of light that are emitting from our bodies are due to the light of the sun and not from God. Proverbs 13:9 says: "The light of the righteous rejoices, but the lamp of the wicked will be put out" (see also: Proverbs 20:20, 24:20; Job 18:5, 21:17). I would like to suggest that when a non-believer dies the little bit of internal light that he had (due to the sun) is lost and being completely disconnected from God, his light is extinguished. However, the believer, just like Adam, will have light emitting from his spiritual body (hence "clothed in light") which is not his own light, but is the absorption and reemission of the Lord's light and so we will be restored to the true image of our Creator. Let's see next how the Scriptures demonstrate that Jesus would come as the second Adam to restore in us the uncorrupted image of God.

CHAPTER THREE

The Genetics of the Incarnation

THE GENESIS PROPHECY spoke of the coming of two seeds—one of the Messiah, the Christ, and the other the Antichrist. In order for us to see how the enemy plans on raising up the Antichrist, we must first understand the genetics of the incarnation of the Lord Jesus.

God promised several things about the coming of the Messiah. First, He promised that through Abraham's seed all the nations of the earth would be blessed. This means that Jesus had to come from the seed of Abraham, which means that there was a genetic link between Jesus and Abraham. Second, we know that Jesus had to be in the blood line of David in order to have the authority to be king of Israel. God promised to David that one of his descendants would be the ruler of all Israel. If Jesus was not related by blood (that is to say genetically) then He would have no right to sit on David's throne. Third, in order for Jesus to be our propitiation (substitution) and also High Priest, he had to be one of us, from Adam's seed. Therefore, the Scriptures declare that the Virgin would conceive and bear a Son. Jesus was connected genetically to His mother Mary as well as to Abraham, David, and Adam.

THE SEED OF ABRAHAM AND OF DAVID

Our first line of evidence concerning the genetic connection comes from the many prophecies that state that from the seed of Abraham and his descendants (with David being the most prominent) the Messiah would come in the flesh. God first announces that from Abraham's seed all the nations would be blessed: "And in thy seed [zarakha זַרְעֲךָ] shall all the nations of the earth be blessed; because thou hast obeyed my voice." Genesis 22:18 (KJV) About one thousand years later, God promises to David in 2 Samuel 7:12 "[...] I will set up your seed [zarakha זַרְעֲךָ] after you, who will come from your body, and I will establish his kingdom." The immediate fulfillment of this verse was realized in Solomon according to 1 Kings 8:19: "but your son who will come from your body, he shall build the temple for My name." However, Peter applies this promise ultimately to the Lord Jesus in Acts chapters 2 and 3:

> Therefore, being a prophet, and knowing that God had sworn with an oath to him that of the **fruit of his body**, according to the flesh, He would raise up the Christ to sit on his throne (Acts 2:30).

> Ye are the children of the prophets, and of the covenant which God made with our fathers, saying unto Abraham, and **in thy seed** [sperma σπέρμα] shall all the kindreds of the earth be blessed (Acts 3:25 KJV).

This ultimate fulfillment of the seed of David culminating in Jesus is also witnessed in the messianic Psalm 89.

> Thy seed [zarakha זַרְעֲךָ] will I establish for ever, and build up thy throne to all generations. Selah ... His seed also will I make [to endure] for ever, and his throne as the days of heaven ... His seed shall endure for ever, and his throne as the sun before me (Psalm 89:4, 29, and 36 KJV).

The New Testament is emphatic that Jesus would be from the seed of David—that is to say, He would be a blood (genetic) relative of David which would also make Jesus genetically related to Adam and hence all of the sons of Adam (humanity). "Has not the Scripture said that the Christ comes from the seed of David [*spermatos David* σπερματος δαβιδ] and from the town of Bethlehem, where David was?" (John 7:42). Paul specifically mentions this fact in his writings and marks that it will be the seed (*sperma* σπέρμα) of David:

- Concerning His Son Jesus Christ our Lord, who was born of the **seed of David** [*spermatos David* σπερματος δαβιδ] according to the flesh (Romans 1:3).

- Now to Abraham and his seed were the promises made. He saith not, and to seeds, as of many; but as of one, and to thy seed, which is Christ (Galatians 3:16 KJV).

- Remember that Jesus Christ, of the **seed of David** [*spermatos David* σπερματος δαβιδ], was raised from the dead according to my gospel (2 Timothy 2:8).

We also see that Levi paid tithes to Melchizedek because he was still in the loins of his father Abraham and of course being a descendant means that one must be genetically connected. Stated plainly, Levi was (genetically) in the testes of his grandfather Abraham when the tithes were paid to Melchizedek.

- And indeed those who are of the sons of Levi, who receive the priesthood, have a commandment to receive tithes from the people according to the law, that is, from their brethren, **though they have come from the loins of Abraham;** for he was still in the loins of his father when Melchizedek met him (Hebrews 7:5, 10).

OUR PROPITIATION

In order for Jesus to be our propitiation and also High Priest, he had to be one of us, which the writer of Hebrews elaborates on:

- Inasmuch then as the children have partaken of flesh [*sarkos* σαρκος] and blood [*haimatos* αιματος], He Himself likewise shared in the same, that through death He might destroy him who had the power of death, that is, the devil [...] For indeed He does not give aid to angels, but He does give aid to the seed of Abraham [*spermatos Abraam* σπερματος αβρααμ]. Therefore, **in all things He had to be made like** His brethren [*opheilin kata panta tois adelphois omoiothenai* ωφειλεν κατα παντα τοις αδελφοις ομοιωθηναι], that He might be a merciful and faithful High Priest in things pertaining to God, to make propitiation for the sins of the people (Hebrews 2:14, 16-17).

- For we do not have a High Priest who cannot sympathize with our **weaknesses** [*astheneiais* ασθενειαις], but was in all points tempted as we are, yet without sin (Hebrews 4:15).

- He can have compassion on those who are ignorant and going astray, since he himself is also subject to **weakness** [*astheneian* ασθενειαν] (Hebrews 5:2).

THE VIRGIN WILL CONCEIVE

Examining Scripture we see that there are many references to Jesus the Messiah as having been connected genetically (through the seed) to David. While it is true that the Bible records two genealogies of Jesus (Matthew's account gives Jesus' line through his adoptive father, Joseph)[39] we learn from the Lukan account that Jesus is a blood descendant of David by way of Mary's line.

Nevertheless, there are some commentators who suggest that Mary acted as an incubator and there was therefore no genetic connection between her and the Lord, or between Him and humanity.

Christ would still be 'made of the seed of David according to the flesh' (Romans 1:3), because His body was nurtured and born of Mary, who was herself of the seed of David. He would still be the Son of Man, sharing all universal human experience from conception to death, except sin. He is truly "the Seed of the Woman" (Genesis 3:15), His body formed neither the seed of the man nor the egg of the woman, but grown from a unique Seed planted in the woman's body by God Himself.

To suggest that Jesus' physical body was a completely unique and new creation and not connected to Mary and hence David, Abraham, and Adam is to ignore the enormity of verses which attest to the contrary. Let's first start with the announcement of the miraculous birth of Jesus made by the angel Gabriel in Luke 1:31-35.

> "And behold, **you will conceive** [*sullepse* συλληψη] in **your womb** [*gastri* γαστρι] and **bring forth** a Son, and shall call His name JESUS. […] and the Lord God will give Him the throne of **His father David** […]" Then Mary said to the angel, "How can this be, since I do not know a man?" And the angel answered and said to her, "The **Holy Spirit will come upon** [*epeleusetai* επελευσεται] you, and the power of the **Highest will overshadow you**; therefore, also, that Holy One who is to be born will be called the Son of God" (emphasis mine).

While this passage is well known, there are several factors that we need to focus on to see conclusively that Mary did not simply act as an incubator for the Lord, but that she was in fact His mother on the genetic level as well. Grasping this important point will give us clarity as we consider the implications of Genesis 3:15. First, we note that Mary was a virgin and had "not known a man." The angel tells her that **she** will conceive and then give birth to a Son. Notice that the angel does not merely say that she will give birth to a Son, but that **she will conceive** (*sullambano* συλλαμβάνω). This is the same language that is used in the well-known verse of Isaiah 7:14 "[…] Behold, the virgin shall conceive [*hara* הָרָה] and bear a Son, and shall call His name Immanuel." The Hebrew word *hara* הָרָה is used fifty seven times in the Hebrew Bible and carries the normative meaning of the word. Basically stated, it is when a child is procreated from the sexual union of a man and woman—that is, it takes two to conceive. Let's consider just a few examples:

- Now Adam knew Eve his wife, and she conceived [*hara* הָרָה] and bore Cain (Genesis 4:1).

- And Cain knew his wife, and she conceived [*hara* הָרָה] and bore Enoch (Genesis 4:17).

- So he went in to Hagar, and she conceived [*hara* הָרָה] (Genesis 16:4).

- For Sarah conceived [*hara* הָרָה] and bore Abraham a son (Genesis 21:2).

- So the woman conceived [*hara* הָרָה] and bore a son (Exodus 2:2).

The implantation of the man's seed is not enough; the woman provides her genetic information (seed) as well. In modern terms this is referring to the reproductive cells, called gametes,[41] which are the seed of the man (sperm) and the Seed of the Woman (ovum). Today we understand that the mother's ovum and father's sperm each provide half of the information (each providing twenty three individual [i.e. haploid] chromosomes) to the zygote (fertilized egg or child) for a total of forty six individual chromosomes. To speak of a woman's seed is extremely precise language (which only serves to authenticate the Bible as being from God). **Thus to speak of the virgin or Mary conceiving means that her ovum (egg) absolutely must account for half of the chromosomes which Jesus' physical body was comprised of.** That being the case then Jesus was genetically connected to His mother Mary and hence His ancestors David, Judah, Jacob, Isaac, Abraham, Shem, Noah, all the way back to Adam.

WHAT IS BIBLICAL SEED?

We know for certain from other Scriptures that when the biblical authors talked about seed (Hebrew *zera* זֶרַע and Greek *sperma* σπέρμα) they were clearly talking about gametes (the reproductive material). Two of the most prominent deserve our attention: After the destruction of Sodom and the loss of their mother, Lot's two daughters saw the need to preserve their father's seed. We read:

> And it came to pass on the morrow, that the firstborn said unto the younger, Behold, I lay yesternight with my father: let us make him drink wine this night also; and go thou in, [and] lie with him, that we may preserve **seed** of our father (Genesis 19:34 KJV).

The second of the two is perhaps as blatant as can be concerning just what is meant by seed: "And if any man's seed [*zara* זֶרַע] of copulation go out from him, then he shall wash all his flesh in water, and be unclean until the even" (Leviticus 15:16 KJV).

In summary, we note that the Scriptures are replete with statements that Jesus would come from the seed of Abraham and his descendants. If the Bible is this specific about the male seed, we ought not to question the Bible when it makes reference to the woman's seed in Genesis 3:15. Therefore the incarnation of Jesus required that He be connected to humanity genetically yet without sin.

THE GENETICS OF THE MESSIAH BECOMING FLESH

The incarnation of Jesus was nothing less than the genetic combination of the celestial (Holy Spirit) and the terrestrial (Mary). We must stress, however, that Jesus as the second person of the Godhead existed from eternity past (Micah 5:2) and did not begin to exist at the Holy Spirit's overshadowing of Mary—He is eternal and has always existed. Nevertheless, the incarnation (becoming flesh) was at the point of conception which was when the Holy Spirit mingled seed (DNA i.e. information) with humanity. After waiting four thousand years the promise of the Seed of the Woman would be fulfilled. From the point of the incarnation God would begin the process of redeeming mankind that so long ago had sinned and corrupted the image of God as well as losing the ability to commune with God. This pivotal moment would then find its fulfillment in the crucifixion and resurrection of this God-man thereby giving men the right to become children of God once more.

JUST WHAT IS A SEED?

Our understanding of genetics and Information Technology (IT) helps us to better understand what it means that we were and are corrupted. The reality is that our DNA is in fact the source code of humanity and it is the essence of the "seed" that Scripture so often talks about. Seed in modern terms is called a gamete which in the male is the sperm and in the female is the ovum. Thus when Mary conceived it meant that her ovum provided twenty three chromosomes and hence the Holy Spirit provided the other gamete (twenty three chromosomes). While it is possible that the Holy Spirit provided actual "sperm," it is unlikely. Sperm (from the male) would be likened to a missile which is carrying a warhead. The warhead is what causes the explosion and the missile simply gets it to the destination. It is not the carrying mechanism which is truly significant for conception, but the "payload"—that is the genetic material (information) that the sperm is carrying. Thus the Holy Spirit provided the twenty three chromosomes without the carrying mechanism. Given that the Holy Spirit (the third person of the Godhead) came upon her, there could not have been any need for millions of seeds. The Holy Spirit must have placed only one gamete (or set of twenty three chromosomes) directly into Mary's ovum, which necessarily resulted in the body for the Lord Jesus.[42]

OUR GENETIC CODE

When most of us come to a computer, we are interested in the applications that we can use to help us do our work, surf the Internet, play games, or watch movies. Underlying those processes is a code that is written with ones and zeros. All of the applications are reduced to a binary (base two) code which a machine can understand. Even the most sophisticated computer program is reduced to a series of ones and zeros. In every living creature there is a coded message that is not a base two but a base four code known as DNA. Dr. Gitt, in his book *In the Beginning Was Information*, describes how DNA is a store of information:

> The storage medium is the DNA molecule (deoxyribonucleic acid) which resembles a double helix. A DNA fiber is only about two millionths of a millimeter thick, so that it is barely visible with an electron microscope. The chemical letters A, G, T, and C are located on this information tape, and the amount of information is so immense in the case of human DNA that it would stretch from the North Pole to the equator if it was typed on paper, using standard letter sizes.[43]

This storage medium is capable of copying itself with astounding precision as Dr. Gitt explains:

> The DNA is structured in such a way that it can be replicated every time a cell divides in two. Both of the two daughter cells have to have identically the same genetic information after the division and copying processes. This replication is so precise that it can be compared to 280 clerks copying the entire Bible sequentially each one from the previous one with at most one single letter being transposed erroneously in the entire copying process.
>
> When a DNA string is replicated, the double strand is unwound, and at the same time a complementary strand is constructed on each separate one, so that, eventually, there are two new double strands identical to the original one [...] One cell division lasts from 20 to 80 minutes, and during this time

the entire molecular library, equivalent to one thousand books, is copied correctly.[44]

The Master Programmer endowed us with perfect code and only at the fall of man did it become corrupted. This chemical code, built on the A, G, T, and C, becomes corrupted as a result of a shuffling of the order of those bits or a loss of one or more bits. Loss of data occurs through replication and through the decomposition of the medium (cf. CD ROM). Adam, as the father of the race and a direct creation of God, had a perfect code. There was no loss of data or corruption of the data in any way. Once he and Eve sinned, death (errors in the genetic code) entered our first parents and those errors have not only been passed to all of their descendants, but the loss of data has been increasing over time as would be consistent with data loss in the world of computers. John Sanford notes that this degradation of data is cumulative and will one day result in the extinction of the human race in his book *Genetic Entropy and the Mystery of the Genome*: "The extinction of the human genome appears to be just as certain and deterministic as the extinction of stars, the death of organisms, and the heat death of the universe."[45]

INFORMATION IS NON-MATERIAL

We must keep in mind that DNA is simply the medium which stores information. Information, however, is something distinct from the medium (or storage device). In his book, Dr. Gitt explains the difference between the two:

> Information requires a material medium for storage. If one writes some information with chalk on a blackboard, the chalk is the material carrier. If it is wiped off, the total quantity of chalk is still there, but the information has vanished. In this case the chalk was a suitable material medium, but the essential aspect was the actual arrangement of the particles of the chalk. And this arrangement was definitely not random, it had a mental origin. The same information that was written on the blackboard could also have been written on a magnetic

diskette. Certain tracks of the diskette then became magnetized, and also in this case there is a carrier for the information.[46]

An average blank CD ROM costs just pennies; it is the information on that disc which can cost hundreds, thousands, or even millions of dollars. However, regardless of how much data is written on the disc, the disc does not change at all in how much it weighs. Thus information is separate from the device holding it. The loss of data by erasing chalk from a chalkboard is analogous to the loss of data in our DNA. Of course, not all of the data in our DNA has been lost but a significant part of the message has been compromised and now the errors are being compounded with every successive generation. Humanity is suffering from an information loss in our own source code.

The most amazing thing about the seed (DNA) is the information that it contains, which was placed there by our Maker (the Master Programmer). What the modern science of Information Technology is just now discovering is that information does not just happen (which, incidentally, is an incredible proof for God and against evolution). Dr. Gitt explains that information is a fundamental entity and is therefore not a property of matter. He formulates several theorems in order to describe information. In theorem 1 he states: "The fundamental quantity **information is a nonmaterial** (mental) entity. It is not a property of matter, so that purely material processes are fundamentally precluded as sources of information" (emphasis mine).[47] In theorem 3 he notes that it is information which "comprises the nonmaterial foundation for all technological systems and for all works of art."[48]

If the information that we originally received from God is being compromised such that one day the entire human race will suffer the ultimate data corruption known as extinction, then we clearly need the Master Programmer to fix the source code. Fortunately, our Maker has provided a way for our code to be corrected. However, it required that the Maker Himself take on our code, mix it with His own, and then offer His blood. Through rebirth we are guaranteed a new body (eternal life) and we have been given the Holy Spirit as the down payment. Thus in the world to come our DNA (our code) will be restored and upgraded.

NORMAL CONCEPTION

Before we try to understand the genetics of the incarnation we need to have a grasp of what happens at the point of a normal conception. During the process of procreation approximately 250 million sperm swim toward the ovum. Both the ovum and the sperm are essentially very similar information. The sperm have a flagellum, which propels them on their quest, but the genetic information they carry inside is what is truly significant.

Our body's cells have forty-six individual chromosomes or twenty-three pairs (diploid). However, the egg and sperm cells have only twenty-three individual chromosomes such that when they combine (during fertilization) they will equal the forty-six individual (twenty-three diploid) chromosomes necessary for human life. The process by which the somatic (body) cells (forty-six chromosomes) are divided is called meiosis. The cells created, which are just the twenty-three individual chromosomes, are called haploid cells. During reproduction, the maternal and paternal gametes (haploid cells), "fuse at conception to produce a zygote, which will turn into a fetus and eventually into an adult human being" according Silke Schmidt writing in the Genetics Encyclopedia.[49] The Encyclopedia Britannica summarizes the process: "When two gametes unite during fertilization, each contributes its haploid set of chromosomes to the new individual, restoring the diploid number."[50]

THE INCARNATION

As we stated before, we need to emphasize that Jesus did not begin to exist at the incarnation—He is eternal and has always existed. Yet, the incarnation was the point at which the Godhead mingled seed (DNA i.e. information) with humanity. Let's consider the mechanics of the incarnation from what we have studied so far. Keep in mind that the following summary does not pretend to account for the entire mystery of what it is for God to take on flesh; nevertheless, we seek to embrace all of the information that God has revealed through His Word. Nor does this explanation account for all the potential reasons the incarnation was necessary. However, looking at the incarnation from a genetics perspective does demonstrate how Jesus could become one of us and yet remain free from sin.

Peter Underhill, in Encyclopedia.com, writes concerning the uniqueness of the Y chromosome and how it is passed from generation to generation unchanged:

> Since normally only one Y chromosome exists per cell, no pairing between X and Y occurs at meiosis, except at small regions. Normally, no crossing over occurs. Therefore, except for rare mutations that may occur during spermatogenesis, **a son will inherit an identical copy of his father's Y chromosome, and this copy is also essentially identical to the Y chromosomes carried by all his paternal forefathers, across the generations**. This is in contrast to the rest of his chromosomal heritage, which will be a unique mosaic of contributions from multiple ancestors created by the reshuffling process of recombination (emphasis mine).

This means that of the twenty-three individual chromosomes (haploid) in the gamete, only one (1/23) could potentially be a Y chromosome. Thus the other twenty-two chromosomes provided by the father's sperm will all be autosomes, or non-sex chromosomes. If the twenty-third chromosome is an X, then the resulting person will be a girl. However, if the sperm is carrying that one Y chromosome then the baby will be a boy. Nevertheless, Peter Underhill has stated that there is essentially no change of the Y chromosome from father to son from generation to generation. The X's in contrast will be a mosaic of his multiple ancestors. Learner.org's online textbook states the peculiarity in another way: "The lack of recombination means that the entire non-recombining portion of the Y is passed intact from father to son. A **male shares the same Y chromosome with his father, paternal grandfather, paternal great-grandfather**, and so on" (emphasis mine). Neil Bradman and Mark Thomas state the significance of implications of this reality perhaps as clearly as possible in light of our study in their article *Why Y? The Y Chromosome in the Study of Human Evolution, Migration and Prehistory.*

> Genesis, chapter 5, records "the generations of Adam": Adam begat Seth, Seth begat Enosh, Enosh begat Kenan ... down to Noah of the flood. Translated into modern genetic terms, the account could read "**Adam passed a copy of his Y chromosome to Seth, Seth passed a copy of his Y chromosome to Enosh, Enosh passed a copy of his Y chromosome to Kenan.**" ... and so on until **Noah was born carrying a copy of Adam's Y chromosome.** The Y chromosome is paternally inherited; human males have one while females have none. What is more, the Y chromosome a father passes to his son is, in large measure, **an unchanged copy of his own** (emphasis mine).

This means that whatever information was encoded in Adam's Y chromosome was passed on unchanged (virtually) to all of his descendants including all of us men alive today! However, if the information in the Y chromosome were faulty, then it would mean that all of his descendants (including us) would also have a faulty code. Discovering the exact make-up of the Y chromosome when Adam was first created is impossible for us to do, however, its current state may tell us something about the fall. The Y chromosome may in fact be a record of an event in the life of our original father. Bradman and Thomas suggest that the Y chromosome contains "a record of an event" in the life the man who passed on the current Y chromosome. However, because Bradman and Thomas are committed to the evolutionary paradigm they believe the event "had no effect on the life of the man in whom the change occurred nor, indeed, **on the life of his descendants**" (emphasis mine). Is it possible that the recorded event is not something that had "little or no effect," but is in some way the record of the genetic fall of our first father? Thus Adam not only died spiritually by virtue of losing the Holy Spirit, but his genetic information (as recorded specifically in the Y chromosome) was corrupted. God stated that in the day that Adam ate of the tree of the knowledge of good and evil he would die (Genesis 2:17).

Death, it appears, entered into Adam's Y chromosome (in some way unique and different than the X) that very moment, causing him to go from being genetically perfect to having serious errors in his code that would eventually cause a "crash." Occasionally people who use computers will experience a scenario where the operating system experiences a "fatal crash." The crash occurs because there is some conflict in the code of the program. Though the program may be able to sustain data loss for a short period, if uncorrected, the program will eventually crash. In Adam's case, that crash took 930 years, but he did eventually experience a complete shutdown.

If that is correct, then the Y chromosome (and all of his chromosomes) must have been complete and whole before Adam fell into sin. We know that he was free from all imperfections because God created him and declared him to be good and because death entered into the world via Adam's sin. Yet, the Y chromosome seems to contain something so deleterious that our Savior could not have shared it. After all, every copy of the Y chromosome (that is, every male descendant of Adam) would necessarily have the same genetic flaw that would also lead to the ultimate crash. In order to save mankind on a genetic level, a new Y chromosome would need to be provided. Furthermore, through the disobedience of Adam all of creation was made subject to corruption as Paul states in Romans 8.

> For the earnest expectation of the **creation eagerly waits** for the revealing of the **sons of God**. For the **creation was subjected to futility**, not willingly, but because of Him who subjected it in

hope; because the creation itself also will be **delivered from the bondage of corruption into the glorious liberty of the children of God**. For we know that the whole creation groans and labors with birth pangs together until now. Not only that, but we also who have the firstfruits of the Spirit, even we ourselves groan within ourselves, eagerly waiting for the adoption, the redemption of our body (Romans 8:19-23).

In some way, Adam's disobedience and subsequent corruption spread to all creation. It could be, though we cannot be sure, that Eve was included under the "creation." In any event women are seemingly not excepted due to the fact that every daughter received twenty-three haploid chromosomes from her biological father who has a Y chromosome and therefore a man, carrying Adam's faulty Y chromosome, was directly involved in her procreation.

THE ORIGINAL DATA LOSS A.K.A. "ORIGINAL SIN"

Scripture testifies to the "blue screen of death" which we could argue has been historically known as original sin. Paul discusses at length that all face the effects of sin (corruption) even though one man was responsible for bringing it into the world. "For since through man *is* the death, also through man *is* a rising again of the dead"(1 Corinthians 15:21 Revised Young's Literal Translation RYLT).[56] Paul then reiterates and summarizes by saying: "for even as **in Adam all die**, so also in the Christ all shall be made alive, and each in his proper order, a **first-fruit Christ**, afterward those who are the Christ's, in his presence" (1 Corinthians 15:22-23 RYLT). Jesus not only rose from the dead, but also mixed with mankind. Thus our resurrection seems to also entail being mixed with the Lord. Bible commentator Thomas Constable notes that the death and resurrection are not just some kind of "spiritual" entities but are in fact physical and literal.

> Adam derived life from another, God; but Christ is Himself the fountain of life. Adam was the first man in the old creation, and, like him, all of his sons die physically. Christ is the first

man in the new creation, and, like Him, all of His sons will live physically (cf. Rom. 5:12-19). [...] Both Adam and Jesus were men. Therefore our resurrection will be a human resurrection, not some "spiritual" type of resurrection. Physical resurrection is as inevitable for the son of Jesus Christ as physical death is for the son of Adam (Constable Notes).

Paul has a longer discussion of how sin came into the world through one man (Adam) and how death, therefore, was passed or spread to all men.

Therefore, just as **sin came into the world through one man, and death through sin**, and so death spread to all men because all sinned—for sin indeed was in the world before the law was given, but sin is not counted where there is no law. Yet **death reigned from Adam to Moses**, even over those whose sinning was not like the transgression of Adam, who was a type of the one who was to come. But the free gift is not like the trespass. **For if many died through one man's trespass**, much more have the grace of God and the free gift by the grace of that one man Jesus Christ abounded for many. And the free gift is not like the result of that one man's sin. **For the judgment following one trespass brought condemnation**, but the free gift following many trespasses brought justification. For if, **because of one man's trespass, death reigned through that one man**, much more will those who receive the abundance of grace and the free gift of righteousness reign in life through the one man Jesus Christ. Therefore, **as one trespass led to condemnation for all men**, so one act of righteousness leads to justification and life for all men. For **as by the one man's disobedience the many were made sinners**, so by the one man's obedience the many will be made righteous (Romans 5:12-19).

Though the sin of Adam was indeed moral in that he broke the command of God, the result was physical as well as spiritual. We have already discussed how his sinning resulted in immediate spiritual death—the loss of the Holy Spirit. However, it also appears from the two above passages that the concept of original sin—that is how we are born in sin—is due to the fact that every child of Adam is also a genetic copy of Adam and Eve (of course with genetic recombination). We might think of it like sourdough bread in which each time a new loaf of bread is made, a little bit of the starter dough is taken and thrown into the mix. In that way, the starter dough is in every new batch.

So it is with Adam's genes: we are all copies of him and therefore whatever coding errors he had would be passed on to us from the very point of conception. The fact that sin is attributed to Adam and not to Eve, though she was the first to break God's command, seems readily explainable. When God formed Eve He took from his side, which of course contains bone marrow. In bone marrow are the stem cells from which all other cells in the body can be replicated. Therefore, God merely borrowed some code from Adam (removed the Y chromosome and added a second X chromosome) and voila—a female clone of Adam. Upon seeing her, Adam even declared: "This at last is bone of my bones and flesh of my flesh; she shall be called Woman, because she was taken out of Man" (Genesis 2:23). Therefore we draw the conclusion that it was the master disc (Adam) that counts when making copies; Eve received her code from Adam. This understanding would certainly not detract from Adam acting as our federal head, but would serve to clarify how exactly that sin was passed and why we are "in sin" from conception.

The solution to the problem is analogous to the problem itself—also an idea that we have already examined in part; John states that "No one born of God makes a practice of sinning, for God's seed abides in him, and he cannot keep on sinning because he has been born of God" (1 John 3:9). The new birth will not merely be a clearing of our debts (though thank the Lord it includes that!) but we will truly be reborn with new bodies. We get to take possession of our new bodies (with their correct DNA, i.e. information) in heaven. Until that time we have the Holy Spirit as a down payment (guarantee).

CONCLUSIONS OF THE INCARNATION

As our understanding of genetics and specifically the Y chromosome stands right now, we are able to conclude that if Adam was corrupted genetically then his descendants would be too and something particular to the data errors in the Y chromosome was especially significant. That means that the data loss was extremely significant and as such crashes in the system will result in time. Since the Y chromosome is passed from father to son (identically), every son will experience the same data loss. Though women do not carry the Y chromosome, they are still under the curse (data loss) because every daughter has a father who is a son of Adam. Therefore, whether son or daughter, all have shared in the genetic loss that Adam first experienced. However in the conception of Jesus' incarnation, the Y chromosome from Adam was not passed on. Therefore Jesus must have (in the flesh) had a perfect Y chromosome! Though while connected genetically to humanity by way of the X chromosomes, Jesus was not a carrier of the Y chromosome which Adam had passed to all subsequent generations. Jesus became the first fruits of the resurrection because one day, by way of the "seed of God" that we have received as believers, we will mingle with our Creator.

We can thus summarize the genetic events of the incarnation as such: Jesus, who, as eternal God, is spirit (John 4:24). As the "source code" [57] of all living things, He is also the prime "data/ information" which is/was non-material. His "information" was put into a medium. In order to encode the information in the physical medium (DNA) the Holy Spirit did apparently one of two options. He either: 1) made ex nihilo the DNA material (amino acids etc.) or 2) used the existing material in the egg as the medium into which Jesus' non-material spirit went into. The Holy Spirit then fused "the Jesus" gamete (spermatocyte) with Mary's gamete (oocyte) (recall that a gamete contains DNA, which is stored information, which is a non-material entity). The fusion of the two gametes is when the incarnation (becoming flesh cf. John

1:14) occurred. The chromosomes from Mary and the Holy Spirit fused to make the (body of the) new Adam. Because Jesus is the second Adam, and because we are genetically connected with the first Adam, we must also be mingled with Jesus' DNA ("He shall see *His* seed," Isaiah 53:10; see also 1 John 3:9; 1 Peter 1:23).

CHAPTER FOUR

Reborn with the Seed of the Messiah

In ISAIAH 53:10 we are given a very important aspect of our salvation. We see that the Lord was pleased to bruise the Messiah and offer Him up for our sakes. The text goes on to say that "He shall see His seed."

> Yet it pleased the LORD to bruise Him; He has put Him to grief. When You make His soul an offering for sin, He shall see His **seed** [*zera* זֶרַע], He shall prolong His days, And the pleasure of the LORD shall prosper in His hand (Isaiah 53:10).

The Hebrew word used for seed (some translations say "offspring") is *zera* (זֶרַע) which is the same word that we looked at concerning the physical and biological offspring (children) of Abraham and David. The word very much meant someone who is descended from another. The question then obviously is how could the Lord Jesus have "seed"? While the Gnostic Gospels suggest that Jesus had sexual relations with Mary Magdalene and consequently had children, such talk is considered to be extremely heretical and anti-biblical.

How, then, can the text be taken literally since it is not referring to the Lord having physical relations with a woman? The answer is found in 1 John 3:9 and 1 Peter 1:23, both of which refer to God having seed: "Whoever has been born of God does not sin, for His seed [*sperma* σπερμα] remains in him and he cannot sin, because he has been born of God," (First John 3:9). First John 3:9 states very clearly that God's seed (*sperma* σπερμα) is in the believer because he has been born again. Said another way, one who is born again has God's seed inside him. That means that all true believers have God's seed in them. Peter confirms this when he says: "having been born again, not of corruptible **seed**[58] but incorruptible, through the word [*logos* λόγος] of God which lives and abides forever" (1 Peter 1:23).

Peter adds that the quality of the seed is not perishable (*phthartos* φθαρτός) but is imperishable (*aphthartos* ᾽φθαρτος). The living and abiding Word of God must refer to the Lord Jesus Himself (and not merely the text of the Bible) since the term Logos [λόγος] is used just like in John 1:1 which declares the Logos to be the One who created everything. John confirms being born of God in his first epistle when he says: "If you know that He is righteous, you know that everyone who practices righteousness is **born** of Him"(1 John 2:29). This statement is then restated: "We know that whoever is **born of God** does not sin; but he who **has been born of God** keeps himself, and the wicked one does not touch him" (1 John 5:18).

REBORN WITH A NEW IMAGE

The fact that we are born again through the Word of God points us back to Isaiah 53:10, which states that the Suffering Servant will see His seed. We are indeed born of God's (or Messiah's) seed which is why we are able to have a part in the age to come. Jesus could not have stressed this enough with Nicodemus when He said that we must be born from above; and if we are not, then we will not have a part in the kingdom of heaven. Jesus wasn't just speaking allegorically. In fact, now with an understanding of Information Technology and also genetics and DNA, we can begin to grasp just a bit of what is going to occur when we come into the Lord's presence. Here and now our DNA remains corrupted, but we who are trusting in the Lord are given the Holy Spirit as a down payment. When we, through the rapture or death, enter into the Lord's presence we will be given our new bodies which will still be "us" but our DNA (our non-material information) will be repaired. In fact, from all that we have gained so far, we can conclude that we will literally be mingled (our DNA [information] combined) with the Lord for only His seed is imperishable (incorruptible). Paul greatly elaborates on this in 1 Corinthians 15, which we have examined already. We must be combined with His seed so that we can be like Him and be with Him forever. It would seem obvious that man and his seed are perishable and corrupted. The fact that everyone eventually dies is proof that man's seed is perishable; but God's seed is incorruptible.

REBORN AS A SON OF GOD

At this point we need to follow the thread of sons of God throughout the New Testament as it pertains to the believer (we will deal with the Old Testament reference to the sons of God in part two). Scripture demonstrates that sons of God are in fact direct creations of God. From Luke we learn that Adam was a son of God. Luke 3:23 gives the genealogy of Jesus in order to show that He is the promised Redeemer. Luke traces His lineage through David and sons, then back to Judah, Jacob, Isaac, Abraham, Shem, Noah, and even Adam. Luke begins:

> Now Jesus Himself began His ministry at about thirty years of age, being (as was supposed) the son of Joseph, the son of Heli, the son of Matthat, the son of Levi, the son of Melchi, the son of Janna, the son of Joseph (Luke 3:23-24).

Luke shows that each person was the son of so and so. Heli was the son of Matthat, (who was) the son of Levi, (who was) the son of Melchi, and so on. He finishes the genealogy by arriving at the beginning of time: "the son of Enos, the son of Seth, the son of Adam, the son of God" (Luke 3:38). Enos was the son of Seth who was the son of Adam who was the son of God. Thus, Adam is declared to be the son of God by Luke. You and I are not naturally born sons of God. We are naturally born sons of Adam, for that is ultimately who our father is. We are not direct creations of God, but a procreation of our mother and father, who were in turn a procreation of their mothers and fathers all the way back to Adam. Thus, we are truly sons of Adam.

Thus far we can deduce that the term son of God is used for beings that are direct creations of God. This conclusion is shared by Bible scholar E. W. Bullinger who states:

> It is only by the Divine specific act of creation that any created being can be called "a son of God." For that which is "born of the flesh is flesh." God is spirit and that which is "born of the Spirit is spirit" (John 3:6). Hence Adam is called a "son of God" in Luke 3.38. Those "in Christ" having the "new nature" which is by the direct creation of God (2 Cor. 5:17, Eph. 2:10) can be, and are called "sons of God" (John 1.13 Rom. 8.14, 15. 1 John 3.1).

> This is why angels are called "sons of God" in every other place where the expression is used in the Old Testament. Job 1.6; 2.1; 38.7. Ps. 29.1; 89.6; Dan. 3.25 (no art.). We have no authority or right to take the expression in Gen. 6.4 in any other sense. Moreover in Gen. 6.2 the Sept. renders it "angels" (The Companion Bible, Appendix 23, emphasis mine).

Adam of course was made in the image and likeness of God. Since the term son of God is used for angels it would seem that they share the image and likeness of God. The main difference between them and Adam, as we have examined, would be that the angels were created as spirits whereas Adam was made of the dust and God's breath (Holy Spirit) was breathed into him.

JUST WHO IS A SON OF GOD?

The Scriptures reveal that sons of God are specifically a direct creation of God. Jesus is referred to as the only begotten (*monogenes* μονογενης) or unique Son of God and so falls in to another category (see discussion on the Triune Nature of God in appendix one). Nevertheless, the term is used to speak of beings that were specially created directly by the hand of God. Let's consider the following: on the sixth day God created Adam. Adam has no human father, rather he is the father of all subsequent humans. Hence all of the descendants of Adam (that includes every person that has and will ever live) are by nature sons (and daughters) of Adam. This is exactly what the Hebrew Scriptures call all humans (*benei Adam*)—sons and daughters of Adam, for that is what we are. Thus to be human is to be a *ben Adam* or son of Adam. And Adam was of course not a son of Adam, for that would be an oxymoron. Adam was, as Luke says, a son of God (*tou theou* του θεου). The common thread between Adam, as a son of God, and the sons of God in the Old Testament, are not that all are human or sons of Adam—in fact, none of them is. The common thread is that they are all direct creations of God.

HOW TO BECOME A BEN ELOHIM

What about the New Testament references to the believer as a son of God? Wouldn't that seem to contradict the conclusion we have just reached? Actually, the contrary is the case. The primary purpose Jesus had in coming to earth was to make it possible for us to become sons of God. In the Gospel of John, we read:

> But as many as **received Him**, to them He **gave the right to become children of God**, to those who believe in His name: who were born, not of blood, nor of the will of the flesh, nor of the will of man, but of God (John 1:12-13).

What we see here is that we who are naturally born as sons or daughters of Adam (*benei Adam*) have the possibility of becoming *benei Elohim* (children [or sons] of God). The power does not lie in us; it is by God's will and not man's. This conversion to a son of God is not through blood (on a physical level), but to those that received Him (and have believed in His name). John's summary statement is evidenced in Jesus' words to Nicodemus, the teacher of Israel who came to Jesus one evening to learn what was required to be part of the kingdom of God. Jesus reproved him for not already knowing what was contained in the Scriptures.

> Jesus replied to him, "Truly, truly I tell you, unless **a person is born from above he cannot see the kingdom of God**. [...] truly I tell you, unless a person is born of water and Spirit he cannot enter the kingdom of God. What is born of the flesh is flesh, and what is **born of the Spirit is spirit**. Do not be astonished that I said to you, 'All of you must be born from above'" (John 3:3-7 ISV).

Jesus clearly states that one must be *born from above* (or "again"). The first birth, earthly, terrestrial, and purely material (as a son of Adam) is not sufficient if one is to be part of the kingdom of God. Paul elaborates on this concept when he states concerning our physical bodies:

> For the trumpet will sound, and the dead [physically] will be **raised incorruptible**, and we **shall be changed**. For this corruptible [body] must put on incorruption, and this mortal [body] must put on immortality (1 Corinthians 15:52-53).

So too, Jesus explains to Nicodemus that we are naturally born corrupted (physically and morally) and a new birth is absolutely necessary. Paul supports this claim by stating: "Therefore, if anyone is **in Christ**, he is a **new creation**; old things have passed away; behold, **all things** have **become new**" (2 Corinthians 5:17). He also says: "For in Christ Jesus neither circumcision nor uncircumcision avails anything, but a **new creation**" (Galatians 6:15). There is simply no way that our current bodies and souls can enter into God's presence "as is"; we have to start over. However, starting over means that we become a direct creation of God (*ben Elohim*) as well as continuing to be a *ben Adam*.

The bottom line is that we have a new nature when we are born again by believing in His name. Jesus states this concerning our new nature (and future nature, see Luke 20:36) "for they cannot die anymore, because they are equal to angels and are sons of God, being sons of the resurrection." Paul also states (Romans 8:14): "For all who are **led by the Spirit of God** are **sons of God**." He also says (Galatians 3:26): "for in Christ Jesus you are all sons of God, through faith." The reverse of Paul's statements are that if one is not led by the Spirit then he is not a son of God and also if one is not "in Christ" then he is not a son of God. All who are not sons of God have only been born once as sons of Adam. Without the second birth as a son of God one cannot see the kingdom of heaven.

Thus before the cross of Jesus there were no sons of Adam (*benei Adam* i.e. humans) who were *also* sons of God. The right for humans (*benei Adam*—sons of Adam) to become sons of God only occurred after the finished work of the cross.[59] Therefore all references to sons of God[60] in the Old Testament (that is to say before the cross and resurrection) were angels. They were angels because they were direct creations of God.

The conception and birth of Jesus to make us into sons of God was only half of the promise that God made to Adam and Eve. He said that her seed would be the one to destroy the enemy, so when God spoke of "your seed" to Satan, we should expect that one will come who will be the opposite of the Messiah. We have seen that seed is used to refer to sperm or ovum (gametes or genetic material). Jesus (speaking of His incarnation) was the perfect fusion between heaven and earth. Given that "her seed" found such a literal and precise fulfillment, should we not then look for an equally literal and precise fulfillment concerning Satan's seed?

PART TWO

PAST ATTEMPTS TO CORRUPT THE IMAGE

CHAPTER FIVE

The Sons of God in the Days of Noah

WE HAVE EXPLORED half of the promise given so many years ago—that "He," that is, the Messiah-Jesus, would bruise the Serpent's head. Jesus came in the flesh from heaven by way of the Holy Spirit who mixed with the seed of woman. If this was true of "her seed," then according the hermeneutical consistency, the seed of the Serpent ought to be interpreted in like manner. What this means is that since Jesus (in His bodily incarnation) was a genetic mix between the heavenly (Holy Spirit) and earthly (Mary), the same ought to be for the other part of the verse and therefore true of Satan's seed; that is to say that he (and his angels) would mix his (genetic) seed (gametes) with a human thereby creating a hybrid between the demonic and human. The Bible calls this kind of progeny Nephilim—that is, fallen ones. We will explore in detail in this section just what happened in the days of Noah and in part three what is happening now and how events will culminate at the time of Jesus' coming.

Jesus gave His disciples an important key to understanding what the last days would be like—they would be like the sudden destruction that came upon the earth in the days of Noah.

> But as the days of Noah were, so also will the coming of the Son of Man be. For as in the days before the flood, they were eating and drinking, marrying and giving in marriage, until the day that Noah entered the ark, and did not know until the flood came and took them all away, so also will the coming of the Son of Man be (Matthew 24:37-39).

What happened in the days of Noah has a direct correlation as to what we ought to expect in the last days. The inhabitants of the earth had been warned repeatedly by Noah, the preacher of righteousness, but they failed to listen. Peter, under the direction of the Holy Spirit, makes this revelation concerning the days of Noah and the destruction that came: "the Divine longsuffering waited in the days of Noah, while the ark was being prepared, in which a few, that is, eight souls, were saved through water" (1 Peter 3:20). In his second epistle Peter writes:

> For if God did **not spare the angels** who sinned, but **cast them down to hell** [*tartarosas* ταρταρώσας the underworld prison] and delivered them into chains of darkness, to be reserved for judgment; and **did not spare the ancient world**, but saved Noah, one of eight people, a preacher of righteousness, bringing in the flood on the world of the ungodly (2 Peter 2:4-5).

Jesus and Peter are telling us more than just the swiftness of the destruction that came upon the earth. Their words give us clues to the condition of the world at that time. We must not miss that the first century Jew, without any apparent exception, believed that in the days of Noah, demons (sons of God) came down to earth and had relations with women, spawning a race of demonic-human hybrids (the proof will be given in the following chapters).

Thus, to fully understand Jesus' statement "as the days of Noah were, so also will the coming of the Son of Man be," we must first understand what life was like in Noah's days. If we fail to understand what this passage means, we will not only miss some very significant historical issues but also our view of the end times will be lacking as well. First of all, let's analyze the text and build our comprehension one level at a time.

When humankind began to multiply on the face of the earth, and daughters were born to them, the **sons of God** [*benei haelohim* בְּנֵי־הָאֱלֹהִים] saw that the **daughters of humankind** [*banot haadam* בְּנוֹת הָאָדָם] were beautiful. Thus **they took wives** for themselves from any they chose. So the LORD said, "My spirit will not remain in humankind indefinitely, since they are mortal. They will remain for 120 more years." The **Nephilim** were on the earth in those days (and also after this) when the **sons of God** were having **sexual relations** with the **daughters of humankind**, who **gave birth to their children**. They were the mighty heroes of old, the famous men. But the LORD saw that the wickedness of humankind had become great on the earth. Every inclination of the thoughts of their minds was only evil all the time. The LORD regretted that he had made humankind on the earth, and he was highly offended. So the LORD said,

> "I will wipe humankind, whom I have created, from the face of the earth—everything from humankind to animals, including creatures that move on the ground and birds of the air, for I regret that I have made them" (Genesis 6:1-7 NET).

At the time of Noah (and the subsequent judgment), the population of the earth grew dramatically. The text says that men (*adam*—this is a general Hebrew expression for men in general, who are of course, sons of Adam in a literal sense) increased in numbers; there were conceivably over ten billion people[61] at the time! As a natural consequence, daughters were born to the race in general but then another group took notice of these female humans, namely, the sons of God. The sons of God took them and fathered offspring known as Nephilim. To understand what was happening then we need to clearly identify the sons of God.

THE SONS OF GOD

The phrase the "sons of God" appears ten times in the Bible (NKJV): twice in Genesis 6, three times in the book of Job, and five times in the New Testament (which we already examined). In Hebrew this phrase *benei haelohim* (בְּנֵי הָאֱלֹהִים) appears four times while *benei elohim* (בְּנֵי אֱלֹהִים) appears once in Job 38:7—the only variation is the definite article. God responds to Job's request to show up and explain the meaning of the tremendous suffering that Job has just endured (chapter 38:7) by asking where he was in the beginning: "When the morning **stars** sang together, and all the **sons of God** shouted for joy?" (Job 38:7).

God makes reference to the fact that Job was not there when He laid the foundation of the earth and the implication is that no human was there for that matter. Therefore we see from the usage here that "sons of God" refers to angels. This is backed by the Septuagint which translates all three of the Job passages as "angels" instead of the Hebrew sons of God—evidently the Jews who translated Job into Greek from Hebrew felt that sons of God were angels and not humans. [62] The NET Bible commentary confirms this understanding: "In the Book of Job the phrase clearly refers to angelic beings" (NET Bible Commentary Genesis 6:2). In the beginning of the book of Job we read:

> Now there was a day when the **sons of God** came to present themselves before the LORD, and Satan also came among them. And the LORD said to Satan, "From where do you come?" So Satan answered the LORD and said, "From going to and fro on the earth, and from walking back and forth on it" (Job 1:6-7).

Again, we note that the Septuagint has translated "sons of God" as "the angels of God" (*oi angeloi tou theou* οι αγγελοι του θεου). To the ancient Jew at least, this phrase was clearly talking about angelic beings. The fact that Satan appeared among their number would suggest that these "sons of God" are fallen angels. After all, from what we read concerning angels in both the Old Testament (Isaiah, Ezekiel, Daniel, etc.) and New

Testament (especially Revelation), angels (that is the good ones) already have access to the presence of God. Thus, to state that one day they came before the Lord would seem a bit odd unless it referred to demons. We should also remember that the term (*malakh* מַלְאָךְ) in Hebrew and (*angelos* αγγελος) in Greek both generally mean "messenger." The messenger can be either good or bad and can be earthly (a man) or heavenly (an angelic being). Jesus at the judgment of the nations: "will also say to those on the left hand, 'Depart from Me, you cursed, into the everlasting fire prepared for the devil and his angels [*tois angelois* τοις αγγελοις]'"(Matthew 25:41). If the devil has angels and they are cast into the lake of fire, then they cannot be good angels. Thus they are fallen angels also known as demons.

From the references in Job and how the term is translated in both the Septuagint and Targumim, we conclude that the term "sons of God" is referring to angelic beings (good or bad). The fact that Satan appeared with the sons of God and the fact that Jesus refers to the devil and his angels leads us to further conclude that the reference in Genesis Chapter 6 is talking about fallen angels (demons).

The New English Translation (NET Bible) commentary discusses the three different positions commonly held and emphasizes that the "angel" interpretation is favorable over the others.

There are three major interpretations of the phrase here. (1) In the Book of Job the phrase clearly refers to angelic beings. In Genesis 6 the "sons of God" are distinct from "humankind," suggesting they were not human. This is consistent with the use of the phrase in Job. Since the passage speaks of these beings cohabiting with women, **they must have taken physical** form or possessed the bodies of men. An early Jewish tradition preserved in *1 En.* 6-7 elaborates on this angelic revolt and even names the ringleaders. (2) Not all scholars accept the angelic interpretation of the "sons of God," however. Some argue that the "sons of

God" were members of Seth's line, traced back to God through Adam in Genesis 5, while the "daughters of humankind" were descendants of Cain. But, as noted above, the text **distinguishes the "sons of God" from humankind (which would include the Sethites as well as the Cainites)** and suggests that the **"daughters of humankind"** are **human women** in general, **not just Cainites.** (3) Others identify the "sons of God" as powerful tyrants, perhaps demon-possessed, who viewed themselves as divine and, following the example of Lamech (see Gen 4:19), practiced polygamy. But usage of **the phrase "sons of God" in Job militates against this view** (NET Notes Genesis 6:2, emphasis mine).

NEITHER MARRY NOR ARE GIVEN IN MARRIAGE

To some people, fallen angels having the ability to take physical form and procreate would seem to create a contradiction in Scripture. In Matthew 22:30 we read: "For in the resurrection they neither marry nor are given in marriage, but are like angels in heaven." This would seem to say that angels are not capable of having offspring and if that is the case, then Genesis 6 could certainly not be referring to fallen angels having some type of sexual relations with women. The parallel passage in Luke sheds more light on the text and seems to be a fuller rendering of what Jesus said on the subject whereas the Matthean and Markan accounts are abbreviated. In Luke we read:

> "But those who are considered worthy to attain to that age and to the resurrection from the dead neither marry nor are given in marriage, **for they cannot die anymore**, because they are equal to angels and are sons of God, being sons of the resurrection" (Luke 20:35-36).

Notice that Jesus says that those who attain that age and the resurrection from the dead neither marry nor are given in marriage "**for** they cannot die anymore." The thrust of the passage is **not** the potential of sexual ability in heaven! Remember, the Sadducees, who denied the resurrection, were trying to pull a fast one on

Jesus by asking whose wife the woman (having seven husbands) would be in heaven. The question and answer had nothing to do with the *ability* to pass on seed but rather to the fact that **there is a resurrection of the dead**; the new order is different than the here and now. God told Adam and Eve to be fruitful (that is to have sexual relations) **and fill the earth**. From Jesus' words we see that there will be no need for anymore procreation (to fill the earth) **"for they cannot die anymore."** However, this verse cannot be used to prove that angelic beings lacked the ability to mingle their seed with the daughters of men. It would seem that they were merely **forbidden** to do so (as we will see from 2 Peter and Jude as well as extra-biblical sources).

CONCLUSION

We saw earlier that the term "sons of God" refers to angels and humans who are direct creations of God. Angels are all by definition sons of God since they do not have parents but were produced directly by God. We therefore conclude that the sons of God in Genesis 6 were in fact angels who had relations with the daughters of Adam. The text in Genesis 6 doesn't say if they were good or bad angels but based on the flood that followed it is safe to assume that they were fallen angels. Nevertheless, how could fallen angels materialize themselves (biblically) in order to have physical relations and propagate their seed?

CHAPTER SIX

The Nature of the Spiritual Dimension

ANGELS OR DEMONS physically materializing themselves in our dimension, let alone having physical relations with women, is a difficult concept for many people to accept. According to the Bible, there is another realm, another dimension that is parallel to our earth-based dimension; it is a dimension filled with beings. Though we can't know all there is to know about that realm, Scripture still gives us many clues to be able to stitch together a decent mosaic of what it looks like.

First of all, we need to define terms—we will start with our dimension since we (generally) understand it intuitively. In the beginning God created the earth, which for simplicity we will just refer to as dirt. God then took some very fine particles of that material (known as dust) and formed Adam. We now understand that all living things are fundamentally composed of carbon atoms. We are earthly because we are made from the earth—dirt if you will. God even pronounces Adam's fate after the fall that he would return to dust because he was made of the dust. "In the sweat of your face you shall eat bread till you return to the ground, for out of it you were taken; for dust you are, and to dust you shall return" (Genesis 3:19).

When it comes to things in the other dimension, we cannot say what they are made of other than that the nature of their composition is spirit. What exactly is spirit? Unlike dirt, which we can put under a microscope and see the individual atoms in it, spirit already seems to be the most fundamental state. Thayer's Greek Lexicon defines *pneuma* (πνευμα) as: "a spirit, i.e. a simple essence, devoid of all or at least all grosser matter, and possessed of the power of knowing, desiring, deciding, and acting" (Thayer's *pneuma*). Ultimately, Scripture itself will serve as the best method of ascertaining the true meaning of things that are of a spiritual nature.

Perhaps the first and most obvious thing that can be said about spirit is that it is non-material—it is not made up of dirt (carbon atoms) or any other material from this dimension. The substance of the spirit is completely from that dimension (the spiritual realm). Jesus said after His resurrection: "a spirit does not have flesh and bones as you see that I have" (Luke 24:39). Beings that are of that realm are not comprised of matter. Psalm 104:4 gives a general description of angels as spirits and their composition: "Who makes His angels spirits, His ministers a flame of fire". Beings from that dimension, however, are able to interact with ours.

SPIRITUAL BEINGS CAN TOUCH US

A number of verses in Scripture describe spirits (angels or demons) touching, moving, throwing, or disrupting a human in some way. In the book of Job we read that a spirit passed by that could not be seen with the eyes but could be felt by the body:

> Then a spirit passed before my face; the hair on my body stood up. It stood still, but I could not discern its appearance. A form [*t'munah* תְּמוּנָה] *was* before my eyes; *there was* silence; then I heard a voice *saying:* 'Can a mortal be more righteous

than God? Can a man be more pure than his Maker? If He puts no trust in His servants, *if* He charges His angels with error, how much more those who dwell in houses of clay, whose foundation is in the dust, *who* are crushed before a moth? (Job 4:15-19).

In this example the spiritual entity brushed by so closely that the hair on the body stood up and there was a form that was indiscernible. Then the contrast is made between mortals, who are of dust, and angels who are spirit. Even though the angel was spirit, there was a particular form that the witness could not make out.

The following verses demonstrate that angels, which are spirit, in some way interact with our physical dimension. The action words in the verses are highlighted:

- Now the two angels **came** to Sodom in the evening, and Lot was sitting in the gate of Sodom. When Lot **saw** [*them,*] he rose to meet them (Genesis 19:1).

- Then David spoke to the LORD when he saw the angel who was **striking** the people (2 Samuel 24:17).

- Then as he lay and slept [...], suddenly an angel **touched** him (1 Kings 19:5).

- An angel who **cut down** every mighty man of valor, leader, and captain in the camp of the king of Assyria (2 Chronicles 32:21).

- My God sent His angel and **shut** the lions' mouths (Daniel 6:22).

- For an angel **went down** at a certain time into the pool and **stirred up** the water (John 5:4).

- An angel of the Lord **opened** the prison doors and **brought them out** (Acts 5:19).

- Now behold, an angel of the Lord **stood** by *him*, and a light shone in the prison; and he **struck** Peter on the side and **raised** him up, saying, "Arise quickly!" And his **chains fell off** *his* hands (Acts 12:7).

- Then immediately an angel of the Lord **struck** him, because he did not give glory to God (Acts 12:23).

- For Satan himself **transforms** himself into an angel of light (2 Corinthians 11:14).

- Do not forget to entertain strangers, for by so [*doing*] some have unwittingly **entertained** angels (Hebrews 13:2).

What we see is that angels, who reside in the spiritual realm, have bodies and can materialize themselves in our dimension on occasion. Thus we can conclude that spiritual things are not nebulous abstractions. In other words, things that come from the realm of the spirit are every bit as real and tangible as things here but they are not of material (earthly) substance.

SPIRITUAL FOOD AND DRINK

This conclusion is proven by Paul in his retelling of the children of Israel passing through the Red Sea. He states: "brethren, I do not want you to be unaware that all our fathers were under the cloud, all passed through the sea" (1 Corinthians 10:1). Here Paul is stating a historical fact which is easily verifiable from the book of Exodus: "And the people of Israel **went into the midst of the sea** on dry ground, the waters being a wall to them on their right hand and on their left" (Exodus 14:22). Paul then states that: "all were baptized into Moses in the cloud and in the sea" (1 Corinthians 10:2). As the Israelites went down along the sea floor with walls of water on both sides of them, they were completely under the water level and were in a way immersed in the sea.

Having started with historical, literal, and verifiable events, Paul then mentions that they: "all ate the same **spiritual food**"

(1 Corinthians 10:3). He is talking about the manna that rained down from heaven which the people lived on during their stay in the wilderness. The manna was food with taste and texture which they collected, turned into various dishes and then ultimately eaten. "It was like coriander seed, white, and the taste of it was like wafers made with honey" (Exodus 16:31). It entered the stomach, being converted to energy necessary to power the body; it was in every way real, "physical," and edible food.

So in what way was it spiritual food? **It was spiritual in that it did not originate from the earth; its source was the spiritual realm.** The psalmist even authenticates this: "Men ate angels' food; He sent them food to the full" (Psalm 78:25). Next Paul says: "and all drank the same **spiritual drink**" (1 Corinthians 10:4). Again, he is referring to events that are verifiable from the book of Exodus where God instructs Moses: "'you shall strike the Rock, and water will come out of it, that the **people may drink**.' And Moses did so in the sight of the elders of Israel" (Exodus 17:6). The action was instructed by God who also brought it to pass and it was witnessed by the people. The water was, like the food, real, physical, and potable water that was able to satiate their thirst. Again, in what way then was it spiritual drink? The origin of the water was not earthly; it originated from the other dimension. There was no hidden spring under the Rock as many would like to argue—for if that were true then there would also need to be some hidden source for the manna in the sky. Rather, the spiritual drink and food came from the other dimension (by God's providence) and did not originate on the earth. Nehemiah confirms this: "You gave them bread from heaven for their hunger, and brought them water out of the Rock for their thirst" (Nehemiah 9:15).

We then come to the last part of his retelling where he makes an important and yet shocking statement—they not only ate the spiritual food (manna) and drank the spiritual water, but the actual Rock was of a spiritual (not of this world) nature and what's even more, the Rock followed them! "For they drank of that spiritual Rock that followed them, and that Rock was Christ" (1 Corinthians 10:4). Not only did the Rock follow them but the Rock was Christ, Paul says. At this point we begin to feel uncomfortable with the conclusion. How could a Rock follow them throughout the desert and how could it be Christ? Certainly Jesus is more than a Rock! First of all, our job is not to decide if it is possible or not; God can certainly do as He pleases. If He was able to part the waters, cause a pillar of fire by night and a cloud by day to protect the people, and even rain down food from heaven, how hard could it be for Him to move a Rock? Second, Jesus Himself said:

> I am the living bread which came down from heaven. If anyone eats of this bread, he will live forever; and the bread that I shall give is My flesh, which I shall give for the life of the world (John 6:51).

Could it be that there is something that we can't quite comprehend? Is it possible for Jesus to be saying that He really was the manna that came down? This question is not easily answered; however, we ought to at least consider that there most certainly are truths that we are not aware of that appear to be impossible to us, but are possible for God. Nevertheless, in light of our study of DNA, if Jesus meant that His seed (data/DNA) will be incorporated into ours, then perhaps the passage can be interpreted literally, physically, and spiritually all at once. Therefore, while we may not be able to conceive how the Rock could literally be the Lord Jesus, we should not deny what the text says. In fact, accepting what Paul is saying literally versus figuratively makes the pieces fit quite well. If we go back to Exodus we note that God said:

> 'Behold, I will stand before you there on the Rock in Horeb; and you shall strike the Rock, and water will come out of it, that the people may drink.' And Moses did so in the sight of the elders of Israel (Exodus 17:6).

God says that He would be before Moses on the Rock which he was to strike, which is clearly a picture of the cross. The next time Moses is just to speak to the Rock (though he fails to do so).

'Take the rod; you and your brother Aaron gather the congregation together. Speak to the Rock before their eyes, and it will yield its water; thus you shall bring water for them out of the Rock, and give drink to the congregation and their animals' (Numbers 20:8).

The interpretation that the Rock (or at least the waters from the Rock) did in fact follow the Jews throughout their wanderings in the wilderness is confirmed by ancient Jewish interpretation. They see the Rock which they call the "well" going with them. Targum Onkelos says:

> And from thence was given to them the well, which is the well whereof the Lord spake to Mosheh, Gather the people together, and I will give them water. Therefore sang Israel this song: Spring up, O well; sing ye unto it. The well which the princes digged, the chiefs of the people cut it, the scribes with their staves; it was given to them in the wilderness. And from (the time) that it was given to them it descended with them to the rivers, and from the rivers it went up with them to the height and from the height to the vale which is in the fields of Moab, at the head of Ramatha, which looketh towards Bethjeshimon (Targum Onkelos 21:17).

The Targum of Jonathan speaks of the same phenomenon,

> The living well, the well concerning which the Lord said to Mosheh, Assemble the people and give them water. Then, behold, Israel sang the thanksgiving of this song, at the time that the well which had been hidden was restored to them through the merit of Miriam: Spring up, O well, spring up, O well! sang they to it, and it sprang up (Targum Jonathan 21:17).

Commentator John Gill also notes the waters of the Rock followed them in the wilderness:

> The waters out of the Rock ran like rivers, and followed them in the wilderness wherever they went, for the space of eight and thirty years, or thereabout, and then were stopped, to make trial of their faith once more; this was at Kadesh when

the Rock was struck again, and gave forth its waters […] And this sense of the apostle is entirely agreeable to the sentiments of the Jews, who say, that the Israelites had the well of water all the forty years [Jarchi in Numb. xx. 2.]. Yea, they speak of the Rock in much the same language the apostle does, and seem to understand it of the Rock itself, as if that really went along with the Israelites in the wilderness. Thus one of their writers on those words, "must we fetch you water out of this Rock?" makes this remark: "for they knew it not, לפי שהלך הסלע, "for that Rock went," and remained among the rocks," And in another place it is said (Bemidbar Rabba, sect. 1. fol. 177. 2) […] when the standard bearers encamped, and the tabernacle stood still, the Rock came, and remained in the court of the tent of the congregation; and the princes came and stood upon the top of it, and said, ascend, O well, and it ascended (John Gill's Exposition of the Entire Bible, 1 Corinthians 10:4).

We therefore conclude that when the Bible speaks of the spirit or things of a spiritual nature, it is not speaking allegorically or figuratively. Spiritual things are not nebulous abstractions; rather, reference is being made to beings or things that do not originate (or perhaps reside) in our dimension. Those entities have their origin in the other dimension known as the spiritual realm. That realm is able to interact with ours in ways that we do not fully understand. Nevertheless, angels and demons having the ability to materialize in our realm and being even able to produce some kind of genetic material is consistent with the pages of Scripture. Should we then find it surprising that all of the ancient (ante-Nicene) Jewish and Christian commentators believed that the sons of God in Genesis 6 were fallen angels who had the ability to procreate and thereby father the Nephilim?

CHAPTER SEVEN

The Sons of God According to Ancient Sources

W E HAVE SEEN that the term "sons of God" refers to a creature that is a direct creation of God in Chapter four. Thus Adam certainly qualified since he had no parents. Believers in the Lord Jesus qualify via the second birth (John 3). Angels qualify as well because they were directly created by God. Prior to the redemption purchased at the cross, there were no (human) sons of God (Adam excepted). The only "sons of God," therefore, during approximately the first four thousand years of world history are of the angelic order (whether good or bad). Not only is this interpretation the most literal and simplest interpretation biblically speaking but it was also believed by all of the pre-New Testament extra-biblical Jewish sources and all Christian commentators until Augustine (who simply and unequivocally denied it).

Ancient extra-biblical sources are important because they act as a type of commentary on the Scripture. What we find from these authors is that they confirm the literal interpretation of Genesis 6:1-4 which is to say that the sons of God were fallen angels (demons) who procreated with women. Again, this is important because when Jesus spoke of the days of Noah, all the listeners would have believed that fallen angels and demonic-human hybrids were rampant on the earth at that time. The ancient Christian and Jewish interpreters confirm that Satan has been seeking to overturn the Genesis 3:15 prophecy and destroy mankind.

FALLEN ANGELS ACCORDING TO THE NEW TESTAMENT

Both Peter and Jude speak specifically concerning the actions of these fallen angels. Peter, in his second epistle, speaks of false teachers with destructive heresies and the destruction they will bring upon themselves. He emphasizes the certainty of their destruction because of how God judged the (fallen) angels and the ancient world.

> For if God did not spare **the angels who sinned**, but threw them into hell [*tartarosas* ταρταρώσας] and locked them up in chains in utter darkness, to be kept **until the judgment**, and if he did **not spare the ancient world**, but did protect Noah, a herald of righteousness, along with seven others, when God brought a flood on an ungodly world, and if he **turned to ashes the cities of Sodom and Gomorrah when he condemned them to destruction,** having appointed them to serve as an example to future generations of the ungodly, and if he rescued Lot, a righteous man in anguish over the debauched lifestyle of lawless men,—if so, then the Lord knows how to rescue the godly from their trials, and to reserve the unrighteous for punishment at the day of judgment, **especially those who indulge their fleshly desires** and who despise authority. Brazen and insolent, they are not afraid to insult the glorious ones (2 Peter 2:4-10 NET).

How can we know for certain that Peter is not merely referring to the initial fall of the angels from heaven? After all, we know that Satan was once in God's presence and fell from his exalted position according to Ezekiel 28 and Isaiah 14.[63] We also learn from Revelation 12 that Satan took one-third of the angels with him when he fell. Couldn't Peter simply be referring to the "sin" of when Satan and the other angels initially rebelled? Peter gives us the answer in Chapter 5 of his first epistle when he says that we need to be on guard because: "your adversary the devil walks about like a roaring lion, seeking whom he may devour," (1 Peter 5:8). We can state with confidence that no angel has sinned worse than Satan himself. Thus why would God cast some of the lesser demons (fallen angels) into hell (a place Peter refers to as Tartarus[64]) and yet leave the majority of the demons, including the king of demons, Satan himself, free to "prowl around"?

We know that during Jesus' earthly ministry there were many encounters between Jesus and demons. During one encounter the demons even asked Him: "What have we[65] to do with You, Jesus, You Son of God? Have You come here to torment us before the time?"[66] (Matthew 8:29). We see that they were free to roam about but that there will be a time when the Lord Jesus will judge them. Jesus speaks of the judgment following the great tribulation known as the Judgment of the Nations in Matthew 25:41 and confirms that the final destiny of all fallen angels is the lake of fire. "Depart from Me, you cursed, into the everlasting fire prepared for the devil and his angels."

Thus the angels that have been cast into hell (*tartaros*) and are locked in everlasting chains waiting until the final judgment must have done something **more** than the initial rebellion. For if the first rebellion was sufficient to require them to be locked up already, why should Satan and so many other demons be allowed to go about freely? Peter provides evidence of just what landed them in everlasting chains so prematurely by his statement in verse 10: "especially those who indulge their fleshly desires [*sarkos en epitumia* σαρκος εν επιθυμια μιασμου] and who despise authority." The Greek term employed by Peter (*epithumia* επιθυμια) is defined by *Thayer's Greek Lexicon* as a great longing

for something, often of things forbidden. This word coupled with
"flesh" (*sarkos* σαϱκος) and "defilement"[67] (*miasmou* μιασμου)
makes a powerful statement—the unrighteous, which includes
(fallen) angels, acted upon a forbidden longing to defile or stain
their flesh.

Jude, most likely basing his own writing on Peter, then elaborates
in what way the angels sinned.

> Now I desire to remind you (even though you have been fully
> informed of these facts once for all) that Jesus, having saved
> the people out of the land of Egypt, later destroyed those
> who did not believe. You also know that the **angels** [*angelous*
> αγγελους] who did **not keep within their proper domain**
> [*arkhen* αϱχην] but abandoned **their own place of residence**
> [*oiketerion* οικητηϱιον], he has kept [There is an interesting
> play on words used in this verse. Because the angels did not
> *keep* their proper place, Jesus has *kept* them chained up in
> another place. The same verb *keep* is used in v. 1 to describe
> believers' status before God and Christ (NET Notes Jude 6).] in
> eternal chains in utter darkness, locked up for the judgment of
> the great Day. So also [*hos* ως] Sodom and Gomorrah and the
> neighboring towns, since they indulged in sexual immorality
> [*ekporeusasai* εκποϱνευσασαι] and **pursued unnatural desire**
> [*sarkos heteras* σαϱκος ετεϱας] **in a way similar to these**
> [*toutois* τουτοις] **angels**, are now displayed as an example by
> suffering the punishment of eternal fire (Jude 5-7 NET).

There are several things that confirm what Peter was saying in
relation to the angels having been equivalent to the sons of God
in Genesis 6. Jude says that the angels didn't keep their proper
domain, *arkhen* (αϱχην). We see this word in a similar context in
the writings of Paul. In Romans 8:38 Paul is confidently stating
that nothing can separate us from God's love: "For I am persuaded
that neither death nor life, nor angels nor principalities [*archai*
αϱχαι] nor powers, nor things present nor things to come."

In writing to the Ephesians Paul makes a bold statement concerning who we are truly warring against.

> For we do not wrestle against flesh and blood, but against **principalities** [*tas arkhas* τας αρχας], against **powers**, against the **rulers** of the darkness of this age, against spiritual hosts of wickedness in the **heavenly** places (Ephesians 6:12).

Paul is stating that the principalities [*archai* αρχαι] are rulers in the kingdom of Satan. Jude on the other hand is referencing what the angels left—that is to say, they left their abode or domain of power and rule (where they acted as principalities of wickedness in the heavenly places).

Jude then goes on to say that in a like manner Sodom, Gomorrah, and the surrounding cities committed an act like these (the Greek text has a masculine demonstrative dative pronoun "to these"). The New American Bible comments on verse 7:

> However, the phrase "practiced unnatural vice"—translated literally as "went after alien flesh"—refers to the desires for sexual intimacies by human beings with angels, which is the reverse of the account in Genesis, where heavenly beings (angels) sought after human flesh.[68]

The NET Bible notes that use of the masculine pronoun refers back to the antecedent "angels" because it is masculine whereas the mention of "cities" (Greek *poleis* πόλεις) is feminine and thus angels must be the antecedent of "to these."[69]

The sin of Sodom and Gomorrah (and the cities of the plain) was so wicked that God destroyed them with fire and brimstone from the sky. However, in order to not let the righteous suffer the same fate as the wicked, God sent two of His angels to rescue Lot and his family. Upon coming to the city the men of the city begin to beat on the door demanding that Lot send out the two men in order that they might have sexual relations with them. At the very least homosexual conduct is being spoken of here. However, with the passage from Jude in view, it is at least possible that God destroyed them not merely for their homosexual conduct, but for previously having relations with angels (of course fallen angels i.e. demons). The notes from the NET Bible offer some valuable insight on the term "strange flesh."

> This phrase has been variously interpreted. It could refer to flesh of another species (such as angels lusting after human flesh). This would aptly describe the sin of the angels, but not easily explain the sin of Sodom and Gomorrah. [...] Another alternative is that the focus of the parallel is on the activity of the surrounding cities and the activity of the angels. This is especially plausible since the participles ἐκπορνεύσασαι (ekporneusasai, "having indulged in sexual immorality") and ἀπελθοῦσαι (apelthousai, "having pursued") have concord with "cities" (πόλεις, poleis), a feminine plural noun, rather than with Sodom and Gomorrah (both masculine nouns). If so, then their sin would not necessarily have to be homosexuality. However, most likely the feminine participles are used because of *constructio ad sensum* (construction according to sense). That is, since both Sodom and Gomorrah are cities, the feminine is used to imply that all the cities are involved. The connection with angels thus seems to be somewhat loose: **Both angels and Sodom and Gomorrah indulged in heinous sexual immorality.** Thus, **whether the false teachers indulge in homosexual** activity **is not the point; mere sexual immorality** is **enough to condemn** them (NET Notes Jude 1:7).

The NET notes nicely draw out the bottom line of the use of the term *sarkos heteras* σαρκος ετερας (strange flesh in the KJV). When this information is coupled with what Paul has to say about the different kinds of flesh in 1 Corinthians 15 the picture becomes incredibly clear that the angels went after something foreign to themselves, as did the inhabitants of Sodom and Gomorrah.

> All flesh is not the same flesh [*sarx* σαρξ], but there is one kind of flesh [*sarx* σαρξ] of men, another [*alle* αλλη] flesh [*sarx* σαρξ] of animals, another of fish, and another of birds. There

are also **celestial bodies** [*somata* σώματα] and terrestrial bodies [*somata* σώματα]; but the glory of the celestial is one [ετερα], and the glory of the terrestrial is another (1 Corinthians 15:39-40).

Paul states that there are different kinds of flesh: men, animals, fish, and birds. Note that all earthly creatures have flesh but it is other or different (*alle* αλλη). Paul then describes the difference between the celestial and terrestrial bodies and states that they are different (*heteros* έτερος of another different kind). After describing the difference between the glory of the sun versus the moon, etc. (1 Corinthians 15:40), Paul then returns to the resurrected bodies that we will possess. There are both earthly bodies and heavenly bodies and they are *"heteros,"* which is the very same word that Jude uses to describe the angels and Sodomites in their going after flesh of another kind.

We learn from Peter and Jude that both the angels (demons) and inhabitants of Sodom and Gomorrah took part in forbidden and debauched sexual conduct. We have seen that the reference by Jesus that in heaven we do not marry but are like the angels does not preclude what fallen angels did in the past. The texts are clear: the (fallen) angels did something that was so heinous that it landed them in everlasting chains in complete darkness until the great day. But we also saw that not all of the fallen angels have been confined there—most conspicuous is Satan himself who still has free reign. Thus, nowhere in the Bible does it say that angels are incapable of mixing their seed with humans. What we learn from Peter and Jude is that they **were not supposed to**. They left their proper domain, i.e. the realm of the prince of the power of the air, and came to earth where they fathered the Nephilim with human women.

ANTE-NICENE CHURCH FATHERS

The conclusions we have reached from the New Testament is backed by all the ante-Nicene church fathers. We will consider all the fathers that mentioned something concerning the sons of God (demons) and their mixing with the daughters of men, and we will see that all of them believed that the sons of God in Genesis 6 were identified as fallen angels.[70]

ATHENAGORAS

Church Father Athenagoras, AD 177, wrote in *Concerning the Angels and Giants* that it was the fallen angels who fathered the giants before the flood.

> Just as with men, who have freedom of choice as to both virtue and vice […], so is it among the **angels**. Some, free agents, you will observe, such as they were created by God, continued in those things for which God had made and over which He had ordained them; **but some outraged both the constitution of their nature and the government entrusted to them**: namely, this ruler of matter and its various forms, and others of those who were placed about this first firmament […] **these fell into impure love of virgins, and were subjugated by the flesh, and became negligent and wicked in the management of the things entrusted to him."**[71]

Notice Athenagoras' description of how these angels outraged (were not faithful) to the government that had been entrusted to them. This language of course corresponds to the language of 2 Peter 2 and Jude of the angels that did not keep their first estate (residence). Athenagoras further commented how these angels could no longer rise to where they once had been (heaven) and the souls of giants, who he says are in fact demons, wander the world.

> These **angels**, then, who **have fallen from heaven**, and haunt the air and the earth, and are no longer able to rise to heavenly things, and the souls of **the giants**, which **are the demons** who wander about the world, perform actions similar, the one (that is, the demons) to the natures they have received, the other (that is, the angels) to the appetites they have indulged.[72]

COMMODIANUS

Commodianus, AD 240, wrote how from angels' seed the giants came about. Again, we see that the ancient Christian interpreter believed Genesis 6 to be referring to the comingling of angels and women which produced a hybrid race of giants; this confirms that when Jesus mentioned "as it was in the days of Noah, so will the coming of the Son of Man be," people would have thought about the Nephilim.

> When Almighty God, to beautify the nature of the world, willed that earth should be visited by **angels**, when they were sent down they despised His laws. Such was the beauty of women, that it turned them aside; so that, being contaminated, they could not return to heaven. **Rebels from God**, they **uttered words against Him**. Then the Highest uttered His judgment against them; **and from their seed giants are said to have been born**. [...] But the Almighty, **because they were of an evil seed**, did not approve that, **when dead, they should be brought back from death. Whence wandering they now subvert many bodies, and it is such as these especially that ye this day worship and pray to as gods.**

THE EXTANT WRITINGS OF JULIUS AFRICANUS

Julius Africanus (AD c. 160?- c. 240?) was the first to tentatively suggest that "sons of God" might be referring to the descendants of Seth and the "seed of men" could **possibly** be referring to descendants of Cain. However, he **also conceded** that it could just be angels as the text he was reading stated. Furthermore, it was by these angels that the race of giants was conceived. Augustine, however, was truly the first to state without a doubt that the sons of God simply meant sons of Seth.

> When men multiplied on the earth, the **angels of heaven** came together with the daughters of men. In some copies I found "the sons of God." What is meant by the Spirit, in my opinion, is that the descendants of Seth are called the sons of God on account of the righteous men and patriarchs who have

sprung from him, even down to the Savior Himself; but that the descendants of Cain are named the seed of men as having nothing divine in them, on account of the wickedness of their race and the inequality of their nature, being a mixed people, and having stirred the indignation of God. But **if it is thought that these refer to angels**, we must take them to be those who deal with magic and jugglery, who taught the women the motions of the stars and the knowledge of things celestial, **by whose power they conceived the giants as their children, by whom wickedness came to its height on the earth**, until God decreed that the whole race of the living should perish in their impiety by the deluge.[74]

PRE-NEW TESTAMENT JEWISH TEXTS

Ancient Jewish sources a century or two before or after Jesus that mentioned the sons of God as fallen angels include texts such as the Book of Enoch, Tales of the Patriarchs (also known as the Genesis Apochryphon), Philo, the Aramaic Targumim of the Pentateuch, the ancient historian Josephus, and others. They consistently accepted the interpretation that fallen angels were capable of producing offspring and therefore had some kind of genetic seed to pass on. This again demonstrates that the phrase "as it was in the days of Noah" was a reference to Nephilim on the earth.

THE GENESIS APOCRYPHON

The Genesis Apocryphon[75], found among the Dead Sea Scrolls, contains accounts purportedly by the ancient patriarchs (Joseph, etc.) from the book of Genesis, but with more detail. Whether or not it goes all the way back to those original patriarchs we may never know, but the book does provide us with some important evidence (at the very least as a commentary) of what pious Jews from Qumran believed about the ancient past, offering valuable insights into what they thought about the sons of God and the Nephilim.

In this fragment Lamech fears the child in his wife's womb is not his but is in fact from the fallen angels known as the Watchers. The child would therefore be a Nephilim or giant.

> I thought, in my heart, that **the conception was the work** of the **Watchers** the **pregnancy of the Holy Ones and that it belonged to the Giants** ... and my heart was upset by this ... I, Lamech, turned to my wife Bitenosh and said ... Swear to me by the Most High, Great Lord {...} I swear to you by the Great Holy One, the King of the heavens ... That this **seed**, **pregnancy**, and planting of fruit comes from you and not a stranger, **Watcher**, or **son of the heaven** ... (Col. 2. [1])

THE WATCHERS

He uses the word "watchers" which is also found three times in Daniel 4. These Watchers we see in Daniel came down from heaven and were also called holy ones.

- I saw in the visions of my head while on my bed, and there was a **watcher**, a holy one, coming down from heaven (Daniel 4:13).

- This decision is by the decree of the **watchers**, and the sentence by the word of the holy ones, in order that the living may know that the Most High rules in the kingdom of men, gives it to whomever He will, and sets over it the lowest of men (Daniel 4:17).

- And inasmuch as the king saw a **watcher**, a holy one, coming down from heaven and saying, "Chop down the tree and destroy it, but leave its stump and roots in the earth" (Daniel 4:23).

The Genesis Apocryphon also qualifies the "watcher" with "son of the heaven." In Second Temple Judaism "heaven" was often used as a circumlocution for "God." Therefore we could see here a reference to sons of God being used to describe heavenly beings. The secondary designation of "holy ones" is parallel to angels, which does not refer only to good angels but to both good and bad of that class of beings. Holy is a word that does not necessarily imply perfection but set apart for a particular purpose.[76]

THE BOOK OF GIANTS

The book of Giants was found among the Dead Sea Scrolls and has been dated to sometime before the second century BC. It is similar to the description of the giants found in the Book of Enoch. Whether or not this book is based on a much older tradition we do not know. But it does act as a commentary on Genesis 6. Only fragments exist of the book so any particular order is somewhat a matter of guesswork on the part of the scholars. Nevertheless we still find some very insightful information concerning the events believed to have preceded the flood. From our first fragment (Qumran cave 1, fragment 23, lines 9, 14, 15) we see the general condition of the earth (brackets here are inserted by the Qumran scholars).[77]

1Q23 Frag. 9 + 14 + 15

> 2[. . .] they knew the secrets of [. . .] 3[. . . si]n was great in the earth [. . .] 4[. . .] and they killed many [. .] 5[. . . they begat] **giants** [. . .] (emphasis mine).

The next fragment appears to speak of taking two hundred different animals and mixing their seed with one another (miscegenation).

1Q23 Frag. 1 + 6

> [. . . two hundred] 2donkeys, two hundred asses, two hundred . . . rams of the] 3flock, two hundred goats, two hundred [. . . beast of the] 4field from every animal, from every [bird . . .] 5[. . .] for miscegenation [. . .]

Apparently from the intermingling of different kinds, strange creatures came about, namely giants and monsters. Whoever the writer was, he was indicating that the cause of the flood was the creation of monsters and giants (unnatural creatures) which came from the mixing of seed. The key word is "corrupted" which refers to a degradation of the genetic code.

4Q531 Frag.

> 2 [. . .] they **defiled** [. . .] 2[. . . they begot] **giants** and **monsters** [. . .] 3[. . .] they begot, and, behold, all [the earth was **corrupted** . . .] 4[. . .] with its blood and by the hand of [. . .] 5[**giant's**] which did not suffice for them and [. . .] 6[. . .] and they were seeking to devour many [. . .] 7[. . .] 8[. . .] the **monsters** attacked it (emphasis mine).

4Q532 Col. 2 Frags. 1 - 6

> 2[. . .] flesh [. . .] 3al[l . . .] **monsters** [. . .] will be [. . .] 4[. . .] they would arise [. . .] lacking in true knowledge [. . .] because [. . .] 5[. . .] the earth [grew **corrupt** . . .] mighty [. . .] 6[. . .] they were considering [. . .] 7[. . .] from the **angels** upon [. . .] 8[. . .] in the end it will perish and die [. . .] 9[. . .] they caused great **corruption** in the [earth . . .] (emphasis mine).

FIRST ENOCH

We next turn to the book of I Enoch. When the Book of Enoch was written is not known. It is entirely possible that some or all of the book was in fact written by Enoch. After all the New Testament book of Jude quoted from I Enoch: "Now Enoch, the seventh from Adam, prophesied about these men also, saying, 'Behold, the Lord comes with ten thousands of His saints' (Jude 1:14). However, we can be certain that it was a central book for the Dead Sea community approximately two centuries before Christ. The book describes in great detail the situation of the earth before the flood and how the sons of God, which the writer clearly identifies, are fallen angels. The text below is from the Book of Enoch, translated from the Ethiopic by R. H. Charles, 1906 (Chapter 9). His comments have been placed in the endnotes.

1. It happened after the sons of men had multiplied in those days, that daughters were born to them, elegant and beautiful.

2. And when the **angels**[78], **the sons of heaven**, beheld them, they became enamored of them, saying to each other, Come, let us select for ourselves wives from the progeny of men, and let us beget children. [verses 3-6].

7. Then they swore all together, and all bound themselves by mutual execrations. Their whole number was two hundred, who descended upon Ardis, which is the top of mount Armon.

8. That mountain therefore was called Armon, because they had sworn upon it, and bound themselves by mutual execrations.

9. These are the names of their chiefs: Samyaza, who was their leader, Urakabarameel, Akibeel, Tamiel, Ramuel, Danel, Azkeel, Saraknyal, Asael, Armers, Batraal, Anane, Zavebe, Samsaveel, Ertael, Turel, Yomyael, Arazyal. These were the prefects of the two hundred angels, and the remainder were all with them.

10. Then they took wives, each choosing for himself; whom they began to approach, and with whom they cohabited; teaching them sorcery, incantations, and the dividing of roots and trees.

11. And the women conceiving brought forth **giants**,

12. Whose stature was each three hundred cubits. These devoured all which the labor of men produced; until it became impossible to feed them;

13. When they turned themselves against men, in order to devour them;

14. And began to injure birds, beasts, reptiles, and fishes, to eat their flesh one after another, and to drink their

blood (emphasis mine).

The details concord quite well with the biblical and extra-biblical evidence that we have already seen. The ancient Jews at Qumran, whether simply the readers of the document or perhaps the authors of it, certainly believed that the sons of God were to be interpreted as fallen angels and that they had sexual relations with women thereby producing the giants. The ancient Jew, if not Enoch himself, understood the Watchers to be angels (whether good or bad), and it was these Watchers (who were also in Daniel 4) who came down and mingled their seed with humanity. Thus according to the author of Enoch, demons mingled themselves with the seed of men and produced a hybrid race.

PHILO`S INTERPRETATION

Philo was a first century Jewish philosopher from Alexandria who was known for trying to make the Bible harmonize with Greek philosophy by way of allegorization. If anyone should have allegorized away the sons of God and the giants it was Philo. However, Philo does nothing of the sort but takes a very literal approach and greatly strengthens our conclusion that the fallen angelic beings were mingling their seed with women.

> And when the **angels of God** saw the daughters of men that they were beautiful, they took unto themselves wives of all of them whom they Chose." [Gen 6:2] Those beings, whom other philosophers call **demons**, Moses usually calls **angels**; and they are souls hovering in the air (emphasis mine).[85]

The text that Philo is quoting from simply interpreted the Hebrew "sons of God" as angels. This is also what the Septuagint did in the book of Job. Philo states very clearly "But sometimes Moses styles the **angels the sons of God"** in his *Questions and Answers on Genesis part 4, note 92.* Note that he also discusses how angels, or sons of God, have on occasion appeared as men. For Philo the giants are absolutely the product of fallen angels and women.

> On what principle was it that giants were born of **angels** and women? The poets call those men who were born **out of**

the earth giants, that is to say, sons of the Earth. But Moses here uses this appellation improperly, and he uses it too very often merely to denote the vast personal size of the principal men, equal to that of Hajk or Hercules. [...] But he relates that **these giants were sprung from a combined procreation of two natures, namely, from angels and mortal women**; for the substance of angels is spiritual; **but it occurs every now and then that on emergencies occurring they have imitated the appearance of men, and transformed themselves so as to assume the human shape; as they did on this occasion, when forming connexions with women for the production of giants.** [...] But sometimes Moses styles the **angels the sons of God**, inasmuch as they **were not produced by any mortal**, but are incorporeal, as being spirits destitute of any body (emphasis mine).[86]

Ironically, Philo takes the text quite literally. In his writings *On the Life of Moses*, I - Part 4, he writes: "they saw that they were very numerous indeed, and **giants** of **exceeding tallness** with absolutely **gigantic bodies**, both as to their magnitude and their strength" (emphasis mine).[87]

TARGUM OF JONATHAN

The Targum of Jonathan is very poignant in just who the sons of God are and even mentions them by name:

Schamchazai and Uzziel, **who fell from heaven**, were on the earth in those days; and also, after the sons of the Great had gone in with the daughters of men [...] (Targum Jonathan Genesis 6:4, emphasis mine).

JOSEPHUS

We next turn to Josephus, the premier Jewish historian of the first century without whose work we would know very little concerning the fall of Jerusalem. In addition to his work entitled *Wars of the Jews*, Josephus also wrote a much longer work entitled *Antiquities of the Jews* in which he plainly states that angels begat sons with women. It is worth mentioning that the piety of Seth and his sons is noted by Josephus. Seth's sons' apostasy is also noted, but Josephus is careful not to suggest that the "sons of men" were in fact the sons of Seth. He maintains the distinction between them.

> NOW this posterity of Seth continued to esteem God as the Lord of the universe, and to have an entire regard to virtue, for seven generations; but in process of time they were perverted, and forsook the practices of their forefathers; and did neither pay those honors to God which were appointed them, nor had they any concern to do justice towards men. But for what degree of zeal they had formerly shown for virtue, they now showed by their actions a double degree of wickedness, whereby they made God to be their enemy.[88]

After reporting on Seth's sons' bad conduct, he then turns his attention to the events which led up to the flood. Josephus specifically states that it was angels that mingled their seed with women.

> **For many angels** of God **accompanied with women**, and **begat sons** that proved unjust, and despisers of all that was good, on account of the confidence they had in their own strength; for the tradition is, that these **men did what resembled the acts of those whom the Grecians call giants** (emphasis mine).[89]

William Whiston, the translator of Josephus, picks up on Josephus' use of the word angel. He states: "This notion, that the fallen angels were, in some sense, the fathers of the old giants, was the constant opinion of antiquity."[90]

THE TESTAMENTS OF THE TWELVE PATRIARCHS

The Testaments of the Twelve Patriarchs are biographies written between 107 and 137 BC. They show what ancient Jews believed about the sons of God and the giants that were on the earth before the flood. In the testament of Reuben, the author discusses how the Watchers were the fathers of the giants. However, in this text it was not only the angels (Watchers) who lusted after women, but the women that also lusted after the Watchers.

> For thus they allured the **Watchers** who were before the flood; for as these continually beheld them, they lusted after them, and they conceived the act in their mind; and the women lusting in their minds after their forms, **gave birth to giants, for the Watchers appeared to them as reaching even unto heaven** (Testament of Reuben 18-20).

SECRETS OF ENOCH

Little is known of this books origin except that in its present form it was written somewhere about the beginning of the Christian era.

> And they said to me: These are the **Grigori** [Watchers], **who with their prince Satanail rejected the Lord of light, and after them are those who are held in great darkness on the second heaven**, and three of them went down on to earth from the Lord's throne, to the place Ermon, and broke through their vows on the shoulder of the hill Ermon and saw the daughters of men how good they are, and took to themselves wives, and befouled the earth with their deeds, **who in all times of their age made lawlessness and mixing, and giants are born and marvelous big men and great enmity.**

SUMMARY

We have seen that the evidence from the New Testament interprets the sons of God in Noah's day as being fallen angels that mixed their seed with women. All of the ante-Nicene church fathers (before the council of Nicaea) believed that the sons of God in Genesis 6 were to be identified as fallen angels. Both Jewish and Christian interpreters believed that a select group of angels, who had previously fallen, took women and fathered children by them. They did not see this as an impossibility nor a problem theologically. In fact, it was the key that solved many riddles. By rejecting the simple and literal interpretation, later interpreters have had to disregard the text in order to make it fit their preconceived notion. The implications for our study are huge: if the fallen angels did that once, then they will do it again as Jesus Himself prophesied: "But as the days of Noah *were,* so also will the coming of the Son of Man be" (Matthew 24:37).

The idea that the sons of God were the supposed sons of Seth is conspicuously absent from these ancient commentators. If the vast majority of interpreters had believed them to be the sons of Seth and the women to be the daughters of Cain, then we might be forced to reconsider our conclusion. The fact is, however, that one hundred percent of them (before Augustine) confirm our conclusion that Satan has been trying to mix his seed with humans and thereby thwart the Genesis 3:15 prophecy. Only when Augustine began reinterpreting the Old Testament allegorically, so that he could reinterpret the literal promises made to Israel and apply them to the church, did the sons of Seth explanation take root.

The Sons of Seth and Daughters of Cain Theory

THE BIBLE IS REPLETE with evidence that the sons of God in Genesis 6:1-4 are fallen angels (demons). All of the ancient Jewish and Christian commentators believed the "sons of God" to be referring to demons (fallen angels) as did all of the ante-Nicene fathers.

AUGUSTINE OF HIPPO

The first, as far as we can see, to definitively deny the sons of God as being angels was Augustine of Hippo of the fifth century, approximately seventy-five years after the drafting of the Nicene Creed. Augustine did much to spiritualize the history of the Bible and twist a simple straightforward reading of the Bible. His method of Bible interpretation made a profound impact and his legacy remains even to this day. Many centuries after Augustine, Thomas Aquinas, a doctor of the Catholic Church in the thirteenth century, quotes in his magnum opus, Summa Theologica, from Augustine's work *City of God* (De Civ. Dei xv) concerning the sons of Seth:

Many persons affirm that they have had the experience, or have heard from such as have experienced it, that the **Satyrs** and **Fauns**, whom the common folk call incubi, have often presented themselves before women, and have sought and procured intercourse with them. Hence it is folly to deny it. But God's holy angels could not fall in such fashion before the deluge. **Hence by the sons of God are to be understood the sons of Seth, who were good; while by the daughters of men the Scripture designates those who sprang from the race of Cain.**[92] Nor is it to be wondered at that giants should be born of them; for they were not all giants, albeit there were many more before than after the deluge. Still if some are occasionally begotten from demons, it is not from the seed of such demons, nor from their assumed bodies, but from the seed of men taken for the purpose; as when the demon assumes first the form of a woman, and afterward of a man; just as they take the seed of other things for other generating purposes, as Augustine says (De Trin. iii), so that the person born is not the child of a demon, but of a man[93]

Just as Augustine fallaciously suggested the sons of God were the so called "godly line of Seth," the daughters of men have been labeled as being from the "ungodly line of Cain." Augustine says, "By the daughters of men the Scripture designates those who sprang from the race of Cain," (Augustine as quoted in *Summa Theologica*, Aquinas). We must ask the important question— where in Scripture does it say such a thing? Augustine makes the claim above that Scripture designates those daughters as coming from the race of Cain, but just where do we see that? The answer is that we simply do not. It was first tentatively considered by Julius Africanus and then completely invented by Augustine and then repeated by all who would follow in his footsteps ever since. If the term "sons of God" refers to the "sons of Seth," as so many suggest, then why does the text not simply state it? Unfortunately neither Augustine nor Aquinas substantiates the claim. They simply presume their statement to be true and offer no biblical proof. Augustine states that "Scripture designates" that the daughters of men "sprang from the race of Cain." But where in Scripture does it say that? Sadly, their unbiblical assertion has left its mark on the modern day, creating a great deal of confusion regarding what the Bible literally teaches.

CALVIN'S INTERPRETATION

John Calvin, in the seventeenth century, carried on the tradition started by Augustine that the sons of God are in fact the sons of Seth. He states in his commentary:

> The principle is to be kept in memory, that the world was then as if divided into two parts; because the **family of Seth cherished the pure and lawful worship of God**, from which the rest had fallen. Now, although all mankind had been formed for the worship of God, and therefore sincere religion ought everywhere to have reigned; yet since the greater part had prostituted itself, either to an entire contempt of God, or to depraved superstitions; it was fitting that the **small portion which God had adopted, by special privilege, to himself, should remain separate from others**. It was, therefore, base ingratitude in the **posterity of Seth**, to **mingle themselves with the children of Cain**, and **with other profane races**; because they voluntarily deprived themselves of the inestimable grace of God. For it was an intolerable profanation, to pervert, and to confound, the order appointed by God. **It seems at first sight frivolous, that the sons of God should be so severely condemned, for having chosen for themselves beautiful wives from the daughters of men.** But we must know first, that it is not a light crime to violate a **distinction established** by the Lord; secondly, that for the **worshippers of God** to be separated from **profane nations**, was a sacred appointment which ought reverently to have been observed, in order that a Church of God might exist upon earth; thirdly, that the disease was desperate, seeing that men rejected the remedy divinely prescribed for them. In short, Moses points it out as the most extreme disorder; when the sons of the pious, whom God had separated to himself from others, as a peculiar and hidden treasure, **became degenerate**, (emphasis mine).[94]

Calvin rightly describes the world as being wicked, but he vainly asserts that the world had been "divided into two parts." Where do we see such an idea in the Bible? He also introduces his deterministic philosophy of predestination by stating that apparently the sons of Seth were adopted by "special privilege." His denial of who the sons of God truly were creates a tremendous amount of confusion that has clouded the interpretation of the text for potentially millions of people over the centuries. Furthermore, nowhere do we see that the daughters of men are from the so-called ungodly line of Cain.

Calvin continues with his unbiblical prohibition of inter-class marriages. Notice that again he does not offer any biblical support for any of his positions. He does not seek to prove his point with Scripture but with opinion and conjecture. Having simply asserted his position, Calvin then ridicules the 'sons of God as demons' interpretation.

> **That ancient figment, concerning the intercourse of angels with women, is abundantly refuted by its own absurdity; and it is surprising that learned men should formerly have been fascinated by ravings so gross and prodigious.** The opinion also of the Chaldean paraphrase is frigid; namely, that promiscuous marriages between the **sons of nobles**, and the **daughters of plebeians**, is condemned. Moses, then, **does not distinguish the sons of God** from the **daughters of men**, because they were of dissimilar nature, or of different origin; but **because they were the sons of God by adoption, whom he had set apart for himself**; while the rest remained in their original condition (Calvin Commentary Genesis 6:1 emphasis mine).

We have already seen how "sons of God" is used in Scripture—furthermore that there were no human "sons of God" before the resurrection of Jesus. However, Calvin introduces great confusion into the text by dogmatically declaring that God's terms are very capricious and that they sometimes mean one thing in one context and quite another someplace else. The simple biblical definition, as we have seen, is that sons of God are direct creations of God. Calvin is unable to define sons of God because of bad exegesis.

> Should anyone object, that they who had shamefully departed from the faith, and the obedience which God required, were unworthy to be accounted the sons of God; the answer is easy, that the honor is not ascribed to them, but to the grace of God, which had hitherto been conspicuous in their families. For **when Scripture speaks of the sons of God**, **sometimes** it has respect to **eternal election**, which extends only to the lawful heirs; **sometimes** to **external vocations** according to which **many wolves are within the fold**; and **though in fact, they are strangers, yet they obtain the name of sons, until the Lord shall disown them**. Yea, even by giving them a title so honorable, Moses reproves their ingratitude, because, leaving their heavenly Father, they prostituted themselves as deserters (emphasis mine).[95]

Now, to support his presuppositions, he must explain away the giants (Nephilim) that are introduced in Genesis 6:4 and are the result of the sons of God (or as he would say the sons of Seth) and the daughters of men (or as he would say the daughters of Cain).

> Moses does not indeed say, that they were of extraordinary stature, but **only that they were robust**. Elsewhere, **I acknowledge, the same word denotes vastness of stature**, which was formidable to those who explored the land of Canaan, (Jos 13:33.) But Moses does not distinguish those of whom he speaks in this place, from other men, so much by the size of their bodies, **as by their robberies and their lust of dominion** (emphasis mine).[96]

He downplays the fact that the fruit of the union between the sons of God and daughters of men were men of extraordinary size. He simply asserts that they were "great" in their evil. His interpretation is unfounded and he is not completely honest here for the word (Nephilim) used in both places is exactly the same. Calvin and numerous others turn to Genesis 4:26 in order to substantiate their case. Hawker's *Poor Man's Commentary* is very typical of those that leap to the conclusion that sons of God must be referring to the Sons of Seth.

> Observe the different expressions: sons of God, and daughters of men. If you turn to Gen 4:26 you there discover that the children of Seth are said to call on the name of the Lord; including both sons and daughters; and hence, therefore, these are meant by the sons of God.[97]

They suggest that this passage in some way proves that the term "sons of God" is really a hidden meaning for sons of Seth. Let's take a look at the passage to see if their claims are valid.

SETH AND HIS SONS

Seth appears a total of seven times in both the Old Testament and the New Testament (NKJV). We get a brief glimpse of his life by stringing together all of the passages[98] that speak of him.

> And Adam knew his wife again, and she bore a son and named him **Seth** [...], And as for **Seth**, to him also a son was born; and he named him Enosh. Then men began to call on the name of the LORD (Genesis 4:25-26).

> And Adam lived one hundred and thirty years, and begot a son in his own likeness, after his image, and named him **Seth**. After he begot **Seth**, the days of Adam were eight hundred years; and he had sons and daughters. **Seth** lived one hundred and five years, and begot Enosh. After he begot Enosh, **Seth** lived eight hundred and seven years, and had sons and daughters. So all the days of **Seth** were nine hundred and twelve years; and he died (Genesis 5:3-4, 6-8).

Here 130 years after creation, Adam has a son named Seth; then 105 years after that Seth had a son named Enosh. Thus we learn that a total of 235 years after creation men began to call upon the name of the Lord. The Hebrew term for Lord is YHWH which is the personal name of God. God told Moses: "I appeared to Abraham, to Isaac, and to Jacob, as God Almighty [*El Shaddai* אֵל שַׁדָּי], but by My name LORD [YHWH יְהֹוָה] I was not known to them" (Exodus 6:3). Thus to think that this was the first time that humans began to worship the Lord is unfounded. Rather we simply read that they began to use his personal name at that point for some purpose. While it appears to have begun with a son of Seth, we should not infer that it was limited to that line. After all, the Hebrew text very literally says *az hukhal likro beshem YHWH* [אָז הוּחַל לִקְרֹא בְּשֵׁם יְהֹוָה] "then was begun (the) calling by (with, in) the name YHWH" (translation mine). The term *hukhal* (הוּחַל) is the passive (hophal) of begin. The subject of the verb *hukhal* is "calling" (*likro'* לִקְרֹא). The word "men" does not even appear in the text. Thus we see that apparently, up until that point, men were not invoking God by His proper name. It could be that they didn't know it, though we cannot be sure. Nevertheless this reading of the verse does not in any way substantiate the notion that Seth's sons were the sons of God. Another reading is possible which may clarify the passage.

A POSSIBLE TRANSLATION

Conversely, the verb *hukhal* (הוּחַל) comes from the root (חלל) the basic meaning is "to profane, defile, pollute, desecrate, begin" according to Brown Driver Briggs'[99] Lexicon of the Hebrew Bible. Thus, the alternative reading would be "then calling by the name of YHWH was profaned." This alternative reading actually finds endorsement by the ancient Aramaic Targumim. Targum Onkelos interprets the passage as:

> And to Sheth also was born a son, and he called his name Enosh. Then in his days the sons of men **desisted** [khalu חָלוּ] (or forbore) from praying in the name of the Lord (Genesis 4:26, Targum Onkelos, emphasis mine).

Targum Jonathan is similar though it amplifies that reading even more:

And to Sheth also was born a son, and he called his name Enosh. That was the generation in whose days **they began to err** [למטעי], and to make themselves **idols**, and **surnamed their idols by the name of the Word of the Lord** (Genesis 4:26, Targum Jonathan, emphasis mine).

While neither "began" nor "profane" supports the sons of Seth theory, the latter would seem to make more sense in light of the entire story of the Bible. The divine name seems to have been known from the very beginning of creation. Adam was familiar with it because he heard the voice of the LORD (YHWH) God in the garden after he had sinned. Calling by the name of the Lord was until that time respected and honored but it was in the days of Enosh when calling by the name of the Lord was defiled. God then destroyed the world because of the continual wickedness. Noah retains knowledge of the name and then apparently at the tower of Babel the name is forgotten or lost. God chooses not to reveal His name again until Moses has the encounter at the burning bush.

THE SONS OF SETH WERE NOT SONS OF GOD

Regardless of which reading we take, there is simply no evidence whatsoever to support the concept that Genesis 4:26 can be used to interpret the sons of God as the sons of Seth. There is no indication that Seth's sons were somehow more godly than the rest of humanity. Furthermore, it must not be missed that Adam lived another eight hundred years after begetting Seth and that he had sons and daughters. Likewise "Seth lived eight hundred and seven years and had sons and daughters" (Genesis 5:7). All of the sons and daughters of Seth as well as the sons and daughters of Cain were in fact sons (and daughters) of Adam. Technically speaking every human ever born on this planet is a son or daughter of Adam; the Hebrew language uses the term to mean "human." Thus the text is driving home the point that there are two dissimilar groups: the daughters of Adam on the one hand and the sons of God on the other. To suggest that the daughters of men were actually the daughters of Cain is fanciful.

Rather, the daughters of Adam are contrasted with the sons of God: the daughters of men were human and the sons of God were not.

Furthermore, we can in no way infer that all of these sons and daughters remained so godly that they would be distinguished from the sons of Cain. After all, only eight people were saved out of the entire world. These sons of Seth must not have been so godly after all. Simply put, the sons of God do not refer to the lineage of Seth but to direct creations of God, which before the redeeming work of Christ was limited to Adam himself and to angels. Therefore, the sons of God in Genesis 6 refers to fallen angels who had relations with human women.

CHAPTER NINE

Who Were the Nephilim?

PREVIOUSLY WE SAW that the sons of God were in fact fallen angels (demons) who had relations with the daughters of Adam. Their union produced unique offspring which the Bible refers to as Nephilim.

> The Nephilim [*haNephilim* הַנְּפִלִים] were on the earth in those days, and also afterward, when the sons of God came in to the daughters of man and they bore children to them. These were the mighty men who were of old, the men of renown (Genesis 6:4 EV).

The Hebrew word Nephilim comes from the root *naphal* meaning to fall. Gesenius in his Hebrew Lexicon notes: "Those who used to interpret the passage in Genesis of the fall of the angels, were accustomed to render *Nephilim* [נְפִלִים] *fallers, rebels, apostates.*" The Greek Septuagint, translated approximately 270 BC translates the word as "the giants" (*oi gigantes* οι γιγαντες). We find that this same word was used in classical Greek literature to refer to men

Figure 3 Demigod Kekrops

or creatures that were half god and half man.[100] Jonathan M. Hall in his book *Ethnic Identity in Greek Antiquity* notes that *gegenes* in fact means "earth born": "From the time of the Iliad, Erekhtheus was treated as a son of the earth, and Herodotus calls him *gegenes* ("earth-born")"[101] "gigantic" or "monstrous."

> In Greek mythology the Giants (from *gegenes*) were the children of Heaven (*Uranos* Οὐρανός) and Earth (*Gaea* Γαῖα) (though some would argue that their father was Tartaros, the hell pit[102]). "The giants of Greek mythology, or Gigantes ('the earth-born') as they are called in the Greek tongue, were a class of oversized and ofttimes monstrous men who were closely related to the gods."[103] Consider also Kekrôps, who according to Apollodorus (iii. 14. § 1, &c.) was the first king of Attica, was known as "a gêgenês, the upper part of whose body was human, while the lower was that of a dragon."[104]

If the translators of the Septuagint didn't want us to think about demigods or men of enormous stature, they sure picked the wrong word! However, if by *gegenes* they understood hybrids between fallen angels ("the gods") and women, then they chose the **perfect** word to describe these ungodly and unnatural creatures which parallels the biblical description of the sons of God (from the heavenlies) coming down to earth and fathering children. Considering the exposure those Alexandrian Jews must certainly have had to Greek literature and the numerous stories of giants, we would be completely ignoring their testimony if we were to understand the word as anything other than creatures who were hybrids of fallen angels and humans—who were also of colossal stature. In fact, in Greek mythology these giants were sometimes thirty feet tall! If the translators had wanted to merely indicate that these men were the offspring of the godly line of Seth and the ungodly line of Cain, they should have chosen a different word.

Targum Jonathan translates Genesis 6:4: "Schamchazai and Uzziel, who fell from heaven, were on the earth in those days."

Shamchazai and Uzziel were fallen angels that we saw in the Book of Enoch as being the ones that took the daughters of men. Targum Jonathan specifically adds "who fell from heaven" giving testimony to how they understood the word Nephilim. Targum Onkelos translates the verse in a similar fashion: "**Giants** were in the earth in those days; and also when, after that the **sons of the mighty** had gone in unto the daughters of men" (Targum Onkelos, Genesis 6:4 emphasis mine). The interpretation of this verse is very consistent in the ancient witnesses: Demons came down from their habitation and took wives and from their sexual union came a race of giants which were hybrids: half-man and half-demon.

If one should ask how there could be Nephilim afterward when they were all destroyed in the flood, the answer is simple: the fathers of the Nephilim were demons. While it appears that the demons that crossed the line when mingling with humans were thrown into the pit, other demons must have taken women and had Nephilim with them after the flood. As a result we discovered that there were Nephilim in the land of Canaan when the children of Israel came to take possession of their Promised Land. Upon seeing the Nephilim they lost faith that God could win the battle for them and so they were taken back to the wilderness where they wandered for another forty years. When they came back to the land forty years later, the Nephilim were still there, but the children of Israel finally trusted in God.

ACCORDING TO THE BIBLE, WHO WERE THE NEPHILIM?

Looking at the ancient translations gives us a solid start as to what the word Nephilim means. Let's now look at what else the Bible has to say about these gigantic half-man, half-demon hybrids. First of all we note that there are a series of verses which act as equations just like saying: A=B=C. Even though each letter is unique and has a different name, the value is the same for all. For example four quarters are equal to ten dimes, which are equal to one dollar. In the same way the verses concerning the

Nephilim show us that they were known by different names in different countries, but they were equal and one and the same.

The following table demonstrates the equation of giants to each other that appears in Scripture. In the left column is the name given to a group of giants (starting with the Nephilim) with an equal sign to the name of the corresponding giants in another place. The right column gives the truncated portion of Scripture that proves the relationship. The complete verses are given in appendix four for review (ESV is used for clarity of the names).

TABLE: CORRELATION OF NAMES OF NEPHILIM THE AMORITES

In addition to the verses above, we see that Abraham was the first to encounter the Rephaim, Zuzim (presumably the Zamzummim), and Emim in the land. They remained there through the days of Joshua and Judges.

NAMES	SCRIPTURES (EMPHASIS MINE)
Nephilim = Anakim	The descendants of Anak came from the giants [Nephilim] (Numbers 13:33)
Anakim = Rephaim = Emim	The **Emim** formerly lived there, a people great and many, and tall as the **Anakim**. Like the Anakim they are also counted as **Rephaim**, but the Moabites call them **Emim** (Deuteronomy 2:10-11 ESV)
Rephaim = Zamzummim = Anakim	It is also counted as a land of **Rephaim. Rephaim** formerly lived there—but the Ammonites call them **Zamzummim**—a people great and many, and tall as the Anakim (Deuteronomy 2:20-21a, ESV)
Og, King of Bashan = Rephaim	**Og the king of Bashan** was left of the remnant of the **Rephaim** (Deuteronomy 3:11 ESV)
Bashan = Rephaim	All that portion of Bashan is called the land of **Rephaim** (Deuteronomy 3:13, ESV)

Sihon of the Amorites = Rephaim = Amorites	For Heshbon was the city of Sihon the king of the **Amorites** (Numbers 21:26 ESV)
Og, King of Bashan = Rephaim = Amorites	His land and the land of **Og**, the king of Bashan, the two kings of the **Amorites**, who lived to the east beyond the Jordan (Deuteronomy 4:47 ESV) What you did to the two kings of the **Amorites** [...] Sihon and Og (Joshua 2:10)
Goliath and his brothers = Anakim = Rephaim	At Gath, where there was a man of great stature, [...] and he also was descended from the giants [**Rephaim**, LXX reads: from the giants, γιγαντων], (2 Samuel 21:20 ESV). **Lahmi the brother of Goliath the Gittite** [Gath]. [...] at Gath, [...] he also was descended **from the giants [Rephaim**, LXX reads: giants, γιγαντες]. [...] These were descended from the giants in Gatt (1 Chronicles 20:5-6, 8 ESV)

- In the fourteenth year Chedorlaomer and the kings who were with him came and defeated the **Rephaim** in Ashteroth-karnaim, the **Zuzim** in Ham, the **Emim** in Shaveh-kiriathaim (Genesis 14:5, ESV, emphasis mine).

- In the land of the Perizzites and the **Rephaim** (Joshua 17:15 ESV, emphasis mine).

- For you heard on that day how the **Anakim** were there, with great fortified cities. It may be that the Lord will be with me, and I shall drive them out just as the Lord said (Joshua 14:12 ESV, emphasis mine).

- The name of Hebron formerly was Kirjath Arba (Arba was the greatest man among the **Anakim**) (Joshua 14:15).

After the battle, which Abram led to rescue his nephew Lot, God showed up and promised to Abram that he would have a son and would inherit the land. He mentions something very interesting concerning the Amorites: "for the iniquity of the **Amorites** is not yet complete" (Genesis 15:16). Notice that the reason that his descendants will come back in the fourth generation is because of the iniquity of the Amorites, suggesting that the Amorites, who were Nephilim, were performing great wickedness in the meantime.

We next encounter the Amorites just after Israel had received the Law at Mount Sinai. Within a year's time, God led them up to the border of the Promised Land and God specifically mentioned that His Angel would go "before you and bring you in to the **Amorites** […] and I will cut them off. You shall not bow down to their gods, nor serve them, nor do according to their works; but you shall utterly overthrow them and completely break down their sacred pillars" (Exodus 23:23-24). We find that the Amorites were still in the land into the time of Judges from the passage "do not fear the gods of the **Amorites** in whose land you dwell" (Judges 6:10).

Finally the moment of truth for the Israelites after coming out of Egypt was when they arrived at the border of the Promised Land, at Kadesh Barnea. They sent in spies to check out the land who returned saying that the land was all that God had said it was.

> "The Amalekites dwell in the land of the Negeb. The Hittites, the Jebusites, and the **Amorites** dwell in the hill country. And the Canaanites dwell by the sea, and along the Jordan." But Caleb quieted the people before Moses and said, "Let us go up at once and occupy it, for we are well able to overcome it." Then the men who had gone up with him said, "We are not able to go up against the people, for they are **stronger** than we are." So they brought to the people of Israel a bad report of the land that they had spied out, saying, "The land, through which we have gone to spy it out, is a land that devours its inhabitants, **and all the people that we saw in it are of great height**. And there we saw the **Nephilim** (the sons of Anak, who come from the **Nephilim**), and we seemed to ourselves like grasshoppers, and so we seemed to them" (Numbers 13:29-33, ESV).

The fact that God commanded the Israelites to destroy man, woman, and child becomes logical if we understand that (as the text says) all people in the land were not merely sons of Adam, but were a mix between the sons of God (demons) and human women just like in the days of Noah.

THE SIZE OF THE NEPHILIM

The spies' report determined the next forty years for the Israelites. Their lack of trust in what God could do denied them the opportunity to see the hand of God work in their lifetime. However, we must not discount the facts of their report. They first of all mention that the people of the land were stronger than they were. It is a land that devours its inhabitants and "**all the people that we saw in it are of great height**." There were not just a few tall people there—but all of the people were enormous. In fact these people were so tall and large that the Israelites likened themselves to grasshoppers compared to these Nephilim: "and we were like grasshoppers in our own sight, and so we were in their sight" (Numbers 13:33).

Having first described the people of the land, they then mention them by name "the descendants of Anak came from the giants [**Nephilim**]" (Numbers 13:33). Notice that Joshua and Caleb do not deny the report. They simply have the faith that God will do what He said. The Nephilim are the reason why the children of Israel did not possess the land right after leaving Egypt. The presence of the Nephilim disheartened the spies who consequently gave a bad report. God, though very upset at the people's lack of trust, nevertheless agreed with the description of the people of the land being of a great height and also agreed with the comparison of the Israelites appearing like grasshoppers. Though years later, in Amos 2:9 God says:

> Yet it was I who destroyed the **Amorite** before them, whose height was like the **height of the cedars**, and he was as strong as the oaks; yet I destroyed his fruit above and his roots beneath (Amos 2:9).

God's endorsement is significant; He states the height of the Amorites was like the cedars and God also likens the tail of the mighty Behemoth[105] to a cedar in Job 40. "Look now at the behemoth, which I made along with you; he eats grass like an ox. See now, his strength is in his hips, and his power is in his stomach muscles. He moves **his tail like a cedar**" (Job 40:15-18). God is clearly not saying that his tail was merely stiff, for any tree might be used to communicate that message. However, the cedar is a tree that was renown in the ancient world and the cedars of Lebanon were famous for their immense height. According to one source cedar trees can grow anywhere from 40-85-feet tall[106] and the cedar of Lebanon being among the tallest. In my book *The First Six Days*, I discuss size of the tail of the mighty behemoth because God there likens it to a cedar of Lebanon. "God states what his bones are like [...] the picture is given that the bones of this creature were of immense strength implying that the creature itself was extremely big to need such strong bones."[107]

The description fits the Sauropod class of dinosaurs extremely well and the dinosaur with the longest tail is thought to be the Diplodocus. One source suggests that the tail[108] may have been up to 46 feet long! God's description of the behemoth is not an exaggeration but consistent with what we currently understand about dinosaurs. It could be that the cedars that Job was associated with measured more in the 40-60-foot range. Thus, just to be as conservative as possible—if we assume the minimum height of the cedar that God had in mind was only 40 feet then we have a likely maximum height for the Amorites. How can we calculate the minimum height of these giants (at that time)?

SIZE OF A CUBIT IN MOSES` DAY

Moses describes the size of the bed of King Og of Bashan, who, as we saw, was one of the Nephilim.

> For only Og king of Bashan remained of the remnant of the Rephaim [NKJV Giants]; behold, his bedstead was a bedstead

of iron; is it not in Rabbah of the children of Ammon? nine cubits was the length thereof, and four cubits the breadth of it, after the cubit of a man (Deuteronomy 3:11 JPS).

Moses clearly says that this man's bed was nine cubits but just how big is a cubit? According to the *Oxford Dictionary* a cubit was:

1. The part of the arm from the elbow downward; the forearm.

2. An ancient measure of length derived from the forearm; varying at different times and places, but usually 18 to 22 inches. The Roman cubit was 17.4 inches; the Egyptian 20.64 inches.

Tim Lovett, an expert on ancient shipbuilding, reviewed the references for cubits from around the world in order to get a firm understanding of how long the cubit was that Noah used in the ark.[109] He notes that the shortest was the Greek Short Cubit of 14 inches (356 millimeters) and among the longest were the Persian (Royal) cubit of 25.2 inches (640 millimeters) and the Arabic (Hashimi) of 25.56 inches (649 millimeters). The cubit varied over the centuries by as much as nearly one foot! However, we can be quite confident of the measure that was being referred to concerning King Og. Clearly, the Greek, Persian, and Arabic Empires were not around in Moses' day, so that immediately eliminates their running in this race; the only empire that fits is Egypt.

Moses had just come out of Egypt and Stephen in Acts 7:22 tells us that Moses was "learned in all the wisdom of the Egyptians." Since we have no record of God instituting a new form of measurement, we can safely conclude that any measurements given would then be in the one that all of the people of Israel would have been familiar with. In fact, considering that they were slaves forced to make bricks and to build store houses, measurements would have been very important for them. The most natural and in fact only measurement that they could have known was the Egyptian. Thus when Moses says that Og's bed measured nine cubits long we are obligated to calculate using the Egyptian standard of that day.

Tim Lovett notes that the original Royal Egyptian[110] cubit had a range of 20.62 inches (523.75 millimeters) to 20.65 inches (525 millimeters) while the average was 20.63/4 (524.00 millimeters). This is corroborated by two places in the Scriptures which make reference to this older and longer cubit. King Solomon used the older measure where we read in 2 Chronicles 3:3: "The length was sixty cubits (by cubits according to the former measure)." In Ezekiel's vision of the future temple the measurement that will be employed will be apparently the older and hence longer measure. "These are the measurements of the altar in cubits (the cubit is one cubit and a handbreadth)" (Ezekil 43:13).

Therefore we can confidently conclude that the cubit Moses was referring to was in fact the Egyptian Royal cubit, which was 20.63 inches.[111]

Multiplying 20.63 inches (524.00 millimeters) by nine (cubits),

http://upload.wikimedia.org/wikipedia/commons/b/bc/Coudée-turin.jpg

we arrive at 185.67 inches (4716 millimeters) for the total length of his bed. Converted into our measurements, it was almost 15 feet 6 inches (15.47 feet, 4.716 meters) long and its width 6 feet 10 inches (6.87 feet, 2.094 meters)! This is one massive bed! Moses also mentions that the bed was made of iron which would preclude the idea that a small man with a big ego slept on it otherwise there would be no need to mention the fact that the bed was physically strong (of iron) in order to support someone of such enormous proportions. Thus we can assume that Og must have been slightly shorter than the bed that he slept on and therefore make him roughly 15 feet (4.55 meters) tall!

However, it is plausible that by "bed" Moses in fact meant his final bed—that is his sarcophagus (coffin). This would make sense from the fact that: a) there is no unique word for sarcophagus in Hebrew other than bed, and b) this "bed" was apparently on display "Is it not in Rabbah of the people of Ammon?" (Deuteronomy 3:11). It would seem strange to just have the bed of their former king lying around apparently on display. However, being able to visit the sarcophagus of their fallen king is very plausible. If that is the case, then it would suggest that the "bed" was not for nightly sleeping but was made just big enough for his body to be placed in. Thus, those dimensions more aptly describe the true size of this Rephaim king who measured nearly 15 feet 5 inches tall and had a shoulder width of almost 6 feet 10 inches.

JUST HOW TALL WAS THAT?

To get an idea of just how massive a person of this size was, consider the chart on the following page. Note that the man on the left is 6 feet, the approximate height for most western men. Next to him stands Goliath measuring about 10 feet, 4 inches tall, the 12-foot man then doubles today's man, and finally King Og, who measured some 15 feet tall dwarfed today's average man!

We must point out that the giants that inhabited the land were not just tall men like basketball players of today. Nor were the ancient Israelites significantly shorter than today and thus upon seeing men over six or seven feet they thought them to be giants as some liberal theologians would suggest! King Og was at least 2.5 times taller than a man measuring six feet tall. These measurements are conceivable if indeed fallen angels took women and procreated the Nephilim according to Genesis 6. However, these measurements are illogical in light of the sons of Seth and daughters of man theory because a godly person and a non-godly person will not have children fifteen feet tall!

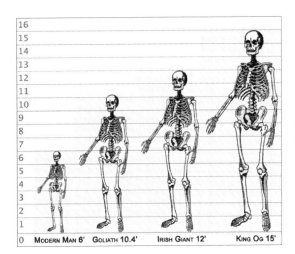

Figure 5
Comparison of Giants

However, demons and humans would presumably produce such enormous children.

HOW HEAVY WAS KING OG?

Let's just consider the implications of a person that tall. Let's assume that he would be equivalent to a man of two hundred pounds—someone who is in shape, but not trying to be a professional athlete and is approximately six feet tall. We know that king Og of Bashan was 2.5 times taller—but how much heavier would he be? Galileo in the early 1600s considered the issue in relation to animals, but the principle is true for people as well. The Indian Institute of Astrophysics notes Galileo's theorization concerning the relation of size to strength (of bone) and structure:

> Consider two animals of different sizes that are geometrically similar. If the larger is twice as long as the smaller animal, it is also twice as wide and twice as high. The larger creature outweighs its smaller counterpart eight times (Indian Institute of Astrophysics 2006).

The above formula is 2 x 2 x 2 = 8. Therefore to calculate King Og's weight we need the cube of 2.5 which is 15.625. That is to say that King Og of Bashan would have weighed 15.625 times more than a six foot man today and thus he would weigh (15.625 x 200 =) 3,125 pounds (1,420 kilograms). Considering that King Og was a warrior, we can presume that he could at least lift the equivalent of his own body weight (a 200 hundred pound man can potentially lift 400-500 pounds or two times his own body weight). Thus, even if he could only lift his own body weight, he still would have been able to lift two war horses (1,500 pounds each) at once with its rider and throw it! In modern terms he could lift a midsize car!

A LAND THAT DEVOURS ITS INHABITANTS

The Israelites also said that it is a "land that devours its inhabitants." It would be easy to suggest that they were simply exaggerating or using hyperbole. However, when we consider how much King Og must have eaten, we begin to see that they were giving an accurate description of what the giants were like! If we use the more conservative weight calculation then he would have needed to consume at least 22,657 calories per day just to stay alive as per the Basal Metabolic Rate[112] which calculates, based on a person's height and weight, how many calories they need to live if they are not doing any significant work per day. Let's put that into perspective to see how he and the other giants his size were devouring the inhabitants, which were presumably animals and hopefully not humans.

First of all today's average American eats about 4,000 calories per day. In 1909 the average American was eating about 3,500 calories per day—about 500 less than today[113] (although the recommended daily calorie intake is only 2,000). King Og, therefore was eating the amount equivalent to about six or seven modern Americans. However, how much was the average person in his day eating? While they didn't leave us detailed records, based on their stature 5'6" to 5'7" and the type of food they had plus the fact that none of today's sugars and processed foods were available, we can estimate that their calorie intake was about 1,600 calories[114] per day. That means that King Og needed, just to stay alive, the same as approximately nine normal sized persons. However, if we convert his needs into pizzas he would need twelve—12 inch pizzas (1,840 calories each). If we convert that to cheeseburgers then he would need sixty three cheeseburgers[115] daily, and converted into lamb he would consume an entire lamb about every two or three days[116] just to just to maintain his daily basic needs. Just imagine if he were having a party or getting ready to go to war! Of course, all of these calculations are only for his Basil Metabolic Rate which is the minimum needed to stay alive each day. His actual consumption was quite possibly double and that is assuming he was not an overeater. Given the fact that he was a giant, he may have just kept eating and eating! He might have had the equivalent of over 30 pizzas or 150 cheeseburgers per day!

Generally the strongest people get first pick on their food preferences; therefore, it would be easy to see how just to feed one giant could easily require numerous animals, plants, fruits, plus water and wine. Therefore, the spies were not exaggerating when they said that it was a land that devours its inhabitants. The Nephilim were certainly eating continually and many animals must have been given to satisfy their nearly insatiable appetites. Therefore we can empathize with the Israelites and the fear they had of the inhabitants of the land who "devoured its inhabitants!" Nevertheless, how sad that they did not (and often we do not) take God at His Word when He exhorted them with these mighty words:

> Therefore understand today that the LORD your God is He who goes over before you as a consuming fire. He will destroy them and bring them [the gigantic inhabitants] down before you; so you shall drive them out and destroy them quickly, as the LORD has said to you (Deuteronomy 9:3).

Approximatelyfive hundred years later David would face the giant Goliath, who was also descended from the Rephaim (1 Chronicles 20:5-6). Goliath, measured a *mere* six cubits (20.6"x6 cubits = 10.3 feet [10′ 4″]). That means that Goliath was 1.72 times taller than a man of six feet. Again, using our cube formula for calculating weight, we need to find the cube of 1.72 which is 5.088 and multiplying that times our two hundred pound man Goliath would weigh 1,068 pounds. Thus King Og weighed about 3,100 pounds and Goliath, who was one-third shorter than Og, weighed approximately 1,000—they were two enormous people which simply underscores the reason the Israelites feared them. The biblical evidence is conclusive that the Nephilim were in fact men of extraordinary stature and that they descended from human mothers and fallen angel fathers.

EXTRA-BIBLICAL CONFIRMATION

Numbers 13 of Targum Jonathan states that the giants were masters of evil:

> The country through which we have passed to explore it is a land that killeth its inhabitants with diseases; and all the people who are in it are **giants**, masters of evil ways. And there we saw the giants, the sons of **Anak**, of the race of the **giants** (Targum Jonathan, Numbers 13, emphasis mine).

The Targum makes reference to the giants of the land as being of the same stock as those that perished in the flood, which again, would prove that they believed them to be Nephilim.

> The Emthanaia dwelt in it of old, a people great and many, and mighty as the **giants**. The giants who dwelt in the plain of Geyonbere were also reputed as the **giants** who perished in the Flood; but the Moabites called them Emethanee (Targum Jonathan, Deuteronomy 2, emphasis mine).

Lastly we see in Targum Jonathan how the ancient Jews believed and understood Moses' saying that the Lord God is "He who goes over before you *as* a consuming fire. He will destroy them and bring them down before you." They understood it as a reference to His Shechinah which is also known as the Word. Notice that the giants were indeed bigger and mightier than the

Israelites. In fact they were so great, God said that He personally would take care of them.

> Hear, Israel: you are this day (about) to pass Jordan to enter in and possess (the country of) nations greater and stronger than you, and cities many, and fortified to the height of heaven. A people (are they) strong and **tall as the giants** whom you know, and of whom you have heard (say), Who can stand before the **sons of the giants**? Know, therefore, today that the Lord your God, **whose glorious Shekinah goeth before you, whose Word is a consuming fire**, will destroy them and drive them out before you; so shall you drive them out, and destroy them quickly, as the Lord your God hath said to you (Targum Jonathan Deuteronomy 9, emphasis mine).

JOSEPHUS AND BARUCH

We next turn to Josephus who described the giants as being extremely large and whose bones were still available even in his day.

> For which reason they removed their camp to Hebron; and when they had taken it, they slew all the inhabitants. There were till then left the race of **giants, who had bodies so large, and countenances so entirely different from other men, that they were surprising to the sight, and terrible to the hearing. The bones of these men are still shown to this very day, unlike to any credible relations of other men** (emphasis mine).[117]

Very much like Josephus, the writer of the book of Baruch mentions their fame and great height. "There were the giants famous from the beginning, that were of so great stature, and so expert in war" (Baruch, Chapter 3:26).

BOOK OF JUBILEES

The book of Jubilees, from the Dead Sea Scrolls, also records the fact of the giants' great height and even gives specific measurements. "But before they used to call the land of Gilead the land of the Rephaim; for it was the land of the Rephaim, and the Rephaim were born (there), **giants whose height was ten, nine, eight down to seven cubits"** (emphasis mine).[118]

TERTULLIAN

We last turn to the church father, Tertullian, who wrote that the giants' bodies were still around in his day. He believed that their remains would contain the needed DNA (germs was the term of his day) to bring them to life again.

> There are the carcasses of the **giants** of old time; it will be obvious enough that they are not absolutely decayed, **for their bony frames are still extant**. [...] the lasting **germs** of that body which is **to sprout into life** again in the resurrection (emphasis mine).[119]

BIBLICAL AND EXTRA-BIBLICAL CONCLUSIONS

Thus we can conclude that Nephilim and all of the other names that are in Scripture for them, were not merely the offspring of a human father with a human mother. There is absolutely no evidence whatsoever that the Nephilim came about as a result of the "good" sons of Seth turning "bad" and then connecting with the bad daughters of Cain. The ancient world believed until the time of Augustine about the Nephilim. Every ante-Nicene interpreter (Jewish and Christian) understood the sons of God to be angels who had sexual relations with women. The offspring of those relationships were the Nephilim. If there were demonic-human (Nephilim) hybrids in the days of Noah and afterward then what will there be at the time of Jesus' return?

CHAPTER TEN

Modern Discoveries of Giants

WE HAVE SEEN that the Bible clearly teaches that the union of demons and women produced a race of hybrids known as the Nephilim, who were on the earth before the flood and afterward. We have also seen that all ancient Jewish and (ante-Nicene) Christian literature (that spoke of the days of Noah) unanimously agreed that demons mingled their seed with women and produced the hybrid race known as the Nephilim. We should expect to find, therefore, some archaeological evidence of the Nephilim.

In addition to the many written modern accounts of explorers and miners discovering men of extremely large proportions, there are also some archaeological findings. However, in our day seeing is not always believing because computer programs like Photoshop can make the unreal look very convincing. Unfortunately there are many photos floating around the Internet that are hoaxes that look fairly authentic. Thus our challenge, short of going out and doing the dig ourselves, is to sort through what is legitimate evidence and what is not. In this chapter I have, with care, selected photos taken before the advent of the computer and news reports from actual newspapers—all of which come from sources which can be verified for the skeptical reader. While the thesis of this book does not stand or fall on such evidence, it is important to help us see that there were giants in those days and afterward, always keeping in mind that Jesus said that His coming would be like the days of Noah.

IRISH GIANT

One way to test the genuineness of pictorial evidence is to find such pictures that were taken before the invention of the computer and Photoshop. That is not to say that the *object* in the picture is *necessarily* real, but the *photograph* itself is **not** something that has been created (or altered) with the aid of a computer. One such example is brought to us by W. G. Wood-Martin, who in 1901 wrote of the Irish Pre-Christian Traditions in his book *Traces of the Elder Faiths of Ireland: A Folklore Sketch* (Volume 1).[120] In his book he includes both textual and photographic evidence of giants. The text is intriguing and corroborates what we have been investigating on giants. Wood-Martin quotes Augusthie from his chapter on "The Lives and Sizes of the Antediluvians" (De Civitate Dei, xv. 9):

> Concerning the magnitude of their bodies, the graves laid bare by age or the force of rivers and various accidents, especially convict the incredulous where they have come to light, or where the bones of the dead of **incredible magnitude** have fallen. I have seen, and not I alone, on the shore of Utica, so huge a molar tooth of a man, that were it cut up into small models of teeth like ours, it would seem enough to make a hundred of them. But this I should think had belonged to some giant, for beside that the bodies of all men were then much larger than ours, the **giants** again far exceeding the rest." Kirby, in his Wonderful (and Eccentric Museum), published in 1820, devotes a chapter to a description of "Gigantic Remains," and states that "all the public prints make mention of an extraordinary monument of gigantic Iniman stature, found by two labourers in Leixlip Churchyard, on the 10th July, 1812. It appeared to have belonged to a man of not less than **ten feet in height**, and is believed to be the same mentioned by Keating—

Phelim O'Tool, buried in Leixlip Churchyard, near the Salmon Leap, one thousand two hundred and fifty years ago. In the place was found a **large finger-ring of pure gold**. There were no inscriptions or characters of any kind upon it. One of the teeth is said to have been as large as an ordinary forefinger" (emphasis mine).[121]

Wood-Martin then includes a story and photograph taken from *Strand Magazine* December 1895 edition and he says to "let the reader judge as to the genuineness of the fossilized Irish giant, which is thus described":

Pre-eminent among the most extraordinary articles ever held by a railway company is the **fossilized Irish giant**, which is at this moment lying at the London and North-Western Railway Company's Broad street goods depot, and a photograph of which is reproduced here ... This monstrous figure is reputed to have been dug up by a Mr. Dyer whilst prospecting for iron ore in County Antrim.

The principal measurements are: entire length, 12 ft. 2 in.; girth of chest, 6 ft. 6 in.; and length of arms, 4 ft. 6 in. **There are six toes on the right foot.** The gross weight is 2 tons

Figure 6 "Irish Giant" taken from Strand Magazine December 1895, C. F. Wood-Martin, 1901:58

15 cwt.; so that it took half a dozen men and a powerful crane to place this article of lost property in position for the Strand magazine artist (*Strand Magazine* December 1895, C. F. Wood-Martin, 1901:58, emphass mine).

Just how much is "2 tons 15 CWT"? Due to the fact that this artifact was measured in England, we must use the Imperial (British) units of measurement. The British ton, known as a long ton, is equal to 2,240 pounds whereas the American ton is 2,000 pounds. The centrum weight abbreviated CWT is equal to 112 pounds[122]. Thus the total weight of two (long) tons is 4,480 pounds and 15 CWT is 1,680. The entire weight in pounds therefore is 6,160. Of course, the man in the coffin did not weigh that much when alive and the fossilization process added to the overall weight. Nevertheless, the Antrim Giant corroborates what King Og of Bashan must have been like. If we return to the original calculation, first made by Galileo, then measuring twice the height of today's man (of 6 feet and optimal weight of 200 pounds.), the Antrim Giant ought to have had a net weight of 1,600 pounds. Not only was this Irish Giant also two feet taller than Goliath, but he also had six toes[123] on the right foot just like the Rephaim (which were counted among the Nephilim).

> Yet again there was war at Gath, where there was a **man of great stature**, with twenty-four fingers and toes, **six on each hand and six on each foot**; and he also was born to the giant [Rephaim, LXX reads: giants, γιγαντες] (1 Chronicles 20:6).

The Fossilized Irish Giant is by no means the only evidence. There are many reports, written and archaeological, that attest to the fact that giants were real. Like the evidence of the Irish Giant, I have sought out evidence that is not subject to Photoshop types of tricks.

PETRIFIED FOOT MORE THAN TWO FEET LONG

A news report from the *Chillicothe Weekly Constitution*, 1917, also speaks of an enormous foot that was found in a coal mine in Iowa.

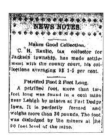

> A petrified foot more than **two feet long** was found in a coal mine near Lehigh by miners at Fort Dodge Iowa. It is perfectly formed and weighs more than **30 pounds**. The foot was dislodged by the miners at the 90 foot level of the mine.

Figure 7 Newspaper *Chillicothe Weekly Constitution*, 1917

The owner of the foot was probably about 13 feet tall (the formula is 6.6 inches in height for every inch of length of the foot).

NEW YORK TRIBUNE: PREHISTORIC GIANT

According to the *New York Tribune*, February 3, 1909, a fifteen-foot human skeleton tall was unearthed in Mexico. We recall that King Og of Bashan was that tall and he was reported to be of the Nephilim.

Figure 8
New York Tribune, 1909

News was received here Monday from Mexico that at Ixtapalapa, a town 10 miles southeast of Mexico City there had been discovered what was believed to be the skeleton of a prehistoric **giant of extraordinary size**.

A peon while excavating for the foundation of a house on the estate of Augustin Juarez found the **skeleton of a human being that is estimated to have been about 15 feet high**, and who must have lived ages ago, judging from the ossified state of the bones.

Romulo Luna, judge of the District, has taken possession of the skeleton which is complete with the exception of the skull. Judge Luna says that as soon as the search for the skull is finished the skeleton will be forwarded to the national museum of Mexico, which has an almost priceless collection of Aztec antiquities. The National museum, it is said, has made arrangements to investigate this "find."

The discovery of the skeleton has revived the old Aztec legend that in a prehistoric age a **race of giants** lived [in the] valley of

Figure 9
NY Tribune Find
Prehistoric Giant

Anahuac, a name given by the aboriginal Mexicans to that part of the Mexican plateau nearly corresponding to the modern valley of Mexico City. These **giants**, known as Quinatzins, the story goes, were afterward destroyed by the Ulmecas, also of **great stature**, who in turn, perished by earthquake, interpreted as an expression of the wrath of God (emphasis mine).[125]

GIANTS OF PREHISTORIC FRANCE

The *Oelwein Register* on November 8, 1894, reported that scientists confirmed the find of a race of giants between ten and fifteen feet tall.

In a prehistoric cemetery recently uncovered at Montpellier, France, while workmen were excavating a waterworks reservoir, human skulls were found measuring 28, 31 and 32 inches in circumference. The bones that the workmen discovered were also of gigantic proportions. The discoveries were sent to the Paris Academy for study. One of the **scientists engaged in examining the skeletons says that they belonged to a race of men who stood between 10 and 15 feet in height"** (emphasis mine).[126]

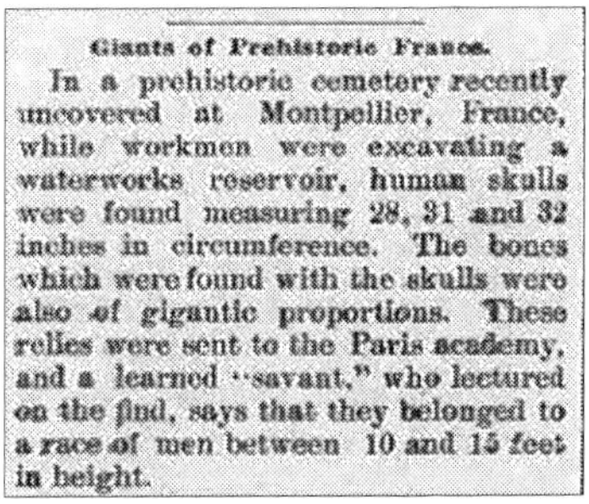

Giants of Prehistoric France.

In a prehistoric cemetery recently uncovered at Montpellier, France, while workmen were excavating a waterworks reservoir, human skulls were found measuring 28, 31 and 32 inches in circumference. The bones which were found with the skulls were also of gigantic proportions. These relics were sent to the Paris academy, and a learned "savant," who lectured on the find, says that they belonged to a race of men between 10 and 15 feet in height.

Figure 10 *Oelwein Register* November 8, 1894

STRANGE FIND BY MINERS OF APOLLO MINE

Appearing in the newspaper *Charleroi Mail*, July 1909 edition, was a news report of a petrified giant whom the finders considered to be absolutely human. The problem is that according to evolution, no human should be found at such a depth as it would indicate the person to be millions of years old. According to the Bible, there were giants on the earth before the days of the flood and hence finding a giant so far below the ground only serves to confirm the veracity of the Bible and the flood.

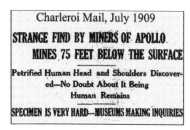

Figure 11
Newspaper *Charleroi Mail* July 1909

"Seventy five feet Below the Surface—Petrified Human Head and Shoulders Discovered—No Doubt About it Being Human Remains—Museums Making Inquiries Specimen is Very Hard."[127]

CONCLUSION

The evidence we have seen in this section confirms what the Bible has said. Given that there are so many fake pictures out on the Internet, it seemed prudent to look for sources that predate things like Photoshop. Therefore we found sources that are copies of old newspapers including testimony and sometimes pictures of strange finds. All of the sources are given for the inquisitive reader to verify the details. Therefore the conclusion that we have arrived at is that there have been extraordinarily large men in the past. Some were found at a great depth under the earth which only serves to confirm that they were buried during a great cataclysm that came upon the earth—which obviously was the flood in the days of Noah.

SUMMARY OF PART TWO:
SATAN'S FAILED FIRST ATTEMPT

Let's recap what we have seen concerning the days of Noah. First, we have seen that men began to multiply on the face of the earth and there were conceivably over ten billion people at the time! We investigated and without reservation concluded that the sons of God were fallen angels; they were the same fallen angels that Jude and Peter spoke about that are kept in chains of darkness reserved for judgment. They came to the daughters of Adam and from their union were born Nephilim, which consisted of human-demonic genetic material. The Nephilim (fallen ones) were known as *gegenes* (of the earth) in Greek.

These were the famous men of the ancient world. The *gegenes* in the Greek traditions were hybrid creatures—half human and half god (demonic). We also saw that all of the ancient Jewish traditions believed the Nephilim to be hybrids—half human and half demonic.

The ancient Christians believed in like manner; the idea that the sons of God were the sons of Seth did not even come about until Augustine. We discovered that Augustine simply asserted that the sons of God were the sons of Seth but he in no way had any supporting evidence (or scripture) to back up his claim. As such, he declared it to be true and since then Bible commentators have repeated his words without offering anymore evidence than he did. We have shown that the sons of God were not the sons of Seth but were in fact fallen angels, and the daughters of Adam (men) were not the daughters of Cain, but were simply women or as the writer of Genesis already put, they were the descendants of Adam. Thus, the contrast is between direct creations of God, which the angels were (and the sons of Seth were not)[128] and between female humans, which were procreations via Adam. With this backdrop do we read that God was grieved by the wickedness of man. Indeed, given that women were having offspring which were half demonic—how could God not be sorry that He had created man?

Without doubt we have seen that fallen angels mingled their seed (genetic information) with humans both before and after the days of Noah (more fallen angels did it again). It is this genetic mixing that makes God's complete destruction of every man, woman, and child in Noah's day reasonable. Without question the Bible says that man's thoughts were constantly wicked and the first four verses of Genesis 6 provide the answer to the question of how they became so wicked; the Nephilim, who had demonic fathers, were on the earth in those days!

It seems incredible, but considering that out of the billions of humans (see Chapter five) on the earth only eight were saved out of it—a major reason for the flood seems to be that many of the human race had been tainted genetically. The Bible tells us that Noah was a just man (*tsadik* צַדִּיק), perfect [*tamim* תָּמִים] in all his generations (Genesis 6:9), meaning that he was without genetic defect. Consider that of the eighty some times *tamim* is used in the Bible, it always refers to an animal without any physical blemish. Thus it would also explain why the Israelites were to destroy the people of the land, every man, woman, and child—that is, they were all tainted because they were Nephilim. Whether or not all but Noah's family were Nephilim is uncertain. However the strong implication is that many, perhaps a majority, were. When the children of Israel saw the Nephilim they lost heart and did not trust that God could overcome the Nephilim.

Among the Nephilim that they had to fight was King Og of Bashan, whom we have seen measured about fifteen feet tall. He also weighed approximately 3,100 pounds. and needed a minimum of about 22,000 calories just to get through each day. Judging from his stature, Canaan was indeed a land that devoured its inhabitants. Lastly, we looked for evidence of such enormous people and found that as recently as one to two hundred years ago, giant mummies, footprints, and accounts all gave witness to the reality of such unnaturally enormous beings. With the thought in mind that the inhabitants of the land were Nephilim, we can understand why God commanded the Israelites to completely exterminate those seven nations. The genetic mingling of demonic and human could not be tolerated. It was not tolerated in the days of Noah and for that reason God commanded the extermination of the inhabitants of the land of Canaan. Everything was to reproduce according to its kind (Genesis 1:24) and the demons clearly broke this commandment. The book of Daniel prophesizes that the mingling of demons with humanity will happen once again and Jesus Himself stated that as the days of Noah were, so the coming of the Son of Man shall be (all hearing those words would have associated the destruction of the world with the Nephilim).

If the sons of God were mingling with the human race in Noah's days then that means that the last days will be marked by a similar occurrence. God gave the human race 120 years until the flood He would bring to destroy the world. During that final time of 120 years until the flood the mingling continued (married and given in marriage) until the very last day when Noah entered the ark and God closed the door. If we are truly in the last days of time then we ought to see biblical proof that events similar to Noah's will repeat. We ought to see the following:

- Demons materializing physically in some manner

- The taking of women

- Demonic-human hybrids

Do we see any of these things happening in our day? Predictably all of these are happening and these are what we will examine in the next section.

PART THREE

THE FINAL ATTEMPT TO CORRUPT THE IMAGE

CHAPTER ELEVEN

Mingling with the Seed of Men

ONE OF THE KEYS to understanding how the image of God will be corrupted in the last days is found in Daniel 2, where we read of the kingdoms that ruled over Israel, beginning with the kingdom of Babylon all the way to the "ten toes." God used King Nebuchadnezzar of the Babylonian Empire to chastise His people for not following Him. The King carried the Jewish people away in three waves of deportation to Babylon, beginning in 606, then 597, and finally 586 BC, when he also destroyed the city of Jerusalem. Among those taken (during the first wave) was a young Jewish man named Daniel. One night King Nebuchadnezzar had a dream about a massive statue of a man made of different materials. God used Daniel to interpret King Nebuchadnezzar's dream, which was in fact a vision of the future kingdoms of the world.

> This image's head was of fine gold, its chest, and arms of silver, its belly and thighs of bronze, its legs of iron, its feet partly of iron and partly of clay. You watched while a stone was cut out without hands, which struck the image on its feet of iron and clay, and broke them in pieces. Then the iron, the clay, the bronze, the silver, and the gold were crushed together [...] And the stone that struck the image became a great mountain and filled the whole earth [...] you are this head of gold (Daniel 2:32-35).

Daniel explained to King Nebuchadnezzar that he was the head of gold and after him would come another three kingdoms ,which are identified as the Medo-Persian Empire, the Grecian Empire, and the Roman Empire.

> But after you shall arise another kingdom inferior to yours; then another, a third kingdom of bronze, which shall rule over all the earth. And the fourth kingdom shall be as strong as iron, inasmuch as iron breaks in pieces and shatters everything; and like iron that crushes, that kingdom will break in pieces and crush all the others. Whereas you saw the feet and toes, partly of potter's clay and partly of iron, the kingdom shall be divided; yet the strength of the iron shall be in it, just as you saw the iron mixed with ceramic clay (Daniel 2:38-41).

The Roman Empire is described in amazing precision by noting that it would become two legs. The Roman Empire was not divided into two parts, Eastern and Western, until AD 285 by Diocletian—over seven hundred years later! However, the kingdom will be governed by a group of ten kings represented by the ten toes. The ten toes are equal to the ten kings found in Daniel 7:24 and Revelation 17:12, and they are partly strong and partly weak. "And as the toes of the feet were partly of iron and partly of clay, so the kingdom shall be partly strong and partly fragile" (Daniel 2:42).

The Roman Empire (or some expression of it) has not yet become ten toes and therefore this is a future fulfillment waiting to happen. When it does it will be partly strong like iron and partly weak like clay. However we are told that "they" will mingle with the "seed of men" in "these days."

> As you saw iron mixed with ceramic clay, **they will mingle** [*mitarvin lehevon* מִתְעָרְבִין לֶהֱוֹן] **with the seed of men** [*bizra' anasha* בִּזְרַע אֲנָשָׁא]; but they will not adhere to one another, just as iron does not mix with clay. **And in the days of these kings** the God of heaven will set up a kingdom which shall never be destroyed; and the kingdom shall not be left to other people;

it shall break in pieces and consume all these kingdoms, and it shall stand forever (Daniel 2:43-44).

THEY ARE MINGLING THEMSELVES

An important clue to understanding this phrase is to understand what is being mixed. This portion of Daniel (Daniel 2:4-7:28) was written in Aramaic because of the direct communication to Nebuchadnezzar, Belshazzar, and their visions (with the vision of Chapter 7 happening during Belshazzar's reign). The word "mingle" [*mitarvin* מִתְעָרְבִין] is a third person plural *hitpaal* (as confirmed by the Westminster Hebrew Morphology Codes). The *hitpaal* is virtually identical to the Hebrew *hitpael*. The basic usage is reflexive which means that the subject is also the object, for example: "I dress myself" is where "I," the subject, do the action (dress), and "I" also receive the action of the verb (being dressed). Thus, the *hitpaal* verb[129] of Daniel 2:43 conveys that same meaning. Therefore "they" are the ones doing the action, but they are also doing it to themselves. Thus, the idea is that "they" (the subject) will mingle themselves (the object of the verb) with something else. This is reflected in the numerous English translations available of Daniel 2:43.

- … **they will combine** with one another in the **seed of men** (NASB).

- … **they shall mingle themselves** with the **seed of men** (KJV, ASV, ERV, WBT, WEB).

- … they are **mixing themselves** with the **seed of men** (YLT).

Bible commentators Keil and Delitzsch note the meaning of the mixing of iron and clay in Daniel 2:43: "The mixing of iron with clay represents the attempt to bind the two distinct and separate materials into one combined whole as fruitless, and altogether in vain" (K&D, Daniel 2:43). In other words, the word is used in Scripture to denote two things that should not be mixed together.

Iron and clay can be put into the same mix but they will not adhere (without heat).

While these don't represent by no means the total consensus of translations, they plausibly provide the preferable (literal) translation based on the grammar. The same Hebrew root (*arab* ערב) is used in five other passages in Scripture. Though there is a slight grammatical difference between the Hebrew *hitpael* and Aramaic *hitpaal*, the root word, nevertheless, is exactly the same in both languages. The first usage we come to outside of Daniel is Psalm 106:35 where the writer recounts the history of Israel noting that Israel, did not destroy the wicked (and ostensibly Nephilim) nations that the Lord had told them to destroy— rather they mingled themselves (via marriage to them). "But were mingled [*vayitarvu* וַיִּתְעָרְבוּ] among the heathen, and learned their works" (Psalm 106:35 KJV). This unfortunately led them to sacrificing their children to demons (Psalm 106:37).

The next usage of the word "mingle" is in Ezra 9:2. Again, the mingling has to do with exchanging seed or genetic material. In this case, the Jews mingled themselves with the people of the land. The concern was that the holy seed (zera זֶרַע) from which the Messiah was to come was being mixed with people who were not of the seed of Abraham, Isaac, and Jacob.

> For they have taken of their daughters for themselves, and for their sons: so that the holy seed [zera זֶרַע] have mingled themselves [*hitarvu* הִתְעָרְבוּ] with the people of [*those*] lands: yea, the hand of the princes and rulers hath been chief in this trespass (Ezra 9:2 KJV).

The holy seed and that of the nations will mix but thereby contaminating the line from which the Messiah will come and therefore the holy seed should not be mixed with seed from outside of the Abrahamic line. The other three instances of the verb appear in the Proverbs, where the idea is not to meddle or mix with the affairs of others.

Coming back to our key verse of Daniel 2:43, we deduce that "they" should not to mix themselves with seed of a different type. Therefore, their type must be something other than the seed of men.[130] Rendering the translation in modern terms will help to grasp the full implications of the verse: **"They will hybridize [mingle, mix, crossbreed] themselves with the genetic material [seed] of mankind"** (translation mine). This rendering is further enhanced when we consider the use of "seed of men," which in Daniel is the Aramaic word for men/mankind [*anasha* אֲנָשָׁא], "the seed of mankind." In Jeremiah 31:27 God declares: "the days are coming [...] when I will sow [*vezarati* וְזָרַעְתִּי] the house of Israel and the house of Judah with the seed of man [*zera Adam* זֶרַע אָדָם] and the seed of beast [*zera behema* בְּהֵמָה זֶרַע]" (Jeremiah 31:27). In this case, God is talking about how He will cause men and animals to flourish in the land of Israel (and Judah). The contrast is made between the seed of men and the seed of beasts (animals), being two distinct kinds. Therefore, if the seed of men refers to humans as a kind (species) then the next question we come to is just who are "they" in Daniel 2:43?

WHO ARE "THEY"?

The text says that "they will mingle themselves." The antecedent of a pronoun usually comes before it, but since there is no other defining noun for "they" we must look at the next possible noun which is "these kings" in verse 44. Thus the word that defines "they" is in fact "these kings." Just like those two materials do not blend well, neither will "these kings" with the seed of men. This cannot be simply referring to the intermarriage of different human ethnicities. We have explored the seed already throughout the Bible and seen that seed is referring to the genetic information contained in the gametes of both men and women. For a man it is the twenty-three chromosomes contained in the sperm and for a woman it is the twenty-three chromosomes contained in the ovum.

Therefore, what is significant about the statement that "these kings" will mingle with the seed of men? After all, every human on the planet originally came from Adam; we are all sons of Adam in a grand sense. When two people (son and daughter of men [Adam]) get married and have children, they literally mingle their seed—which is what procreation or child-bearing is all about (recall our discussion of the genetics of the incarnation). So, to say that these kings will mingle with the seed of men **must necessarily** mean that they are different from men. That is, **they are not** of the seed of men. After all, there really is no need to mention that a son and daughter of Adam (Aramaic *Enosh* אֱנָשׁ) are mixing their seed; even though procreation is miraculous, it is nonetheless "normal" and "ordinary." Therefore to say "they will mingle with the seed of men" must mean that "they" are not themselves of the seed of men, which is to say that **"they" are not human**. If they are not human, then what are they?

They (the ten kings) must be some beings that are able to mix their seed with mankind but are different from mankind and just as we saw in the Jude 1:7 passage, the strange flesh reference (mingling with a different kind) seems to be referring to demons (fallen angels) having sexual relations with women. Daniel, in fact, records the answer of who these kings are in Chapter 10. As we examined before, an angel[131] visited Daniel, who described him as:

> His body was like beryl, his face like the appearance of lightning, his eyes like torches of fire, his arms and feet like burnished bronze in color, and the sound of his words like the voice of a multitude (Daniel 10:6).

This angel (possibly Gabriel who visited Daniel in chapter 9) says to Daniel:

> Do not fear, Daniel, for from the first day that you set your heart to understand, and to humble yourself before your God, your words were heard; and I have come because of your words, But the prince [*sar* שַׂר] of the kingdom of Persia withstood me

twenty-one days; and behold, Michael, one of the chief princes [*hasarim harishonim* הַשָּׂרִים הָרִאשֹׁנִים], came to help me, for I had been left alone there with the kings [*malkhei* מַלְכֵי] of Persia (Daniel 10:12-13).

This "man" that Daniel saw, who we would classify as an angelic being, whose "face was like lightning," was stopped by a being of a similar likeness and power known as the prince of Persia. The word "prince" (*sar* שַׂר) used to describe the one who withstood is the same word used to describe Michael, the chief prince (*sar* שַׂר). The man states that not only had he been stopped by the prince of Persia, but that he remained alone with the kings (*malkhei* מַלְכֵי) of Persia. The Septuagint interprets the kings simply as rulers or princes [*arkhontos* αρχοντος], which is the same Greek word in Ephesians 6:12. He then mentions that he must also fight against the prince of Greece.

Then he said, "Do you know why I have come to you? And now I must return to fight with the prince [*sar* שַׂר] of Persia; and when I have gone forth, indeed the prince [*sar* שַׂר] of Greece will come. But I will tell you what is noted in the Scripture of Truth. (No one upholds me against these, except Michael your prince [*sar* שַׂר] (Daniel 10:21).

These princes and kings are the demonic power and influence behind the earthly kings and empires. The kings in Daniel 10 must necessarily be demon kings and not human kings for not even any number of human kings would be able to imprison one (good) angel as witnessed when just one angel killed 185,000 mighty Assyrians in one night (2 Kings 19:35).

In the book of Revelation we find another evil angelic king named Abaddon in Hebrew and Apollyon in Greek. "And they had as **king** over them the angel (*angelos* αγγελος) of the bottomless pit, whose name in Hebrew is Abaddon, but in Greek he has the name Apollyon" (Revelation 9:11). Angelic beings (good or bad) are referred to both as princes and also as kings. Therefore "these kings" who "mingle with the seed of men" in Daniel 2 are in fact of the angelic order; the fact that they are destroyed proves that they are not good angels but are fallen angels.

TEN TOES, HORNS, AND KINGS ARE DEMONS

Lastly, we note that the four empires in Nebuchadnezzar's dream are parallel to those in Daniel chapter 7. Therefore, the ten toes of Daniel 2:43 are identical to the ten horns in Daniel 7:7 (and Revelation 13:1) and from Revelation 17:12 we learn that the horns are kings. Note the following verses:

- And *as* the **toes of the feet** *were* partly of iron and partly of clay, […] **they** will mingle with the seed of men; […] And in the days of **these kings** the God of heaven will set up a kingdom which shall never be destroyed […] (Daniel 2:42-44).

- And the **ten horns** that *were* on its head, and the **other** *horn* **which came up**, before which three fell, namely, that horn which had eyes and a mouth which spoke pompous words, whose appearance *was* greater than his fellows (Daniel 7:20).

- The **ten horns** *are* **ten kings** *who* shall arise from this kingdom. And another shall rise after them; He shall be **different** from the first *ones,* and shall subdue three kings (Daniel 7:24).

- And another sign appeared in heaven: behold, a great, **fiery red dragon** having **seven heads** and **ten horns**, and **seven diadems** on his heads (Revelation 12:3).

- […] And I saw a beast rising up out of the sea, having **seven heads** and **ten horns**, and on his **horns ten crowns**, and on his heads a blasphemous name (Revelation 13:1).

- The **ten horns** which you saw are **ten kings** who have **received no kingdom as yet**, but they receive authority for one hour as kings with the beast (Revelation 17:12).

We see that the ten toes are the ten horns, which are the ten kings—and these ten kings are demon kings and not specifically human (though human rulers are probably controlled by them). This squares well with the fact that we are told in Revelation 12:3 that Satan has ten horns.[132] The same heads, horns, and diadems, which the dragon has, are also on the beast. This presents somewhat of a challenge in that the beast sometimes appears as an empire and sometimes as an individual entity; perhaps both are true. At least part of the time the beast must refer to an individual entity because he is eventually thrown into the lake of fire along with the false prophet (Revelation 19:20). Throwing an empire into the lake of fire appears to be impossible in that an empire is not a living entity, but is a collection of individuals performing the wishes of the leader.

REVELATION 17:12

The final proof that the toes/horns/kings are demons comes from Revelation 17:12, which we already considered as proof that the kings are equal to the horns. However, if we zoom in just a bit we notice[133] something important; the ten horns "**are** ten kings" (*deka basileis eisin* δέκα βασιλεῖς εἰσιν) which "have received no kingdom **as yet**." John was told that there **are** kings (current to his day) that do **not yet** have a kingdom. However, these same kings (alive in John's day) will receive their kingdom when the Beast rises to power. It has been nearly two thousand years since John received the Revelation from Jesus on the island of Patmos. What human kings have been alive for two thousand years? Clearly the answer is none! Therefore, the only option left are kings that do not die but continue—demons do not physically die and therefore the ten kings were present back in John's day, had no kingdom but will receive the kingdom when the Beast comes, and so we conclude that the kings are **necessarily** demonic kings. We know that the understanding of "are kings", signifying that they were alive then in John's day, must be right because Jesus used the same grammatical argument against the Sadducees to prove the resurrection: "I am the God of Abraham, and the God of Isaac, and the God of Jacob'? He is not God of the dead, but of the living" (Matthew 22:32).

Thus we see that in the last days, rulers of this dark age (Ephesians 6:12) will mingle their seed with humans just as they did in the days of Noah and also when the children of Israel went into the Promised Land. So, just as Jesus predicted, the days of His return would be like the days of Noah. The sons of God took women and the fruit of their union was the Nephilim. So too the last days will be marked by the coming of these Nephilim. In fact we see that these days have already begun to be fulfilled and so our Lord's return cannot be far away.

CHAPTER TWELVE

The Demonic Deception

"There is no neutral ground in the universe.
Every square inch, every split second
is claimed by God and counter claimed by Satan."
- C. S. Lewis

ACCORDING TO WALTER MARTIN

THE RESPECTED and late Bible expert Walter Martin said in a 1968 interview: "At some point in the near future UFO occupants would begin to interact extensively with people. Their message? We are superior beings—advanced far beyond you earthlings. Look at our technology. But we have come to help and guide you."[134]

Walter Martin did not believe in little green men from the other side of the universe and neither do I, for the Bible in no way teaches such things. Martin was simply discussing the "alien" deception—that is **that demons have been masquerading as "aliens,"** "extraterrestrials" that have come from a distant galaxy and are here to help. He goes on speaking of the theology of these would be "aliens."

A vital clue to the UFO mystery is this: **UFO theology— gained from the so-called close encounters—is diametrically opposed to Christianity**. The world of the occult and the people involved in it speak constantly of contact with UFOs and their occupants, and the theology derived from UFO contact is most revealing. **Extraterrestrials** (according to those who claim to have spoken to them) do **not believe God is a personal being; they do not believe Jesus Christ is the only Savior, and they do not believe the Bible alone is God's Word to the world.** They do not believe in eternal punishment, and they do not believe in bodily resurrection. The reincarnation of the Hindus, Kabbalah, and New Age philosophies gains a new perspective when viewed through the eyes of extraterrestrials: it transforms into planetary reincarnation, where people evolve from planet to planet in order to reach perfection.

It would be an amazing thing, from the world's perspective, if an advanced technological civilization arrived upon the earth, claiming to be the savior of mankind and the Creator of *Homo sapiens*. **It is not beyond the realm of possibility that with all of the fanfare of scientific accomplishment, the ultimate deception could reveal itself at the end of the ages as our deliverer.** In 2 Thessalonians 2:3-9, we are told that when **Satan appears in human form, he appears as the Antichrist who leads men**, through deceit, to destruction. Those who refuse the knowledge of the truth of Jesus Christ will believe him (emphasis mine).[135]

Martin is suggesting that the powerful delusion, spoken of by Paul in 2 Thessalonians 2:11 is in fact the appearance of the so-called aliens (demons) on the world scene someday.

The coming of the lawless one will be accompanied by the power of Satan. He will use every kind of power, including miraculous signs, lying wonders, and every type of evil to deceive those who are dying, those who refused to love the truth that would save them. For this reason, God will send them a **powerful delusion** so that they will believe the lie (2 Thessalonians 2:9-11 ISV).

ACCORDING TO RESEARCHERS

The fact is that many Bible researchers believe the alien phenomenon to be happening but that the so-called "aliens" are in fact demons masquerading as intelligent life from other parts of the universe. Author David Hunt said: "UFOs […] are clearly not physical and seem to be **demonic manifestations** from another dimension, calculated to alter man's way of thinking" (emphasis mine). [136] Bible researchers John Ankerberg and John Weldon said: "**the fact that all UFO phenomena are consistent with the demonic theory**, indicate that this explanation is the best possible answer for the solution to the UFO mystery" (emphasis mine).[137] William Goetz, in his book *UFOs Friend, Foe, or Fantasy*, stated: "I am quite convinced that the evidence reveals **UFOs to be demonic**," (emphasis mine)[138]. This conclusion is echoed by Dr. Pierre Guérin, senior researcher at the French National Council for Scientific Research: "UFO behavior is more akin to magic than to physics as we know it […] the modern **UFOnauts and the demons of past days are probably identical**" (emphasis mine).[135] Even the atheist John Keel in his book *UFOs: Operation Trojan Horse*, concludes that the UFO phenomenon is demonic and not beings from another planet: "The **UFO manifestations** seem to be, by and large, merely minor variations of the **age-old demon-ological** phenomenon."

The identification of these "aliens" as demons is clear to those who study the Bible. In fact, the entire study in this book has been pointing in this direction. The fallen angels, a.k.a. demons (sons of God), came to earth once and caused havoc and Jesus said that the last days would be like the days of Noah. Today, however, most people of the world have been so influenced by Darwinian-evolutionary thinking that they do not believe in God and certainly do not believe in demons. The change has come slowly over several decades and now has come to fruition. The *Cutting Edge Newsletter* # 1912 offers six points how people have gone from having at least a general belief in God or Jesus to accepting aliens as real. They note how once people begin to reject the truth of Jesus they will stop reading the Bible and applying it to their lives. This will then lead them to believe that the Bible is just a collection of myths, there are no supernatural beings, and only what we can observe through our senses are real. Next Satan convinces man that if it works then it must be true and therefore when people are exposed to some form of demonic power they accept it though not believing its origin is demonic. The *Newsletter* concludes with Satan proceeding "in stages of ever-increasing frequency and power, to his final Alien deception. Alien beings and UFO phenomenon begin to appear with increasing frequency and contact." Because men no longer believe in demonic beings, they generally accept the lie that "they are an Alien race from another world. This other world is supposedly more technologically and spiritually advanced than Planet Earth."[140]

Bible teacher William Frederick, in his book, *The Coming Epiphany* (2009), suggests that the purpose of the UFOs is to condition people to accept the Antichrist and to turn people away from God and abandon Christianity. He states:

> I believe that they are going to be used to deceive many people into believing the lie that Jesus was an alien, and that UFOs started life on earth. And I also believe that the coming antichrist will, with great signs and wonders, get people to believe this lie and may even proclaim himself as the alien who started life on earth. In other words he will proclaim himself as god. [...] As the return of Christ draws near the deception will get stronger and gain greater acceptance.[141]

THE PROPAGANDA

In reality, there is a powerful propaganda machine working continuously to cause people to believe that one day the aliens will come to earth and this propaganda is rapidly increasing. The foundation of the propaganda was set via the theory of evolution which has programmed the modern person to accept the possibility of aliens showing up. Evolution has made man believe that if he could evolve against all odds, then, considering the trillions upon trillions of stars in the universe, there must be another hospitable planet that could also have given rise to the evolution of life. Modern-day scientists like Stephen Hawkingconfirm this notion that since we evolved, then it is just a matter of time before aliens will show up—based simply on the numbers. He warns, however, that they might not necessarily be nice when they do show up: "To my mathematical brain, the numbers alone make thinking about aliens perfectly rational [...] The real challenge is to work out what aliens might actually be like."[142]

The academic speculations concerning the existence and arrival of aliens are then continually reinforced in the media with their stunning special effects. The media has brought us the message over the years with various angles of how we should expect these aliens. H. G. Wells' classic *War of the Worlds*, first broadcast over radio, left millions panicking that aliens truly had invaded the earth seeking to destroy humanity. Steven Spielberg's blockbuster film *Close Encounters of the Third Kind* revealed a more benevolent alien—one who had come with peaceful motives and sought to help us rather than destroy us. The litany of global saviors is growing and the public loves it. Superheroes like Superman, Iron Man, Spider Man, and X-Men have also become earth's heroes and saviors. Thanks to commercialism and incessant marketing, we see the images of these heroes many times a day—far more than we see references to Jesus or the Bible.

"ALIENS" SAVE THE HUMAN RACE

The 2009 film *Knowing*, starring Nicholas Cage, envisions an apocalyptic scenario where earth is going to be destroyed by a solar flare of immense proportions. Throughout the movie some rather dark-looking individuals are in pursuit of a boy and girl, whom they eventually convince to go with them before earth is destroyed. Nicholas Cage, who plays the father of the little boy, finally realizes that there is no hope for earth and so letting his son go with these individuals is the only option. As he hands him over to the aliens, they transform themselves from their simple (but dark) human bodies into radiant beings of light, which only serves to remind us all too well of where Scripture declares that Satan and his angels can transform themselves into angels of light (2 Corinthians 11:14-15). All throughout the movie various characters make reference to God and Jesus in a fairly positive light. However, at the end of it all, the earth is destroyed and God and Jesus do absolutely nothing for humanity. Selected boy-girl couples (and two of every creature) are safely transported to other planets where they will begin again. If it were not for the oversight of the aliens, the entire human race would have been lost forever. The message is powerful that God and/or Jesus are impotent (or do not care) to help, but the aliens, who have never asked anything from us, are the ones who in fact are superintending the continuation of the human race. The last scene even subtly implies that it was the aliens who originally planted humanity on earth in the same manner as they then planted the children on distant planets.

FALLEN

As part of the propaganda that is intended to influence public sentiment—perhaps even to the point of empathizing with the demons and/or their offspring, ABC TV introduced a movie and series called *Fallen* in the fall of 2006. The concept of the story is that angels, who have fallen from heaven, will one day make it back via the "redeemer" who is a hybrid with a fallen angel and human mother—a race that the sequel calls "Nephilim."[143] When we consider that ABC Family's *Fallen* had approximately two million viewers weekly (according to TVGuide.com) we begin to see that the propaganda machine is in full motion.

We might classify ABC's series *Fallen* as sympathy for the Devil. While it is true that Lucifer remains a bad guy in the series, the other fallen angels (who, biblically, are demons and do his bidding) are made to look as if they have been given a bad rap. The series causes the viewer to wonder if perhaps God isn't being unfair in some way. More importantly, it creates fascination and perhaps even desire for some to be a Nephilim (a hybrid) as well. The conditioning of the viewer's mind to not be shocked at the thought of fallen angels mingling themselves with the seed of men is masterfully executed in the series. Lastly, we must not miss the most important element of all: it will be a demonic-human hybrid who will redeem the fallen angels and gain them access back into heaven. Could this be an allusion to Genesis 3:15 in which Satan's seed will incarnate? Could this be why the Antichrist is often called the Beast in that he is not fully human but is a hybrid? This series and the many other TV series and movies all program mankind into accepting in the future what are today's far-out concepts.

CHAPTER THIRTEEN

Witnessing the Return of the Fallen Angels

"We all know that UFOs are real.
All we need to ask is where do they come from."
- Captain Edgar D. Mitchell
Apollo 14 Astronaut

THE DECEPTION of the coming "aliens" to save the planet in one form or another is not only found in the movies and popular media, but in "eyewitness" accounts as well. Over the past sixty years numerous people all over the world have testified to seeing some type of unknown objects in the sky. According to an ABC News poll conducted in 2000, "nearly half of all Americans and millions more globally believe we're not alone [...] 40 million Americans say they have seen or know someone who has seen an unidentified flying object, or UFO, a growing number believe they've actually met aliens."[144] Among those millions both in America and abroad, are presidents, scientists, astronauts, and others whose testimonies concerning such things should be above reproach. While we might be able to dismiss easily the proverbial simple farmer, can we really outright dismiss the numerous testimonies from people of such caliber?[145] To deny that something is going on in the skies is to stick your head in the sand.

U.S. LEADERS

Ronald Reagan, 40th president of the United States, said the following to newsman Norman C. Miller, then Washington bureau chief for the *Wall Street Journal*, in relation to his 1974 encounter with an unidentified flying object:

> I looked out the window and saw this white light. It was zigzagging around. I went up to the pilot and said, have you ever seen anything like that? He was shocked and he said, "Nope." And I said to him: "Let's follow it!" We followed it for several minutes. It was a bright white light. We followed it to Bakersfield, and all of a sudden to our utter amazement it went straight up into the heavens. When I got off the plane I told Nancy all about it.

Several years later as president, he made the following comment on December 4, 1985, speaking to the students of Fallston High School in Fallston, Maryland, concerning his discussions with General Secretary Gorbachev:

> I couldn't help but say to him, just think how easy his task and mine might be in these meetings that we held if suddenly there was a threat to this world from some other species from another planet outside in the universe. We'd forget all the little local differences that we have between our countries and we would find out once and for all that we really are all human beings on this earth together. Well, I do not suppose we can wait for some **alien race** to come down and threaten us (emphasis mine).

President Reagan made a very telling statement to a full session of the United Nations on September 21, 1987. He stated clearly that an alien force was already among us.

In our obsession with antagonisms of the moment, we often forget how much unites all the members of humanity. Perhaps we need some outside, universal threat to make us recognize this common bond. I occasionally think, how quickly our differences worldwide would vanish if we were facing an **alien** threat from outside this world. **And yet, I ask is not an alien force already among us?** There are only a handful of people who know the truth about this (emphasis mine).

He also made several other comments throughout his presidency that reflect his clear admission to the United Nations in 1987. In 1988 he made the following remark: "But I've often wondered, what if all of us in the world discovered that we were threatened by a **power from outer space**, from another planet" (emphasis mine).

Ronald Reagan was not unique among presidents. President John F. Kennedy made the following statement concerning UFOs: "The US Air force assures me that **UFOs pose no threat** to National Security" (emphasis mine). In 1966 (future) President Gerald Ford recommended an official investigation of UFOs:

I strongly recommend that there be a committee investigation of the UFO phenomena. I think we owe it to the people to establish credibility regarding UFOs and to produce the greatest possible enlightenment on this subject.

While campaigning for the presidency in 1976, Jimmy Carter admitted that he too had witnessed a UFO: "I do not laugh at people anymore when they say they've seen UFOs. I've seen one myself!" In 1965 Senator Barry Goldwater, who was also a retired Air Force Brigadier General and pilot, made the following admission: "I certainly believe in aliens in space, and that they are indeed visiting our planet. They may not look like us, but I have very strong feelings that they have advanced beyond our mental capabilities."

Even General Douglas MacArthur was firmly convinced of the existence of extraterrestrials. On October 8, 1955, he boldly declared:

> You now face a new world, a world of change. We speak in strange terms, of harnessing the cosmic energy, of ultimate conflict between a united human race and the **sinister forces** of some other **planetary galaxy**. The nations of the world will have to unite, for the **next war will be an interplanetary** war. The nations of the earth must someday make a common front against attack by people from other **planets** (emphasis mine).

WORLD LEADERS

Air Marshall Roesmin Nurjadin, Commander-in-Chief of the Indonesian Air Force, wrote in a letter to Yusake J. Matsumura (5/5/1967)—"**UFOs sighted in Indonesia** are identical with those sighted in other countries. Sometimes they pose a problem for our air defense and once we were obliged to open fire on them" (emphasis mine).

Mikhail Gorbachev, as reported in the Soviet Youth magazine, May 4, 1990 (reported in CIA declassified FBIS) stated: "The phenomenon of **UFOs does exist**, and it must be treated seriously" (emphasis mine). In 1994 Hungarian Minister of Defense *György* Keleti was quoted in the *Népszava*, Bupadest (8/18/1994 edition) in response to the question: "Are You Afraid of a UFO Invasion?" He stated:

> Around Szolnok many **UFO reports have been received** from the Ministry of Defense, which obviously and logically means that they [UFOs] know very well where they have to land and what they have to do. It is remarkable indeed that the Hungarian newspapers, in general newspapers everywhere, reject the reports of the authorities (emphasis mine).

ASTRONAUTS AND SCIENTISTS

It seems logical that if anyone should have any information concerning the existence of UFOs, it would be pilots and those from NASA. In 1971 Captain Edgar D. Mitchell, Apollo 14 Astronaut, made two insightful statements: "We all know that UFOs are real. All we need to ask is where do they come from." His testimony is confirmed by many in his field. Colonel L. Gordon Cooper, Mercury 7 Astronaut, made the following statement in a letter to the United Nations in 1978: "I believe that these extraterrestrial vehicles and their crews are visiting this planet from other planets which obviously are a little more [...] advanced than we are."

Mercury Astronaut Captain Donald Slayton disclosed in a 1951 interview his experience:

> I was testing a P-51 fighter in Minneapolis when I spotted this object. I was at about 10,000 feet on a nice, bright, sunny afternoon. I thought the object was a kite, then I realized that no kite is gonna fly that high. As I got closer it looked like a weather balloon, gray and about three feet in diameter. But as soon as I got behind the darn thing it didn't look like a balloon anymore. It looked like a saucer, a disk. About the same time, I realized that it was suddenly going away from me—**and there I was, running at about 300 miles per hour. I tracked it for a little way, and then all of a sudden the thing just took off. It pulled about a 45-degree climbing turn and accelerated and just flat disappeared** (emphasis mine).

Maurice Chatelain, former chief of NASA Communications Systems, put it this way:

> **All Apollo and Gemini flights were followed**, both at a distance and sometimes also quite closely, by space vehicles of extraterrestrial origin—**flying saucers, or UFOs**, if you want to call them by that name. Every time it occurred, the astronauts informed Mission Control, who then ordered absolute silence.

Physicist Michio Kaku, professor of *Theoretical Physics* at University of New York, candidly stated in an ABC News Quote:

> In my mind, there is no question that they're out there. My career is well established. My textbooks are required reading

in all the major capitals on planet earth. If you want to become a physicist to learn about the unified field theory, you read my books. Therefore, I'm in a position to say: Yes, most likely they're out there, perhaps even visited, perhaps on our moon.

Can there be any question that something is happening in the heavens? Could this be what Jesus was referring to when he said in Luke 21:11 "there will be fearful sights and great signs from heaven"? We have seen numerous testimonies from extremely credible witnesses. The fact that beings whom we have identified as demons are manifesting in the sky is undeniable. The question remains, what is their intent?

CHAPTER FOURTEEN

The Counterfeit Rapture

NOT ONLY ARE DEMONS (sons of God) manifesting in the heavenlies, but they are also sending messages to many on earth, which reveals their true character. In general the entities are communicating that the earth will soon go through a period of cataclysmic changes. The descriptions they give are what the Bible refers to as the great tribulation. However, these so-called "aliens" are nothing more than demons pretending to be from some other galaxy. Their messages, as we will see, consist of some basic ideas that are the diabolical mirror to the Bible.

- Cataclysmic events will come upon the earth

- They will help us overcome those events

- They will take those that can't or won't evolve to the next level

- Those that remain get to evolve to the next level now

- A man from among us will be raised up with special powers and knowledge

In historical studies, the strongest type of witness we can have is what is referred to as a hostile witness. A hostile witness is when someone's enemies (or perhaps competition) are forced to admit certain things about that person that are not in their best interest to say.[146]

Satan, in a sense, has proven the rapture event by the messages that his horde have been giving over the years. Clearly, their messages, as they are given, are full of lies. Nevertheless, they do include some elements of truth, which is always the point of a deception. That there will be an "evacuation" of the earth is certain as we learn from Scripture: "Then we who are alive *and* remain shall be caught up together with them in the clouds to meet the Lord in the air" (1 Thessalonians 4:17). The truth of that verse is proven by the lies that are being told by the "aliens." In effect, they are getting the world ready for what is coming so that when it does happen people will not likely consider the biblical rapture as an option.

The enemy undoubtedly will have a counter explanation ready for when that happens; after all, he has read the Bible too. "Missiologist Ralph Winter estimated in early 2001 that there are 680 million *'born again'* Christians in the world, and that they are growing at about seven percent a year. This represents about eleven percent of the world's population and thirty-three percent of the total number of Christians (based on the UN projected world population of 6.301 billion for mid-2003.)"[147] In 2010 the population was 6.856 billion and assuming (conservatively) that the percentages had stayed the same, then 754 million people were born-again followers of Jesus. These followers will be taken from the earth in a flash.

While born-again followers of the Lord Jesus Christ will not be here to see what follows, we can safely conclude that some time shortly after the rapture, the demons will most likely appear to the world as the saviors of the world and will provide an answer for the disappearance of over 700 million people worldwide. Many believe that the aliens/demons will say that they were the ones who seeded the planet (were the Creators of man) and have returned to help in our hour of greatest need. The reason that most of the world will not immediately turn to the God of heaven and earth following the rapture is because the enemy has been conditioning people for just such an event. The rapture is certain in that God has clearly said it would come to pass; therefore, Satan (as the father of lies, cf. John 8:44) must have some type of event in place to deceive the world when the event actually occurs. Sometimes the message is that the people evacuated will be resettled to another planet. Sometimes the "aliens" tell us not worry about where the ones taken will go. And sometimes we see it is the bad aliens who have come to catch people up into their spaceships; those brave enough to resist will survive, as portrayed in the 2010 movie *Skyline,* whose motto is "do not look up" because those that look at the light will be taken. Jesus told us to "look up" (Luke 21:28) when we see all these things beginning to come to pass. Could it be that Satan has found a clever way to encourage people to do just the opposite?

THEIR MESSAGES

The various messages were first compiled by researcher Brad Myers who did much of the research for the bestselling book *Alien Encounters*[148] by Drs. Chuck Missler and Mark Eastman. The research in their book is impressive; however, rather than simply quoting their book, I searched out the sources for myself and scrutinized the authenticity of each statement. In some cases I found other supporting evidence from the stated authors or from others not mentioned in their book.

In her book *Aliens Among Us,* Ruth Montgomery writes of how the "aliens" have communicated: "We are coming in great numbers, not with any intention of harm, but to **rescue the earth from pollution and nuclear explosions**" (emphasis mine).[149] Some like Barbara Marciniak, a popular New Age author and channeller, in her book *Bringers of the Dawn,* writes of *messages* which she claims she received from extraterrestrials from the star system Pleiades. She discusses the disappearance that is coming upon the world:

> The people who leave the planet during the time of Earth changes do not fit in here any longer, and they are stopping the harmony of Earth. When the time comes that perhaps 20 million people leave the planet at one time there will be a tremendous shift in consciousness for those who are remaining.

It should be clear that Satan and his legions are making great preparations to have a counter explanation once the rapture occurs. She also shares another "message" from the ETs regarding the rationale for why millions of people will be taken.

> If human beings do not change—if they do not make the shift in values and realize that without Earth they could not be here— then Earth, in its love for its own initiation and its reaching for a higher frequency, will bring about a cleansing that will balance it once again. **There is the potential for many people to leave the planet in an afternoon.** Maybe then everyone else will begin to wake up to what is going on.[150]

After the explanation for the disappearance of millions, which the Bible truthfully calls the rapture, she goes on to speak of apocalyptic events that are extremely reminiscent of the words of Jesus some two thousand years ago when He spoke of wars and rumors of wars and nation rising against nation.

> As we see it, as the probable worlds begin to form, there will be great shiftings within humanity on this planet. **It will seem that great chaos and turmoil are forming, that nations are rising against each other in war, and that earthquakes are happening more frequently.** It will seem as if everything is falling apart and cannot be put back together. Just as you sometimes have rumblings and quakings in your lives as you change your old patterns and move into new energies, Earth is shaking itself free, and a certain realignment or adjustment period is to be expected. **It will also seem that the animals and fish are departing Earth.** Those animals are now moving over

to the new world as it is being formed. They are not ending their existence, they are merely slipping into the new world to await your joining them."[151]

WARNINGS FROM ASHTAR

New Age writer Thelma Terrell claims to have received messages from Ashtar, the leader of an "alien confederation," concerning the evacuation of millions around the globe. Those familiar with the Bible immediately see that Ashtar is nothing more than the same demon from Bible times (Asherah/Ashtoreth) but with a message that modern man wants to hear. In former days Ashtar was considered a god, but now such talk is, for the most part, out of style. Therefore, Ashtar has come back as an "alien" to warn the citizens of earth of the impending rapture. However, the true reason for the evacuation of the planet is never given. When the rapture does occur, the demonic realm will be ready because they have been warning people of just such an event. Ashtar has communicated that **"Earth changes will be the primary factor in mass evacuation of this planet."** [152] **Therefore** because of the impending events coming upon the earth, the "alien" ships will come in close enough to lift people off the earth "in the twinkling of an eye,"—even the terminology is borrowed from the Bible concerning the rapture.

> Our rescue ships will be able to come in close enough in the **twinkling of an eye to set the lifting beams in operation in a moment**. And all over the globe where events warrant it, this will be the method of evacuation. **Mankind will be lifted, levitated shall we say**, by the beams from our smaller ships. These smaller craft will in turn taxi the persons to the larger ships overhead, higher in the atmosphere, where there is ample space and quarters and supplies for millions of people.[153]

The demons who are posing as "aliens" will try to convince mankind that they in fact are the saviors. We have seen the conditioning in the movies and people's minds will remember those stories when the event occurs. Ashtar states that great preparation and care has gone into the rescue of mankind: "There is method and great organization in a detailed plan already near completion for the purpose of **removing souls from this planet, in the event of catastrophic events making a rescue necessary**."[154] However, there will not be any advanced notice of the event and it will happen in a flash. **"The Great Evacuation will come upon the world very suddenly.** The flash of emergency events will be as a lightning that flashes in the sky. So suddenly and so quick in its happening that it is over almost before you are aware of its presence."[155]

The demons/"aliens" need to reassure those left behind that they in fact are the ones getting the better deal since then the aliens will return for "the children of all ages and races. The implication is that those taken were not part of the "children of all ages and races":

> Phase I of **the Great Exodus of souls from the planet will take place at a moment's notice** when it is determined that the inhabitants are in danger. Phase II: This second phase immediately following the first. The second phase is vital, **as we return for the children of all ages and races**. The child does not have the power of choice in understanding nor personal accountability.[156]

However, some people might begin to wonder if such awful events are coming upon the world, then why were they not taken as well? Ashtar assures them to not take it personally as everyone will have a part to play:

> Do not be concerned nor unduly upset if you do not participate in this first temporary lift-up of souls who serve with us. This merely means that your action in the plan is elsewhere, and you will be taken for your instructions or will receive them in some other manner. Do not take any personal affront if you are not alerted or are not a participant in this first phase of our plan. Your time will come later, and these instructions are not necessary for you at this time.[157]

Ashtar has communicated this message to others with the twist that those taken will have to remain in the third dimension whereas those that are left will then be free to evolve to the fourth dimension. The website Gateway to Oneness speaks of one named Cristah, the light worker, who receives messages from Ashtar. Cristah relays Ashtar's message: "those who do not believe, will be left in the 3rd dimension," and "those that are not of the light must stay and learn here in the 3rd dimension." Cristah adds that Ashtar "says that the fate of earth's inhabitants" will be handled on an individual basis."[158] The idea is that the disappearance of millions around the globe will be due to them being left in the third dimension and those that then find themselves on the earth have transitioned to the fourth dimension.

Ashtar has been leaving messages with other channellers as well in order to make sure that his message is heard and spread. Johanna Michaelson is a former New Ager who is now a Christian. In her book *Like Lambs to the Slaughter: Your Child and the Occult,* she writes about the well-known New Age guru John Randolph Price who also receives messages from Asher (a variation of Ashtar). Michaelson relays that, according to John Randolph Price, as many as two billion people could be wiped off the planet. This seemingly refers to the trials coming upon the earth versus the evacuation, nevertheless, the impact will be "we told you so" once the events begin to occur.

> Asher, the spirit guide of John Randolph Price, a moving force behind the New Agers' 'World Instant of Cooperation' (on December 31, 1986, in which thousands of mediators worldwide simultaneously concentrated on world peace hoping to cause a critical mass launching into the New Age) told him that **two billion people who didn't go along with the New Age would be wiped off the face of the Earth during the coming cleansing.**"[159]

New Age author and channeller Kay Wheeler, who goes by the name Ozmana, describes how Mother Earth is fighting for her life and is in critical condition, which she says is "why you see the many crises in the world." She states that Mother Earth must fight for her survival and we as light bearers can help her:

> **Mother is cleansing**. It is all she knows to do at this time to clear herself of the pollution that exists within her body. But you **as light bearers** can help your Mother cleanse in such a way that does not destroy all life on this planet.[160]

As part of the cleansing process, many people will be removed from the planet so that the planet can move into the fourth dimension. "Earth's population needs to be decreased to bring forth the necessary changes upon this planet to move into the fourth dimension." She states that the changes are coming and "those who plan to stay must be of this vibration." The reason that many will leave the planet is because they are not able to go to the fourth dimension. She says that we should not feel sad for them but rather rejoice for them and also that now the beings on earth can move forward:

> Many of these beings who are leaving this planet at this time have completed that which they came to do. It is a time of great rejoicing for them. Do not feel sad about their leaving. They are going home. Many are waiting to be with them again [...] Many beings must move on, for their thought patterns are of the past. They hold on to these thoughts that keep Earth held back.[161]

SUMMARY AND CONCLUSION

The messages from the "aliens" and the New Age are clear: major earth changes and cataclysms are coming upon the earth. As a result many will be removed from the earth in the twinkling of an eye by the "aliens" or will remain in the third dimension while everyone else moves into the fourth dimension. The rapture is certain and Satan has prepared for the event through the movies and through channellers receiving messages from "aliens" of the impending event. Unfortunately, for many the rapture will not be an event that makes them look up to God but to the "aliens" posing as man's savior.

CHAPTER FIFTEEN

The Coming Nephilim

LOOKING BACK AT GENESIS 6:4 we recall that the text said "The Nephilim were on the earth [...] when the sons of God were having sexual relations with the daughters of humankind, who gave birth to their children" (Genesis 6:4 NET). We know that we are in the days like Noah's because what was happening then is happening now. Just as the fallen angels took women and engendered children by them, so too is this happening today. Demons, who are masquerading as "aliens," are in fact taking people to create Nephilim hybrids, just like in the days of Noah. This phenomenon has been documented by numerous researchers working with thousands of people who claim that they were abducted and were exploited for their ovum or sperm.

Dr. Jacques F. Vallée is an important voice in the study of UFOs. Professionally, he has worked a lot on the development of the Internet and is the author of many books on Information Technology. However, he has done a great deal of research in the area of "aliens" and UFOs also. Back in 1975 he offered some potential reasons why the "entities" may be abducting people though the exact reason remained elusive to him. He states:

> **In order to materialize and take definite form, these entities seem to require a source of energy [...] a living thing [...]**

a human medium. Our sciences have not reached a point where they can offer us any kind of working hypothesis for this process. **But we can speculate that these beings need living energy which they can reconstruct into physical form.** Perhaps that is why dogs and animals tend to vanish in flap areas. Perhaps the living cells of those animals are somehow used by the ultraterrestrials to create forms which we can see and sense with our limited perceptions.[162]

In his book *Dimensions* he ponders: "Are these races only semi-human, so that in order to maintain contact with us, they need crossbreeding with men and women of our planet?"[163] He also observes the hostile element of the abductions in his book *Confrontations*:

The **'medical examination' to which abductees are said to be subjected, often accompanied by sadistic sexual manipulation**, is **reminiscent of the medieval tales of encounters with demons**. It makes no sense in a sophisticated or technical framework: any intelligent being equipped with the scientific marvels that UFOs possess would be in a position to achieve any of these alleged scientific objectives in a shorter time and with fewer risks.[164]

The symbolic display seen by the abductees is identical to the type of initiation ritual or astral voyage that is imbedded in the [occult] traditions of every culture [...] the structure of abduction stories is identical to that of **occult initiation rituals** [...] the UFO beings of today belong to the same class of manifestation as the [occult] entities that were described in centuries past.[165]

JOHN MACK

Harvard University Professor of Psychiatry, John Mack, discussed in an interviewed with NOVA how he came to his conclusions about so-called "alien" abductions from a clinical position. He did not start his investigations as a "believer" but came to see that the only satisfactory explanation for the experiences that people were having was that non-human creatures or "aliens" were taking them against their will. Mack is an excellent witness because he has non-religious motivations. And his reputation is at stake. Becoming a so-called believer in the "alien" abduction phenomenon is not something that Ivy League professors generally want to do. The Dean of Harvard was so concerned about Mack's endeavors that he appointed a committee of peers to critique Mack's case but they could find no fault with him. They then issued a statement that Dr. Mack "remains a member in good standing of the Harvard Faculty of Medicine."[166]

Thus we have first-rate testimony from a man who did his best to disprove the abduction phenomenon. He states that he simply had little place in his mind to accept or take seriously the idea that there were "other" worldly beings that could have a physical effect on our world. As a result he worked hard to try to find a different conclusion other than that of alien abductions. He states in the NOVA interview that he: "came very reluctantly to the conclusion that this was a true mystery."[167] He also notes that he did everything he could "to rule out other sources, or sexual abuse" (all subsequent quotations from Mack are from the NOVA interview).[168]

Dr. Mack has worked with well over one hundred "experiencers" intensively, which involved an initial two-hour screening interview. He notes how he has been impressed "with the consistency of the story, the sincerity with which people tell their stories, the power of feelings connected with this, the self-doubt—all the appropriate responses that these people have to their experiences." As a former skeptic himself, Dr. Mack notes that there are aspects of the abduction phenomenon which we are justified in taking literally: "UFOs are in fact observed, filmed on camera at the same time that people are having their abduction experiences." Mack also says that he is convinced that aliens are creatures from a distant planet and does not consider them to be demons as we have discovered in our study. He does, however, believe there is a spiritual dimension to the abductions.

> People, in fact, have been observed to be missing at the time that they are reporting their abduction experiences. They return from their experiences with cuts, ulcers on their bodies, triangular lesions, which follow the distribution of the experiences that they recover, of what was done to them in the craft by the surgical-like activity of these beings.

> All of that has a literal physical aspect and is experienced and reported with appropriate feeling, by the abductees, with or without hypnosis or a relaxation exercise.

> It's both literally, physically happening to a degree; and it's also some kind of psychological, spiritual experience occurring and originating perhaps in another dimension.

He discusses the various phenomena that occur when someone undergoes an encounter. He notes that "a **blue light** or some kind of energy paralyzes the person, whether they're in their home, or they're driving a car. They can't move."

> They feel themselves being removed from wherever they were. They floated through a wall or out a car, carried up on this **beam of light** into a craft and there subjected to a number of now familiar procedures which involve the beings staring at them; involves probing of their body, their body orifices; and a complex process whereby **they sense in the case of men, sperm removed; in the women, eggs removed; some sort of hybrid offspring created which they're brought back to see in later abductions.**

He states the harvesting of eggs and sperm is to bring about some hybrid species which will carry human evolution forward:

> **To produce some kind of new species to bring us together to produce a hybrid species which**—the abductees are sometimes told—**will populate the earth or will be there**

**to carry evolution forward, after the human race has
completed what it is now doing,** namely the destruction of
the earth as a living system. So it's a kind of later form. **It's
an awkward coming together of a less embodied species
than we are,** and us, for this evolutionary purpose. [...]
**it may be that these hybrids we're told is what will have to
be.** It's a kind of insurance policy if the earth continues to be
subjected to the exploitation of its living environment to the
point where it can't sustain human and other life as it's now
occurring.

We must note the mention of evolution because evolution is what
will drive man to desire to become greater through changing his
own DNA—a concept that we shall discuss in the next chapter.

Mack also discussed how those who report to have been
abducted are shown cataclysmic events on large television
screens. The cataclysms are the same type of propaganda that
we see in the movies and the same dire messages that the New
Age channellers have been receiving.

People are shown on television screens a **huge variety of scenes
of environmental destruction of the earth polluted;** of a kind
of post-apocalyptic scene in which even the **spirits** have been
routed from their environment because they live in the same
physical and **spiritual** environment that we do; and canyons
are shown with trees destroyed; pieces of the earth are seen
as breaking away—portions of the East Coast or West Coast.
[...] These experiences often occur in literal consciousness.
Not in a hypnogogic or dreamlike state. The person may be in
their bedroom quite wide awake. **The beings show up. And
there they are and the experience begins. That they're not
occurring in any dreamlike state.**

Mack stresses that any theory that would explain these claims
as a purely mental or psyche (from the brain) experience, must
explain the following factors:

- The extreme consistency of the stories from person to person, which you would not get simply by stimulating the temporal lobes.

- There is no ordinary experiential basis for this. In other words, there's nothing in their life experience that could have given rise to this, other than what they say.

- The physical aspects: the cuts and the other lesions on their bodies.

- The tight association with UFOs, which are often observed in the community, by the media, independent of the person having the abduction experience, who may not have seen the UFO at all, but reads or sees on the television the next day that a UFO passed near where they were when they had an abduction experience.

Mack continues by stating: "**I didn't believe anything when I started**, I do not really believe anything now. **I've come to where I've come to clinically.** In other words, I worked with people over hundreds and hundreds of hours and have done as careful a job as I could to listen, to sift out, to consider alternative explanations." He continues: "**No one has found an alternative explanation in a single abduction case.**"

What is further confirmation for Mack is that this phenomenon is not just occurring in the United States but is happening worldwide. He states that it has been happening among the Native Americans, people in South Africa, Brazil, and Malaysia. His professional research is alarming and yet consistent with Bible prophecy.

DAVID M. JACOBS

Another person who has committed his career to investigating the abduction phenomenon is Dr. David M. Jacobs. He is a professor at Temple University and is the author of several books. He has spent more than thirty years investigating "alien" abductions. He has performed nearly 900 hypnotic regressions with over 140 abductees. During most of that time, he was quite upbeat about the prospect of "aliens" visiting the planet. Recently, however, he was able to put the pieces together and has come to a startling conclusion. The "aliens" are not merely conducting experiments but have a plan to create hybrids from themselves and us (a conclusion also suggested by Dr. Mack). Dr. Jacobs is not a Christian and so his conclusions are not influenced by the Bible, yet they reflect what the Bible has predicted. We must keep in mind that he truly believes that the entities are not demonic but visitors from another world. What the Bible has predicted concerning the days of Noah he has discovered independently of the Bible—just like Dr. Mack.

INTERVIEW WITH DAVID JACOBS ON HIS BOOK "THE THREAT"

Dr. Jacobs' testimony, given in a 2003 interview with Sean Casteel,[169] profoundly demonstrates the demonic events that are happening in our day. Dr. Jacobs shared how in all the years that he had studied the "alien" phenomenon, he had never, until then, been pessimistic about the future prospects of what the "aliens" hope to do but that he despaired concerning what he had discovered.

> I've been involved with UFO research for about 32 years now, since about 1965, and I have never been downcast or depressed about the phenomenon. I have never been pessimistic about it. But I must say that now that I've learned as much as I have learned [...] **I am very, very unsettled and upset by what I see.** I do not like what I see. I wish I didn't see this. **I wish I hadn't uncovered this. I despair of it.** It's thrown me into a tremendous sense of concern about the future and unease. [...] I do not want to be this way. [...] I could not have ever imagined that I would come to this position (all subsequent quotes from Dr. Jacobs are from the 2003 interview, emphasis mine).

He notes that the "aliens" are not here to simply examine us but they have a program, which is in its last phase, to create a hybrid race and how, because the phenomenon is worldwide, all humans will become second-class citizens.

> **And the program ultimately is not abducting people.** Abductions, you have to remember, are a means to an end. **They're abducting people for a purpose, for a reason.** The physical act of abducting people, which is the abduction phenomenon, really is only part of the program. […] So what we have here is **an abduction program, a breeding program, which accounts for all the reproductive activity** that we see, and a **hybridization program**, which is why people see hybrids all the time—as babies, as toddlers, as adolescents, and then as adults.
>
> And then, finally, **I think all this is leading to an integration program in which ultimately these hybrids, who look very human, will be integrating into this society.** And who will eventually, I assume, be in control here because they do have superior technology and superior physiological abilities that we do not have. We would therefore be sort of second-class citizens, I think.
>
> Now, I find this to be very disturbing. […] I know that people feel it's positive and it's wonderful, and they're here to help us. But **in the cases that I've investigated, very carefully, very thoroughly, for a very long time, I have not had people discuss that. When people discuss the future, generally speaking, they are discussing this integration program that they're confronting, and we're all confronting.**
>
> As you know, the UFO and abduction phenomena is very, very widespread. And people have seen tens of thousands, hundreds of thousands, maybe millions of UFOs around the world for a long time now, at least through the 20th Century, and certainly since 1947.

Jacobs notes another disconcerting aspect is that the "aliens," which we recall are demons in disguise, are trying to keep their hybrid activities a secret. "**They do not want us to know what they're doing.** They do not want us to interfere. This is a consciously-arrived-at and successful secrecy program to prevent us from knowing." He also comments that one doesn't have to be a rocket scientist to see what is happening, though admittedly, he himself did not realize the implications until he put the pieces together.

> **It's been worldwide with millions of people for 50 years.** Day in, day out, 24 hours a day. […] Why they would want to do it in the first place? What's the point? We do not really know that. But I think this is certainly a hypothetical answer to the UFO puzzle. I think pretty much we've answered it […] and therefore **I think we're looking at a very difficult future.**

Jacobs then discusses the "Disaster Scenario that abductees keep talking about over and over again," which he and others had heard about for years. He confesses that he personally is not sure whether they will be a disaster or not but something **"the aliens and abductees call 'The Change,' is going to take place."** The cataclysms that are mentioned are "**all sorts of disaster scenarios**, which includes atomic war. It includes asteroids hitting the earth. It includes **floods, plagues, famine**, whatever. It's sort of a generalized disaster […] I do not think the specifics are all that important, but the **idea of a disaster is the most important thing.**"

Jacobs summarizes the interview with the awful sense of dread that he is experiencing: "I've spent my entire adult life studying this subject intensely. […] **And I've never really felt the despair I feel now that I think that we've broken it open and we're looking at it and examining it.** And it's just not what I expected. It's not what anybody expected." [170]

If we summarize Jacob's main points, we note the following:

- People are taken

- Sperm and ova are being harvested

- People are constantly told of impending disasters

- The beings will be with us and over us

- They are currently mingling with us

- They do not have good intentions

Jacobs is not a believer in the Bible and yet he has discovered and documented phenomena which the Bible prophesizes. Mack and Jacobs have both documented that the abduction phenomenon is worldwide and thanks to an Israeli reporter we know that it is happening in Israel as well.

THE GIANTS RETURN TO ISRAEL

Israeli author and reporter Barry Chamish, in his book *Return of the Giants*, has documented how strange, rather unexplainable phenomena have been occurring in Israel as early as 1980 (all of the quotations below are from his book). Well over a dozen "alien" visitations have been reported and even sightings of demons have been reported by a number of Arabs.[171] He states: "of the seven best documented close encounters with alien beings probably connected to UFOs, six involved giants. These giants were determined to leave evidence of their arrival in the form of cadmium-imbued landing circles, miles of impossible boot tracks and deliberate communication with witnesses." Chamish believes that the giants people are seeing are related to the biblical Nephilim, Anakim, and Rephaim.

While serving in the Israeli Air Force in the Sinai Peninsula, Chamish and Private Adam Reuter witnessed strange lights in the sky that continued for three months. Both men had been trained to identify all kinds of aircraft and to recognize satellites. Chamish recalls: "What we were seeing was nothing like anything taught in our skywatching classes." The unexplainable objects he says were "highflying, soundless dots in the upper atmosphere that flew in squadrons, stopped in the middle of their flight, joined together then split off in different directions and turned at impossible angles."

Many other sightings were to follow his and after some time of examining the physical evidence and interviewing other witnesses, Chamish came to the conclusion that what has been happening in Israel is unique. He notes: "the giants thoughtfully chose reliable contactees as witnesses, allowed their craft to be filmed and left in their wake ample physical evidence. In fact, what characterizes the current Israeli UFO wave from others in the world, is the sheer abundance of physical evidence left behind by the visitors."

One witness of an "alien" visitation is Shosh Yahud who "awoke to see a seven-foot, round faced being in silvery overalls circling her bed as if "floating on his shoes." The creature assured her he was not there to harm her and she became relaxed. After a few minutes the being "floated through her wall outside." She relates how she thought the whole thing was a dream until she looked out her window only find "a 4.5 meter crop circle in her backyard [comprised of] silicon and cadmium."

Another witness is Ada, a medical electronics technician, from Kfar Saba which is where several unidentified flying objects were recorded on video. In the summer of 1993 she went to her bedroom for an afternoon nap when she saw "a three-dimensional being less than a meter" away from her. She notes that he was tall and was "wearing a 'space suit' of silver and green. The being emitted white beams from his waist area." The emission of light reminds of us the Bible's warning that even Satan's is able to transform himself into an angel of light (2 Corinthians 11:14-15). In order to set the stage for the grander deception that is coming upon the world, Satan needs to condition the world that the beings that are coming are glorious and have magnificent bodies.

The hardest evidence to dismiss that fallen angels are appearing in Israel comes from the village of Yatzitz, twelve miles east of Rishon Letzion. Chamish reports:

> Herzl Casatini, the village security chief and his friend Danny Ezra were sharing conversation when they heard an explosion and felt Ezra's house shake. Herzl opened the door and stood face to face with a nine-foot tall creature in metallic clothes whose face was hidden in "a haze." He shut the door and called the police. They arrived and discovered deep boot tracks in the hard mud. The tracks sunk 35 centimeters into the ground meaning whoever made them had to have weighed, literally, a ton. […] The tracks carried on for 8 kilometers. […] Sometimes the distance between tracks was twelve feet (picture available at douglashamp.com).

Just like Mack and Jacobs, Chamish forecasts that the arrival of these beings will have dire consequences: "The biblical giants were God's enemy and Israel's armies were the means to their utter destruction. There is a legitimate reason to contemplate the recent re-arrival of giants in Israel with a good measure of dread." The entities appear to be none other than the fallen angels (sons of God) who, in the days before the flood, took the daughters of men and produced the Nephilim/giants by them. The in-depth research of Mack, Jacobs, and Chamish indicates that the prophecy of Daniel 2:43 ("they will mingle with the seed of men") has already begun.

THEY FLEE AT THE NAME OF JESUS

There is one final proof that these so-called "aliens" are in fact demons who are hell bent on destroying humanity—and that is the fact that they flee at the name of Jesus. Abduction researchers David Ruffino and Joe Jordan discuss in their book *Unholy Communion: The Alien Abduction Phenomenon, Where It Originates—And How It Stops* how the phenomenon of abductions is real but the entities commonly referred to as "aliens" are in fact demons. They have counseled and documented more than

300 actual test cases of people that claim to have been abducted and have encouraged many of those abductees to put their faith in Jesus. After doing so, many found that the abductions ceased forever and if the entities returned then just mentioning the name of Jesus would cause them to flee.[172] The entities in question, therefore, are demonic and not truly "aliens" from some other world but are trying to deceive the world of the impending rapture of believers before the beginning of the tribulation.

This conclusion is noted in an article from March 2007 entitled *Alien Abductions Stopped by the Name of Jesus Christ,* by Stephen Yulish. He states that he believes that "extraterrestrials are not aliens from another planet or galaxy, but are instead fallen angels here to undertake a diabolical plan that is more sinister than any alien invasion."[173] He notes that ultimately the UFO battle is not for the planet but for the soul of man. He writes: "These extraterrestrial fallen angels are setting us up for the coming great deception where those people left behind when the body of Christ is caught up to be with Him in the air during the *harpazo* (rapture) will believe that those who have suddenly vanished were abducted by UFOs."[174] Yulish is likewise convinced that the current UFO "alien" deception is nothing new; it is just a repeat of how things were in the days of Noah.

CONCLUSION

Based on the extensive investigation of many researchers, among them John Mack from Harvard, who interviewed on numerous occasions over one hundred abductees, we see the demons have been harvesting eggs from women and sperm from men for many years. According to the testimony of some abductees, they are using the genetic material to create hybrid babies—that is a mix between themselves and humans. This is also the dire conclusion of researcher Dr. David Jacobs who has determined that the "aliens" are not just experimenting on humans but have a specific program that they are working to accomplish. Their goal, according to him, is to create an "alien"-human hybrid race and take control of the planet. Thus, we have come full circle to the days of Noah. Once again Satan and his hordes are attempting to corrupt the image of man by mixing their seed with humans. However, whereas the abductee cases are limited to a number of people, a time is coming when they will attempt to mingle their seed with all of humanity on a global scale, which we will see in chapter seventeen.

The most obvious conclusion is that we are currently living in the days that are just like the days of Noah. Though people are going about their business thinking that everything is fine and will go on indefinitely, judgment is quickly approaching. It is approaching quickly because of what is happening behind the scenes; the sons of God have returned and have resumed their devilish program wherein they see that the daughters of men are good and are taking them as wives (think: their seed and for their incubation) in order to create Nephilim. As the many abductees have testified, the "aliens" are using their sperm and eggs to create a new race (post human). The demons are mingling their seed with the seed of men, just like the book of Daniel prophesied. In the Jewish book of Giants we read that the demons also mixed the seed of different animals together (miscegenation) and created monsters and giants. Could this really happen in our days? The fact is it has already begun.

CHAPTER SIXTEEN

Man Becoming His Own God

"We are going to become Gods, period [...]
but if you are going to interfere with me becoming a God,
you're going to have trouble. There'll be warfare."
- Transhumanist Richard Seed

IN THE BEGINNING GOD established that everything should reproduce according to its kind. We find the phrase *according to its/their kind* five times in Genesis chapter 1. God founded the fundamental principle from the beginning of time that everything should reproduce after its own kind.

> Then God said, "Let the earth bring forth the living creature **according to its kind**: cattle and creeping thing and beast of the earth, each **according to its kind**"; and it was so. And God made the beast of the earth **according to its kind**, cattle **according to its kind**, and everything that creeps on the earth **according to its kind**. And God saw that it was good (Genesis 1:24-25).

While a German shepherd can mate with a Golden Retriever, for example, they are both from the same kind—that is the dog (technically wolf—canus lupus) species. Thus, mixing goats and let's say—spiders—should never happen as it would violate God's law. Yet, this sort of manipulation of the kinds is exactly what is happening today. Genetic scientists have actually mixed a goat and a spider together at the DNA level. Though the percentage of spider is only $1/70,000^{th}$, the resulting creature is still one that is not completely according to its own kin anymore.

Genetic scientists have incorporated selected spider DNA into goat embryos to engineer a hybrid spider goat. The result is a goat that looks like a goat, acts like a goat, BUT produces milk which contains proteins which, when treated, produce a very close imitation of the valuable spider silk. A single goat only produces small amounts of the desired material, so an extremely large herd is required to acquire useful quantities.[175]

Figure 12
Hybrid Spider Goats
photo courtesy of
www.scienceray.com

While we can understand the desire to harvest spider silk for its great strength, mixing two different kinds violates God's principle and will ultimately end poorly. This kind of technology raises the question of whether one day we will actually try to make a real-life Spider Man.

GREEN EGGS AND HAM

Mixing spiders and goats is not all that is happening. Taiwan researchers have mingled the seed (genetic material) of pigs with jellyfish that glow in the dark to create real life green eggs and ham! "They claim that while other researchers have bred partly fluorescent pigs, theirs are the only pigs in the world which are green through and through. The pigs are transgenic, created by adding genetic material from jellyfish into a normal pig embryo."[176]

Whereas God commanded the land to bring forth the animals into existence He formed Adam from the dust of the ground with His own hands and then blew His Spirit into Adam, and thus made him in His own image. Therefore, to mix man with an animal must be infinitely more offensive to God since it would

Figure 13
Green glowing pigs,
photo courtesy of BBC

be a direct and deliberate violation of his law and an affront to His glorious image, "Nor shall you mate with any animal, to defile yourself with it. Nor shall any woman stand before an animal to mate with it. It is perversion" (Leviticus 18:23).

Then God said, "Let Us make man in Our image, according to Our likeness; let them have dominion over the fish of the sea, over the birds of the air, and over the cattle, over all the earth and over every creeping thing that creeps on the earth" (Genesis 1:26).

THEY EXCHANGED THE GLORY

In the book of Romans we see that man should have known about God but suppressed that knowledge and thereby became a fool, though he thought that he was most wise. Man's foolishness would cause him to exchange the brilliance (and image) of the true God for images looking like animals and such.

> Although they claimed to be **wise**, they **became fools** and **exchanged** the glory of the immortal God for **images** made to look like mortal man and birds and animals and reptiles (Romans 1:22-23).

Even though Paul's primary thought is probably idols and the statues that accompany them, we could certainly see how evolution could also be included in that. Rather than teach

Figure 14
Scientific American

that we are in God's image, evolution teaches that we came from microbes and then other lesser creatures until finally and accidentally we evolved to become human. The teaching of evolution which began 150 years ago is now having its full impact. Man for the most part is generally committed to the belief that we humans evolved from animals and that God does not even exist. With God removed, we can understand how mixing two different kinds of animals in order to "evolve" to a new level raises very few flags for most people. After all, they say we came from animals. National Geographic News published an article in 2005 discussing how the lines between human and animal are becoming blurred by creating human-rabbits, pigs with human blood, and mice with human brains.

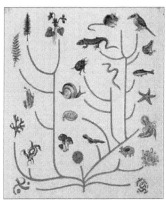

Figure 15 Evolutionary Tree of Life

> Scientists have begun blurring the line between human and animal by producing chimeras—a hybrid creature that's part human, part animal. Chinese scientists at the Shanghai Second Medical University in 2003 **successfully fused human cells with rabbit eggs**. The embryos were reportedly the first human-animal chimeras successfully created. **They were allowed to develop for several days in a laboratory dish before the scientists destroyed the embryos to harvest their stem cells.** In Minnesota [...] researchers at the Mayo Clinic created pigs with **human blood** flowing through their bodies. And at Stanford University in California an experiment might be done later this year to create **mice** with **human brains** (emphasis mine).[177]

In 2008 Britain granted licenses to create human-pig embryos according to onenewsnow.com. Dr. Mark Mostert of Regent University, who was interviewed in the article, notes that "British law requires that the human-animal embryos be killed after 14 days."[178] Yet he predicts that "some researchers will violate that statute and let them grow even further."[179] He makes the important observation concerning what is really happening and where it will most likely end. He elaborates:

> Species were created to procreate among those of like kind, and now this takes us a step closer to essentially saying, 'well, whatever the Bible says or whatever a Christian perspective is doesn't really matter.' We have now completely divorced what we do in biology and in human engineering from acknowledging that we as human beings are creations of God and that other species are made by the Creator. Now we're saying we are taking that role. [180]

Mostert argues that the creation of human-pig embryos will create beings that God never intended to be.

FORSAKING THE IMAGE OF GOD THROUGH TRANSHUMANISM

Man now believes that he can take his "evolution" into his own hands and direct it for his own good. This belief was stated boldly by Juan Enriquez, Chairman and CEO of Biotechonomy, who was featured in an article by Ken Fisher of artestechnica. com entitled, "We are becoming a new species, we are becoming Homo Evolutis." He states:

> **Humanity** is on the **verge of becoming** a new and **utterly unique species**, which he dubs *Homo Evolutis*. What makes this species so unique is that it "takes direct and deliberate control over the evolution of the species." Calling it the "ultimate reboot," he points to the conflux of DNA manipulation and therapy, tissue generation, and robotics as making this great leap possible [...] The day may come when we are able to take the best biology of the known animal kingdom and make it

part of our own. This isn't just about being a bit stronger, or having perfect eyesight our whole lives. All of our organs and limbs have weaknesses that can be addressed, and there are also opportunities to go beyond basic fixes and **perform more elaborate enhancements.**"[181]

This ultimate reboot, as Enriquez puts it, is in fact in direct conflict with what God has offered freely, which we considered in the first chapters of this book. Through the cross, Jesus has made a way that we can obtain the epitome of "ultimate reboots." We can be born again—that is as good as it can get! Sadly, however, rather than submit to God's plan to fix man genetically and spiritually, Man prefers to believe the lie that he can fix himself. In fact the theory of evolution has paved the way for man to shake off the philosophical inhibitions of seeking God. Man has come to the point that he believes that having evolved this far, he can take himself to the next level. The Scriptures are plain, "Know that the LORD Himself is God; it is He who has made us, and not we ourselves" (Psalm 100:3 NASB). In spite of that man believes that he can become his own God.

Dr. Ray Kurzweil is the Creator of numerous inventions including the electronic piano keyboard. He is at the forefront of the transhumanist movement and is a major visionary of where we are headed. Fully convinced of the supposed fact of evolution, he states in his publication *The Singularity Is Near: When Humans Transcend Biology*:

> Evolution moves toward greater complexity, greater elegance, greater knowledge, greater intelligence, greater beauty, greater creativity, and greater levels of subtle attributes such as love. In every monotheistic tradition God is likewise described as all of these qualities, only without any limitation: infinite knowledge, […] and so on. […] So **evolution moves inexorably toward this conception of God**, although never quite reaching this ideal. We can regard, therefore, the freeing of our thinking from the severe limitations of its biological form to be an essentially **spiritual undertaking.**[182]

Time Magazine, in December of 1997, reported on Dr. Richard Seed, a physicist from Chicago who became well known for his announcement of plans to start human cloning. He declared:

> God intended for man to become one with God. We are going to become one with God. **We are going to have almost as much knowledge and almost as much power as God**. Cloning and the reprogramming of DNA is the first serious step in becoming one with God (National Public Radio, emphasis mine).[183]

Seed's words are not intended in any biblical sense but to declare that we too will become as God—that we can be our own gods. A week later Seed elaborated in an interview on CNN: "Man will develop the technology and the science and the capability to have an indefinite life span."[184] Eleven years later he would make an even more radical statement; whereas the first was to become like God, his latter statement was for man to become a god.

> **We are going to become Gods**, period. If you do not like it, get off. You do not have to contribute, you do not have to participate but if you are going to **interfere with me becoming a God**, you're going to have trouble. There'll be warfare (emphasis mine).[185]

Seed's words are not just isolated radical ideas but part of the much larger and well-funded movement known as transhumanism (or posthumanism). While probably most in it would not proclaim that they want to become "gods," the goal is the same. They are playing with the human source code in ways that are extremely dangerous. Biblical and transhumanism researcher Dr. John P. McTernan puts it this way: "Evolution also detaches man from his Creator and being created in God's image and likeness. Man is now a free agent to tamper with his DNA under the guise of advancing evolution."[186] Therefore, man sees himself as the captain of his own destiny. He is going to overcome death, disease, and human "limitations." Rather than live with the image of God that he has and receive the cure for his fallen state, man would rather pretend that God does not exist and attempt his own cure. Even the difference in the sexes is no longer considered to be God-given.

According to the publication Mail Online (dailymail.co.uk), scientists have succeeded in creating male eggs and female sperm. The article is titled boldly: "No men OR women needed: Scientists create sperm and eggs from stem cells." It goes on to say:

> Human eggs and sperm have been grown in the laboratory in research which could change the face of parenthood. [...] But it raises a number of moral and ethical concerns. These include the possibility of **children being born through entirely artificial means**, and men and women being sidelined from the process of making babies. [...] The science also raises the possibility of **'male eggs' made from men's skin and 'female sperm' from women's skin.** [...] This would allow gay couples to have children genetically their own" (emphasis mine).[187]

Mankind is racing toward changing the very image that we were created in to disconnect us from God forever. Dr. McTernan describes very well what is going on in the mind of the evolutionist and the path that they are on.

> The natural progression is to enhance the human race by sharpening the senses. If the DNA is now understood and can be manipulated, why not increase the eyesight and hearing? With the addition of eagle DNA man could see like an eagle [...] For strength the introduction of gorilla DNA could give super strength, and for speed how about ostrich DNA!

> The evolutionists believe they are rapidly advancing evolution by manipulating the DNA. Many scientists believe they are enhancing evolution by improving man. Because, through evolution, man has no fear of God and thus no restraints on tampering with DNA, any attempts to stop this tampering will be met with cries from the scientists. [188]

He then states what he believes God's response to man's actions will be once man corrupts his image with that of animals which happened in Noah's day.

> The creation of a chimera is in direct violation of the Bible. The mixing of DNA from two different species violates this law [of reproducing according to its kind]. When God created man, He stated that man was made in His image and likeness. The human DNA is what physically carries this image and likeness. The addition of animal DNA means that man is no longer in God's image. It is extremely serious to tamper with the integrity of man as transmitted through his DNA. This is, in part, what triggered the flood in Noah's day. All of the hybrid humans were destroyed during the flood, and God then started over with Noah.[189]

Dr. McTernan offers a very sobering perspective of where we have been and where we are going as a species. Apparently Satan's ultimate plan will be to persuade and/or force man to change his genetic makeup so that he is no longer fully in the image of God. Once we give up the code we have been made with, we in fact will be forsaking the image of the One who created us. Not only does this violate the "according to its kind" principle that we just discussed, but it also has the radical consequence of man changing himself from God's image.

Thomas Horn, who owns his own news agency, has amassed a great deal of evidence that the research is already taking place. In the United States, similar studies led Irv Weissman, director of Stanford University's Institute of Cancer/Stem Cell Biology and Medicine in California to create mice with partly human brains, causing some ethicists to raise the issue of "humanized animals" in the future that could become "self-aware" as a result of genetic modification.[190] Senior counsel for the Alliance Defense Fund, Joseph Infranco writes:

> The **chimera** in Greek mythology was a monster with a lion's head, a goat's body, and a dragon's tail. It was universally

viewed by the Greeks as a **hideous creature**, precisely because of its **unnatural hybrid makeup**; Prince Bellerophon, who was assigned the unhappy task of fighting the creature, became a hero when he slew it. If we fast-forward to today, the chimera, or combination of species, is a subject of serious discussion in certain scientific circles. [191]

We are well beyond the science fiction of H. G. Wells' tormented hybrids in The Island of Doctor Moreau; we are in a time where scientists **are seriously contemplating the creation of human-animal hybrids**. The hero is no longer Bellerophon who killed the creature; it is, rather, the scientist creating it.

Horn also points out that in 2007 National Geographic magazine stated that within ten years the first transhumans would walk the earth. He continues by citing Vernor Verge who recently discussed the meaning of life and then stated for H+ (Transhumanism) Magazine: "Within thirty years, we will have the technological means to create superhuman intelligence. Shortly thereafter, the human era will be ended."[192] Summing up the stark reality of transhumanism Nick Bostrom, director of the Future of Humanity Institute and a professor of Philosophy at Oxford University, in his online thesis *Transhumanist Values*, describes the "current human sensory modalities are not the only possible ones, and they are certainly not as highly developed as they could be."[193] He notes how man could be mixed with animals in order to acquire some of their abilities:

> Some animals have sonar, magnetic orientation, or sensors for electricity and vibration; many have a much keener sense of smell, sharper eyesight, etc. The range of possible sensory modalities is not limited to those we find in the animal kingdom. There is **no fundamental block to adding say a capacity to see infrared radiation** or to perceive radio signals and perhaps to add some kind of telepathic sense by **augmenting our brains**" (emphasis mine).[194]

In his book *Life, Liberty, and the Defense of Dignity: The Challenges of Bioethics*, former chairman of the President's Council on Bioethics Leon Kass cautioned:

> **Human nature itself lies on the operating table, ready for alteration, for eugenic and psychic 'enhancement,' for wholesale redesign.** In leading laboratories, academic and industrial, new Creators are confidently amassing their powers and quietly honing their skills, while on the street their evangelists are zealously prophesying a posthuman future. **For anyone who cares about preserving our humanity, the time has come for paying attention** (emphasis mine).[195]

The "wholesale redesign" of humanity is what Satan has been planning for millennia. Leon Kass is correct that if anyone cares about preserving our humanity, the "time has come for paying attention." What the rapidly growing transhumanist (and posthumanist) movement demonstrates to a large degree is how man feels about his Maker. It shows in general that:

1. Man has no fear of God which is only natural if people feel that God has been disproven through evolution and of course, if there is no God, then …

2. There is no need to submit to His Word. Having rejected the author of the Word, man is under no obligation to accept the statements in His book nor is he seeking the solution to man's problems prescribed in the book

3. Believing that he has evolved this far and the complexity of the human body is due to evolution, man believes that he should carry on his own evolution.

4. Man desires to direct his own destiny and rewrite his source code by mixing it with creatures.

5. By rewriting his DNA according to his own wisdom man rejects the image of God which is coded in his DNA.

6. Should the right opportunity arise, man might be willing to go through the ultimate upgrade and thereby completely reject the image of God.

SATAN'S NEXT MOVE

To understand Satan's next move and to see how man will be persuaded to take such an improvement, we will need to review just a little. We have seen conclusively that Satan has tried many times throughout history to mingle his seed with men. He started in the days of Noah, which resulted in God destroying the demonic-human hybrids (Nephilim) in the flood (Genesis 6), then he polluted the land of Canaan with the demonic-human hybrids when the children of Israel first came to possess it (Numbers 13:33; Deuteronomy 3:11). We hear of the last of the Nephilim with the destruction of Goliath and his brothers (2 Samuel 21:18-22). Daniel's interpretation of Nebuchadnezzar's dream prophesied that one day ten kings would mingle themselves with the seed of men but would not adhere (Daniel 2:43). Finally, Jesus Himself warned that at the time of His coming conditions would be as they were in the days of Noah (Matthew 24:37). Just as the demons mixed with humans in the days before the flood, so too they will mingle their seed with humanity in the days before the second coming. If the reason for destroying the world via the flood was the mingling of the demons and humans (which grieved God's heart in that their thoughts and actions were continually wicked), then a major reason the Lord will again judge the world may be due to the demons once again mingling themselves with the seed of men.

Man now possesses the power, via transgenics and transhumanism, to direct his own evolution. Tinkering with his code at the genetic level (DNA) is not only possible, but is currently being done. Strange animal hybrids are being made in the laboratory and even humans and animals are being experimented with; man is certainly open to improving himself in any way possible.

From all of the testimony that we have seen, we know that transhumanism is of course not the real goal. For the very concept of it is "trans"—that is, to be transhuman—to go beyond being human. The mixing of human seed with animals is merely a stepping stone to something far more sinister that Satan has been planning for a very long time, and in fact, has already attempted several times. Daniel 2:43 predicts that such a scenario is going to happen again and we saw that it has already begun. Thus, man mingling himself with animals is detestable, but not the deal breaker. Transhumanist activity is only the stepping stone to an even grander deception. We have noted that after the rapture, the Enemy will have a counter explanation and the "aliens" will take credit for it. The Bible tells us that a man with fierce countenance will arise and he will have all the power, authority, and working signs of Satan to deceive the world and to cause them to take on his mark. Could the science of transhumanism and transgenics play a role in the rise of the Antichrist and the Mark of the Beast? Could technology allow Satan to create one from his own seed as Genesis 3:15 predicts? Satan's end game has been in the making now for many decades and will very soon be put into play. We will explore how this will happen in the next chapter.

CHAPTER SEVENTEEN

The Genetics of Satan`s Seed

THE GENESIS 3:15 PROPHECY speaks of two seeds: the Seed of the Woman (her seed) and the seed of Satan (your seed). Jewish and Christian interpreters were convinced that the reference to her seed found its culmination in Jesus the Messiah, and we fully examined just how that was possible genetically. Because the fulfillment of "her seed" was the genetic mixing of the earthly (Mary) with the heavenly/divine (Holy Spirit) then it follows that the fulfillment of "your seed" will follow in like manner. Therefore, because the incarnation of the Messiah was Mary's seed plus the Holy Spirit (human seed + spiritual seed), the embodiment of the anti-Messiah ought to be a mingling of human seed plus Satan (who is opposed to the woman). We conclude therefore that **the Antichrist will genetically be the son of Satan.**

How could that be possible? We recall that Adam and Eve were made in God's image and emitted light like a garment. The image was tainted at the fall and they lost the light garments. God promised a Redeemer to restore the image and restore the light garments. The Messiah mixed genetically with humanity to rescue us and upon resurrection we get our new bodies with the image restored. However, only those who follow Jesus (by dying to self) will receive the restored image.

Concurrently, Satan attempted to destroy the image genetically with the Nephilim both before the flood and after the flood (the sons of God returned). Daniel 2:43 prophesied of a mixing of the seed (distortion of the image). We have learned that the "alien" (demonic) abductees report their seed being harvested and that the "aliens" (demons) are creating a hybrid race between them and us. All the while they (demons) are warning of impending cataclysms coming upon the world and are purporting that they will raise up a superhuman leader in our time of need. Lastly, we saw that the transhumanist movement is seeking to improve man by way of changing his genetic code and via recombinant DNA it is possible to alter an adult individual at the most fundamental level.

THE LITTLE HORN RISING

The key to unlocking the genetic connection between the Beast (Antichrist) and Satan is found in Daniel and Revelation. We formerly considered who the ten toes (ten kings) were in Daniel 2:43 and we came to the conclusion that they are not humans but demons. We also demonstrated how the kings in Daniel 10 must necessarily be demon kings and not human kings for not even any number of human kings would be able to imprison one (good) angel as witnessed when just one angel killed 185,000 mighty Assyrians in one night (2 Kings 19:35). The ten toes of Daniel 2:43 are identical to the ten horns in Daniel 7:7 and Revelation 13:1 and from Revelation 17:12 we know that the horns are kings. Given that the horns are demons, the little horn rising up among them takes on a new significance.

> I was considering the horns, and there was another horn, a little one, coming up [*silkat* סִלְקָת] among them, before whom three of the first horns were plucked out by the roots. And there, in this horn, *were* eyes like the eyes of a man, and a mouth speaking pompous words (Daniel 7:8).

The term "coming up" (among them) is the Aramaic word *silkat* (סִלְקָת), which means "to ascend or come up" (cf. BDB Hebrew Lexicon). The implication is that if the ten horns are demonic, then the little horn ascends to their level; he rises up in likeness to them. In other words, the little horn becomes of a like nature to the ten horns: **he is transformed from simply human to a genetic hybrid between Satan and human—he becomes the Beast**. Daniel Chapter 8 supports this conclusion.

THE LITTLE HORN IN DANIEL CHAPTER 8

In Daniel chapter 8, Daniel sees a vision of Alexander the Great coming and attacking with great velocity the Medo-Persian Empire. In the vision, Alexander is represented as a male goat: "the male goat grew very great; but when he became strong, the large horn was broken, and in place of it four notable ones came up toward the four winds of heaven" (Daniel 8:8). The angel explains that out of the one, four come up. We know that after Alexander's death his four generals took over the empire. We of course need to keep in mind that behind each of these kingdoms is a spiritual ruler, per Daniel 10. Nevertheless, out of one of the horns would come Antiochus IV (Epiphanes): "And out of one of them came a little horn which grew exceedingly great toward the south, toward the east, and toward the Glorious *Land* (Daniel 8:9). Thomas Constable in his commentary states "almost all scholars recognize that Antiochus Epiphanes fulfilled what Gabriel predicted in these verses (cf. 1 Maccabees. 1:10)." He notes that many students of the verses in question "have noticed striking similarities between Antiochus Epiphanes as described here and another political leader predicted to appear in the future." He concludes that he (and other students of Daniel) take the verses to be prophetic of Antiochus **and** the Antichrist.

> It seems that Antiochus did on a smaller scale what Antichrist will do on a larger one. Apparently in the much later period of the rule of these kings, namely, the end times, transgressors will have run their course even more completely. The Antichrist will oppose the Prince of princes, God the Son, who will break him without human agency (Psalm 2; Revelation 19:19-20).[196]

Thus we conclude as well that the passage of Daniel 8 was true in many aspects of Antiochus IV but will be completely fulfilled through the person of the Antichrist. The little horn in Daniel 8:9, therefore, is the same horn as in Daniel 7:7. We then continue reading concerning this little horn:

> And it **grew up** [*vatigdal* וַתִּגְדַּל] to the **host** [*tzevah* צְבָא] of **heaven**; and it **cast down** *some* of the **host** [*tzavah* צְבָא] and *some* of the **stars to the ground**, and trampled them. He even **exalted** *himself* as high as the Prince of the host; and by him the daily *sacrifices* were taken away, and the place of His sanctuary was cast down. Because of transgression, an **army was given** over *to the horn* to oppose the daily *sacrifices;* and he cast truth down to the ground. He did *all this* and prospered (Daniel 8:10-12).

The Hebrew[197] word *vatigdal* (וַתִּגְדַּל) comes from the lexical form *gadal* (גדל) meaning to "grow up, become great, to be magnified." The idea is that the little horn goes from a lesser state to a greater state. He becomes so great that he even grows up to the angelic/demonic realm which the Bible commonly refers to as the "host of heaven." The host of heaven refers to the army of heaven—which is to say the angelic and/or demonic host. However, the word "host" simply means "army," which refers to either human or angelic/demonic. We first note that God is commonly referred to as YHWH *tzevaoth* (LORD of hosts/armies).

Isaiah 34:2-3 states that: "For the indignation of the LORD is **against all nations**, and His fury against all **their armies**; He has utterly destroyed them, He has given them over to the slaughter. Also their slain shall be thrown out; their stench shall rise from **their corpses**, and the mountains shall be melted with their **blood**." We then find this contrasted in the next two verses with the host of heaven—which is referring to the demonic armies (which we learned about in Daniel chapter 10).

> **All the host of heaven shall be dissolved**, and the heavens shall be rolled up like a scroll; all their host shall fall down as

the leaf falls from the vine, and as fruit falling from a fig tree. For My **sword shall be bathed in heaven**; indeed it shall come down on Edom, and on the people of My curse, for judgment (Isaiah 34:4-5).

On that day the Lord will **punish the host of heaven, in heaven**, and the **kings of the earth, on the earth**. They will be gathered together as prisoners in a pit; they will be shut up in a prison, and after many days they will be punished (Isaiah 24:21-22).

ANGELS AS STARS

The next phrase of Daniel 8:10, reiterates and expands upon that with a parallel statement that He will cast some of the host and stars down to the ground. Scripture frequently refers to angels as stars. We know that it must not be referring to what we call stars today, i.e. burning balls of gas in space, for that would require Him to move many of them and of course the entire earth and all therein would be instantly dissolved. In the book of Job, stars represent angels where the term "morning stars" is in parallel with "sons of God," which we have already studied in depth: "When the morning **stars** sang together, and all the **sons of God** shouted for joy?" (Job 38:7). This same imagery is used of Lucifer himself in Isaiah 14:12-13:

> How you are **fallen from heaven**, O Lucifer, son of the morning! [*How*] you are cut down to the ground, you who weakened the nations! For you have said in your heart: "I will ascend into heaven, I will exalt my throne above the **stars** of God; I will also sit on the mount of the congregation on the farthest sides of the north."

Likewise in Revelation the dragon took one third of the stars with him to the ground which we see in verse 7 is a reference to angels.

> His tail drew a third of the **stars** of heaven and threw them to the earth. […] And war broke out in heaven: Michael and his

angels fought with the dragon; and the dragon and his **angels** fought (Revelation 12:4, 7).

The reason angels are so often referred to as stars is because they literally shine. We can see this proven when the disciples went to the tomb and found Jesus' body missing. They were visited by two men in shining garments (Luke 24:4)—the word used to describe the "shining" garments is *astrapto* (αστραπτω) which is the same linguistic root as a "star"—that is just as a star shines, so too do the garments of angels. Thus, we see graphically why the angels are referred to as stars occasionally in the Bible.

EXALTED TO THE HEAVENLY HOST

Next we note that this king will be exalted as high as the prince of the host (*sar-hatzavah* שַׂר־הַצָּבָא). This could be a reference to Michael, who is referred to as the chief prince (*sar* שַׂר) though it could also refer to the Lord Jesus. In any event, this king will be exalted[198] or will exalt himself up to the spiritual realm. Again, the impression is that this king somehow goes through a transformation from a lower state to a higher state. The angel then gives the interpretation of this coming king.

> And in the latter time of their kingdom, when the transgressors have reached their fullness, a king shall arise, having fierce features, who understands **sinister schemes**. His **power shall be mighty**, but **not by his own** power; he shall destroy fearfully, and **shall prosper and thrive**; he shall destroy the mighty, and *also* the holy people. Through his **cunning He shall cause deceit to prosper** under his rule; and he shall exalt *himself* in his heart. He shall destroy many in *their* prosperity. He shall even rise against the Prince of princes; but he shall be broken without *human* means. And the vision of the evenings and mornings which was told is true; therefore seal up the vision, for *it refers* to many days *in the future* (Daniel 8:23-26).

The keys aspects of this coming king as seen in the vision and the interpretation of the vision given by the angel are the following:

- His coming will be at a time of great transgression reminiscent of Jesus' prediction that "the love of many will grow cold" (Matthew 24:12), and Paul's prediction of the coming apostasy (2 Thessalonians 2:3)

- The king will have fierce features

- He will understand sinister schemes (riddles or enigmatic sayings)

- He will have great power but the source is from another (Satan)

- He will war against the holy people (see also Revelation 12)

- He will exalt—declare himself to be god (see also 2 Thessalonians 2:4)

- He will stop the sacrifices (Daniel 11:31, 37-38)

- He will be destroyed supernaturally (literally "without a hand he will be broken" [*b'ephes yad yishaver* יָד יִשָׁבֵר בְּאֶפֶס]. (see also 2 Thessalonians 2:8; Isaiah 11:4).

Therefore the composite we draw is that this person will be exalted, though not by his own power, to the level of the demonic realm (the stars, host, horns). He will share some common features with the horns (demons), first of all because he is known as the little horn. Secondly, he will rise up to the host of heaven and will even cast down some of the host and some of the stars (demons). Therefore, we see that the man will rise up to the level of demons; he will become part horn, which we have seen is demonic. Therefore, he will be a hybrid which points us back to Genesis 3:15 where we saw that Satan's seed will become the Antichrist (Beast). The man known as the Beast will take on the DNA (seed of Satan) and will go from being a regular human and will become a hybrid (Nephilim).

SON OF PERDITION

End times researcher Tom Horn reaches a similar conclusion that the Antichrist/Beast will be the progeny of the demonic realm based on his reading of 2 Thessalonians 2:3.: "Let no one deceive you by any means; for *that Day will not come* unless the falling away comes first, and the man of sin is revealed, the son of perdition [*apoleia*]" (2 Thessalonians 2:3). He notes that Greek word *apoleia* (perdition) is the same root as *Apollyon / Apollo* all of which mean "perdition" or "destruction." Horn states:

> Antichrist will be the progeny or incarnation of the ancient spirit, "*Apollo.*" Numerous scholarly and classical works identify "Apollyon" as the god "Apollo"—the Greek deity "of death and pestilence," and *Webster's Dictionary* points out that "Apollyon" was a common variant of "Apollo" until recent history.

> Revelation 17:8 also ties the coming of Antichrist with Apollo, revealing that the 'Beast' shall ascend from the bottomless pit and enter him. "The Beast that thou sawest was, and is not; and shall ascend out of the Bottomless Pit, and go into *perdition* [*Apolia*, Apollo]: and they that dwell on the Earth shall wonder, whose names were not written in the Book of Life from the foundation of the world, when they behold the Beast that was, and is not, and yet is" (Revelation 17:8).

> *Abaddon* is another name for Apollo (Revelation 9:11), identified historically as the king of demonic "locusts" (Revelation 9:1-11). This means among other things that Apollo is the end-times angel or "King of the Abyss" that opens the bottomless pit, out of which an army of transgenic locusts erupts upon earth.[199]

Horn's idea has tremendous merit and would appear to corroborate the evidence that we have examined concerning Genesis 3:15. Thus, if the linguistic connection is correct,[200] then the Holy Spirit inspired Paul to confirm the Genesis 3:15 prophecy, thereby further substantiating that the Antichrist/Beast will be a hybrid or the ultimate Nephilim.

We conclude therefore that the little horn (Antichrist/Beast) will begin as a man and then become the genetic son of Satan. It is important to note that he will begin as a regular man: Though the Lord will use him to in part judge the world, he was not predestined to be the Antichrist but he will choose to become a hybrid (Nephilim) with Satan to fulfill his purposes.[201] He will have free choice all the way until the Lord Jesus returns to destroy him. We know that he begins as a man from several clues in Scripture:

- The beast rises out of the sea (Revelation 13:1).

- Waters (like sea) are defined as peoples multitudes, nations and tongues (Revelation 17:15).

- Satan gives or bestows his power and authority to him (Revelation 13:2).

- He demonstrates that he is a god in 2 Thessalonians, thereby suggesting that he needs to prove it because he was not always so.

- The ten horns which are ten kings receive authority and then give it to the Beast. We recall that Satan would give all of his power and authority to the Beast—thus the horns/kings (demon kings) receive authority from Satan and then give it to the Beast (who did not begin as a hybrid).

Satan will give all of his authority and power to this individual but just what would cause Satan to give anyone all of his authority, his throne, and his power? Conservative scholars frequently refer to the unholy trinity wherein the role of the Father is Satan, the role of the Son is the Antichrist, and the role of the Holy Spirit is the False Prophet. However, rather than this unholy trinity merely being a relationship of mutual interest, the Antichrist (the argument could be made for the False Prophet as well) will in fact share genetic information with Satan and thus will truly be the son of Satan. Therefore, just as God the Father committed all authority to Jesus ("All authority has been given to Me in heaven and on earth" Matthew 28:18), who is of like substance to the Father (*homoousios*), in like manner will the Antichrist be given all authority and power of his father and he will take on Satan's traits.

- The coming of the [*lawless one*] is **according to the working of Satan, with all power, signs, and lying wonders** (2 Thessalonians 2:9)

- The **dragon gave him [the Beast] his power, his throne, and great authority** (Revelation 13:2).

- So they worshiped the **dragon who gave authority to the Beast**; and they worshiped the beast, saying, "Who [*is*] like the beast? Who is able to make war with him?" (Revelation 13:4).

Nevertheless, we are left with the question of how this could be. If our conclusion is correct, then just how could Satan mingle his seed with a grown man? The virgin birth of Jesus Christ was truly one of the greatest miracles in the Bible—even today the concept of the virgin birth is just too much of a stretch of the imagination for many people. How then could Satan perform that same miracle? Just as with the many plagues in Egypt Satan was able to empower the Egyptian magicians so that they could mimic the miracles, so too Satan will mimic the virgin birth. However, as we have discovered, no woman is necessary for this genetic transfer.

THERION

The fact that the Antichrist is referred to as the Beast (exclusively in Revelation) ought to cause us to pause and consider that this person will not be an average human. The Greek word for beast is *therion* (θηρίον) and according to the *Liddell Scott Jones Classical Greek Lexicon*, it generally means an animal as opposed to men and a "beast, esp. as hostile and odious to man; monster, creature, of sharks." Aristotle used the word to signify "either above or below the nature of man."[202] Lastly, in Sophocles' *Ichneutae* the term *therion* (θηρίον) was used to refer to mythological creatures known as satyrs, which according to the *Encyclopedia Mythica* "are deities of the woods and mountains. They are half human and half beast; they usually have a goat's tail, flanks and hooves. While the upper part of the body is that of a human, they also have the horns of a goat."[203] Though the Beast in Scripture may not be classified as a satyr, the usage of the word to describe a human-like entity is extremely significant—that is, the Antichrist will not be fully human and today we have the technology to make this happen.

THE GENETICS OF THE DECEPTION

The technology known as recombinant DNA in fact now makes it possible for a grown man or woman to be altered at the genetic level. If a non-human gene were introduced into the human genome then the person would no longer be fully human but would by definition become a hybrid. The ancient name for a creature that is composed of different kinds is known as a chimera and that is also the name given to hybrid creatures by scientists today. We considered some strange creatures in a previous chapter such as the spider goat and the green glowing pigs to name a few.

RECOMBINANT DNA

Recombinant DNA is "hybrid DNA that has been created from more than one source."[204] The basic procedure is where a DNA strand is opened up and then a gene from another organism is inserted, making a new strand of DNA. Then the RNA replicates the new strand and it is passed into the entire system. "When recombinant DNA is then further altered or changed to host additional strands of DNA, the molecule formed is referred to as a "chimeric" DNA molecule, with reference to the mythological chimera that consisted as a composite of several animals."[205] By means of recombinant DNA, Satan may be able to convince humanity to insert demonic genes, perceived as desirable, into the human genome. The genetic composition of the person, therefore, would result in that person becoming a chimera.

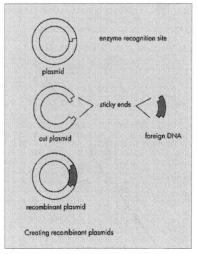

Figure 16
Plasmids and Foreign DNA

Using recombinant DNA, a fully mature man could inject himself with the selected gene or genes of another species. The process, which is really just a matter of copying and pasting, is explained by T. Wakayama et al. in the July 1998 issue of *Nature:*

> In the late 70s, **Dr. Stan Cohen** (Stanford) studying antibiotic resistance plasmids in E. coli, and **Dr. Herb Boyer** (UCSF) studying restriction enzymes [...] realized that they could use restriction enzymes to cut **both** plasmid DNA as well as DNA containing a gene of interest, and combine the DNAs so that the "sticky ends" of each DNA could be joined, or "spliced," to make a **recombinant DNA** (i.e. bacteria human).[206]

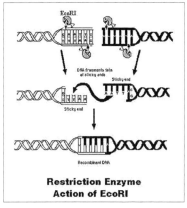

Therefore, we can see how a man with access to technology and to Satan's seed could then merely inject it into his DNA; then once inserted his own RNA would copy the new strands with

Figure 17
Restriction Enzyme and Sticky Ends

the foreign gene(s) and it would spread throughout his entire system. Once the process of replication was complete the man would no longer be a mere human; he would in essence be a chimera, a hybrid; he would be a beast!

HIS IMAGE

And it was allowed to **give breath to the image of the beast, so that the image of the beast might even speak** and might cause those who would not **worship the image of the beast to be slain** (Revelation 13:15).

Approximately three and a half years after coming to power, the Beast will require everyone to take his mark, the number of his name, and to worship his image. Exactly how that will be realized is impossible to know. We can suggest however that the image that the False Prophet gives breath to could be some transhuman or transgenic creature or some form of synthetic biology—the important thing to note is that it will truly have breath and will not simply be a clever trick. The technology already exists to make some version of the image. This image is what will then cause all to take the mark.

HIS MARK

Also it [the image of the beast] causes all, […] to be marked on the right hand or the forehead, so that no one can buy or sell unless he has the mark, that is, the name of the beast or the number of its name. This calls for wisdom: let the one who has understanding calculate the number of the beast, for it is the number of a man, and his number is 666 (Revelation 13:16-18).

Transhumanist and end-times researcher Tom Horn has written a great deal about the coming consequences of man changing himself at the source code level.[207] Horn's wife Nita has suggested that recombinant DNA (RDNA) may be the means by which the mark of the Beast is introduced onto an unsuspecting world[208] through the rewriting of one's DNA so that the person is no longer fully human but is part beast (Antichrist).[209] The suggestion appears valid in light of all that we have learned.

Presumably some point after the rapture, humanity, in an effort to not be removed from the planet (like those taken) and to be able to evolve to be like the Beast (the supposed leader of the "aliens"), will allow their DNA to be rewritten thus altering their image—that image that was in God's image (though fallen) will therefore become genetically like the Beast and of course Satan and his angels. The mark then would simply be the proof (or perhaps the means by which) one has undergone the genetic transformation. This action of taking the mark will condemn them to hell forever because they will no longer be in the image of God. How sad it is to realize that what man will trade his soul for, God was willing to give for free. Man wants to augment himself with greater powers and to go on living forever—but without God. God, however, has already made a way for man to have those powers and eternal life if he will simply humble himself and ask.

CONCLUSION

To whom would Satan be willing to give of his own genetic material? Crossing the line of mixing "different kinds" is against the natural law of God. The sons of God that did so in the days of Noah got themselves thrown into the pit/abyss/Tartarus as testified by Peter who says: "[...]God did not spare the angels who sinned, but threw them into hell and locked them up in chains in utter darkness, to be kept until the judgment," (2 Peter 2:4). The penalty for crossing that barrier is ostensibly imprisonment until the final judgment. We know that Satan will find himself thrown into the abyss right after the great tribulation and perhaps "fathering" his own son is the line that he is not permitted to cross. Therefore, Satan must be very selective of this person. We can presume that this person will have all of the worldly advantages possible: the best education, all the power, riches, and technology. He will worship Lucifer and will lust for the ultimate power to have greater than human capacity. This person will indeed be the one that Jesus spoke of who gains the whole world but loses his soul (Matthew 16:26). The kingdoms of the world that Satan offered to Jesus this person will possess, (see appendix five for a socio-economic sketch of the Antichrist).

He will obtain Satan's own genetic material and then insert it into his body using recombinant DNA. His body's own RNA will then cause the Satanic strain to be replicated into various parts of his body and once completed, his genetic makeup (DNA) will be a new code—a code not strictly from Adam (even in Adam's fallen state), but will be augmented code that has been mixed with Satan just as God declared in Genesis 3:15. Satan will have finally succeeded in imitating the incarnation. This man will literally become the genetic son of Satan because he will have Satan's seed mingled in with his own. This conclusion fulfills Genesis 3:15 plus it is consistent with what other fallen angels did in Noah's day. It is consistent with Daniel 2:43 and also explains how the little horn rises up to where the other horns are and how he is able to cast them to the ground. It is consistent with the technology of transhumanism, in that dissimilar kinds can now be mingled, and it is also consistent with the research of John Mack and David Jacobs, that the "aliens" want to create a hybrid race. Lastly, it squares with the expectation that "aliens [...] will select a human person and endow him with superhuman powers and knowledge. This man will lead us to world government and world peace."[210]

It is reasonable and probable that the mark of the Beast will also be an imitation of what the Lord wants to do for believers. He will restore us spiritually and genetically: we will be like Him, we will be in His image, we will be conformed to His glorious body, we will have God's seed in us. By Satan giving his genetic material to the Beast (who "replaces" Jesus) and then the Beast offering (forcing) all to take of his altered genetic material, Satan will be perfectly imitating our salvation. Probably one reason people will desire to take of his seed is because of the powers they are promised. We have seen both in the movies and by real life personal testimony the "aliens" appear as beings of light. Of course, believers in Jesus will actually receive true bodies of light—but the Beast will promise glorious bodies which he will ultimately not deliver. However, those transformed with the DNA change (mark of the Beast) will receive traits of Satan. Perhaps they will not be able to die which we see when the locusts torment mankind for five months and though they seek death it will flee from them (Revelation 9:6)—this could be because they possess traits from Satan (who does not die).

Some two thousand years after the true incarnation and six thousand years after the fall of man in the garden, Satan, the Serpent, will have fulfilled the prophecy that God spoke to him of the enmity between his seed and her seed. Having his own seed mingled with a son of Adam and with today's technology, Satan can finally try to replicate his own seed in every last person on the planet. If he can accomplish this then perhaps his own fate can be averted; perhaps he can succeed in his war to destroy the image of God genetically contained in man.

Satan's long war to destroy the image of God will ultimately fail. Though he will successfully deceive many and even apparently be just moments away from success, the Lord will in the end intervene. More than likely victory will appear to be just on the verge of achieving—very much like how it was in the days of Noah. Every human on the planet, except Noah and his family, were corrupted morally and perhaps also genetically as well. With only eight standing in the way, Satan must have felt that victory was his—only to watch his entire devilish work gasp for air and then perish in the flood. So too will the return of the Lord most likely be. Just at the last moment, the Lord Jesus will return to save the Jewish people and all others who trusted in Him during the great tribulation. He will destroy the Antichrist and the False Prophet in the lake of fire and Satan and his angels will be bound for one thousand years in the pit. The Lord will

THE GENETICS OF SATAN'S SEED

also judge the nations and set up His kingdom which will last for one thousand years initially and then forever. It is during the millennium that the conditions that were lost in the garden of Eden will be restored to the earth, to the animals and to man himself. In the end, Jesus will crush the head of the serpent once and for all.

NARRATIVE: THROUGH THE EYES OF THE BEAST

The time is moments after the rapture—over 700 million people have just been removed from the earth. The "aliens" appear as bright lights in the sky around the globe simultaneously. Shortly after this worldwide phenomenon their leader, who was originally born in the area known formerly as the Roman Empire (a vast area of land stretching from west North Africa up to England and then as far as the Middle East) and who is a hybrid between man and demon ("alien"), comes on the scene to lead the world to accept his father Lucifer.

Because of the position and influence this man holds as well as the circles he is involved in, he knows that there are no such things as aliens. He is acutely aware that the so-called "aliens" are in fact demons and he has for many years of his life attempted to harness the power of the spiritual realm of the demons and Lucifer. He thinks that Lucifer is the one who wants to give humanity freedom and now he thinks he will lead the world to ultimate freedom—unshackled from the image of God.

The man had attained everything a person could want: money, power, influence—all because of his loyalty to his master Lucifer. However, he had not been satisfied. He had lusted for more power—the ultimate power; he had desired to be like his ascended masters—to become like one of them! His father Satan realized his commitment to the ways of darkness and his lust for the greatest of all power and because the dark lord's own time was short, he decided that he would be the one to receive the "Lucifer strain"; Satan's very own "seed." Using the dark, blood- filled rituals that his order practiced, he and his followers were able to have Satan materialize physically. In reality, the practice was similar to what the sons of God of old had done and even similar to how the so called "aliens" had been materializing. Satan then gave him his seed, his own genetic material.

With the Lucifer strain gathered, he took it and inserted the genes into his own body using recombinant DNA. Oh how he remembered that moment, the sense of awe and power he felt—even from the first moment that his father's genes were grafted into his own DNA strands. Then his RNA worked in their normal fashion and replicated the new enhanced strands; one cell at a time he was being transformed from the inside out. With each moment that passed he felt greater and greater strength and power flow through his body. He was literally being transformed into a new type of being. All the while the image of the Creator was being undone! Soon the process would be complete and every cell in his body would be transformed. Then the physical limitations that had shackled him would be completely gone—he would see directly into the spiritual realm, communicate telepathically, bring down fire from the sky, move things with his thoughts, and would even direct the spiritual host of wickedness. He would fully share the qualities of Lucifer. The seething energy of Lucifer would be completely his! The dark power would be his to command! On top of that Satan himself possessed the man as a "down payment" to guide him until the transformation was complete. He was becoming the Beast, the son of perdition, the seed of the Serpent.

The man had been well aware of the plan of Adonai, his arch enemy, and how there would be a "lifting away" of millions of souls. To prepare for this attack, his cunning father had for many years spread lies via movies, "alien" channellers, New Age channellers, evolution, and the like so that when the rapture, did occur the dwellers of the earth would not assume it was the work of the Enemy. Rather they would attribute it to the "aliens." Satan had commanded his legions to manifest for many hours in the sky all around the world simultaneously at the moment of the "snatching up." Then they would repeat the many lies they had told up to that point about how they, the "aliens," were taking away those that could not or would not evolve to the next level. Even details like the trumpet that the Enemy said would precede the rapture they had twisted—so that people wouldn't understand it as the Enemy's last trump of people leaving for heaven, but they would believe it to be the blast of the coming of the Maitreya, the Christ to Earth—it would announce his coming.

Now the millions had been finally taken and he, the Beast, a true mingling of human and Satan, a hybrid of the kingdom of hell and earth, would come to the world to offer his guidance. With his body transforming into the ultimate hybrid and his father Satan possessing him, the world would never see what hit them. He would quickly take control of the world, which had over many centuries been prepared for his coming. He would explain to the frightened world how he was in fact the leader of the so-called "aliens" and that he and his people had been observing planet earth for a long time, waiting for the time of troubles to come. He would explain how he and his "people," out of their great love for humanity—for the race that they had seeded—had been watching over them knowing that this moment would come and how they were now here to help.

His job at first would be to convince the world of who he is. His abilities would be easily and quickly noted for indeed, he is superior to humans. His father Satan would be directing him and giving him every benefit ever known to any man (though he was no longer simply a man).

With the disappearance explained and "peace" established, phase two would begin: construction of the temple in Jerusalem—the place that his father so deeply desired and for which he had prepared for so long. For there, on that mount and in that temple, he would finally demonstrate the greatness of his father Lucifer and he would declare himself to be god and prove it with all signs and wonders. Now that man's technology had caught up with the dark knowledge of hell, it would be possible to demonstrate that the Enemy was not the only clever one. His father Lucifer was able to make life as well: synthetic biology, transgenics, and transhumanism—all the genius of his father. Even the virgin birth was possible to repeat because of recombinant DNA. They would show the world that the Enemy was not so special or even necessary after all. They would set up an image that they would bring to life—it would breathe and speak and with it they would enforce their will upon man along with the 200 million army of hybrids created via the abductions. (See Daniel 8:12, Revelation 9:16)

However, they would also make man an offer that he could not refuse—they would offer him the opportunity to transform himself from the weak image of the Enemy to the Beast's own image! He, the Beast, would offer his own genes, now a combination of his original genes and those of Satan, his genetic father, to humanity so that they could mingle themselves together with him. In so doing they would finally overcome the image of the Creator—every last person on the planet would be transformed to no longer be according to the Creator's image and likeness but according to Satan's. Together they would recreate the earth as it ought to be—a place without the Creator! If any would not accept such a liberating offer to transform their image, they would be exterminated. And those that did gratefully accept would be given a mark on their right hand or forehead to demonstrate that they had now forever given up the image of the Enemy. But why would any refuse? Immortality, powers beyond their wildest imagination, and the knowledge of the universe awaited them! With his genes that were themselves mixed with his father Lucifer's, they could become like him. By taking the Lucifer strain, the cataclysmic changes coming upon the earth would not affect them; at least that is what Satan told him. This time, they would succeed unlike during the days before the flood. They had learned so much and even so, the Enemy was bound by a promise to never flood the earth again. Nevertheless, man's technologies (many inspired by his father) would safely get the marked beyond the time of trouble. Nothing and no one would stop them this time.

EPILOGUE

Restoring the Image

THROUGH ADAM'S EYES

For ADAM, the resurrection was indeed sweet—oh so sweet. Though after he died he went to a place in the grave where he was comforted, he and those with him, who had anticipated the Seed of the woman, were not in the delightful presence of their Father, the blessed One who created them! They remained there for four thousand earth years until suddenly one day, the Seed of the woman, the Redeemer, stood there before him—how beautiful He was to behold—and Adam's heart raced with joy at that moment. After the Redeemer rebuked those spirits who were disobedient in the days of Noah, He then led all those who had been captive in that place up to the Creator's abode in heaven. There they remained for another two thousand earth years, which seemed like mere days, in that exalted place in the Creator's presence. Yet still, he and all the others who had been rescued were mere spirits, souls if you will, without bodies. Though being there was blissful, something still felt like it was missing without the body he had been created in.

Then after those two thousand years, Adam finally heard the blast of the anticipated last trump and those who were asleep bodily were raised! At last! After six thousand years his glorious body with its covering of light was restored to him. Oh, the joy to have his gloried light emitting body. He felt whole again—like the day when he was created, yet now it was even far greater than that day. Now he understood the depth of the love that His Creator had for him—that he would send His only begotten Son to die on that despicable cross so that he, Adam, the very one who brought sin into the world and because of sin, death, could be restored to the uncorrupted and pure image of the One who made him.

The Seed of the woman, the great King, and Creator mounted up on His white horse and all those in heaven did likewise and then they rode toward the earth. They entered into earth's dimension just over Egypt in a great cloud of glory. They then proceeded north toward Teman and then to Bozrah where the great King treaded the nations in His anger—so much that He even splattered His garments with their blood!

Over there! Over there! There he was—the Wicked One! Adam remembered so vividly the words spoken there in the garden "I will cause enmity between you and the woman and between your seed and her Seed. He will strike your head and you will strike His heel." So this was the prophesied seed of the Serpent, the "Beast," who had gathered together the kings of the earth and their armies, and was leading them to make war against Him who sat on the horse and against His army.

So this was the finality of that prophecy! Adam remembered how some two thousand years ago the serpent struck the heel of the Seed of the woman, Messiah Jesus, and now the serpent and his seed would be struck on the head! Adam noticed the horror on the face of the Beast as he saw the great King coming toward him with what appeared to be a sword coming from His mouth. The Beast tried to flee but was captured, and with him the False Prophet who in his presence had done the signs by which he deceived those who had received the mark of the Beast and those who worshiped his image. They were thrown alive into the lake of fire that burns with sulfur, never to be seen again.

With the Wicked One, the seed of the Serpent vanquished, Jesus directed His horse to the Mount of Olives and there His feet touched down and all of those with Him. There for the first time in six thousand years, Adam returned to the world where he was created. However, the world he was returning to was utterly destroyed and would never rise again. Jesus, his King and Redeemer, said that in seventy-five days He would establish the new age upon the earth. For Adam, the journey was just beginning.

TWO PATHS AND TWO IMAGES

It is at this point that you the reader have to make a decision:there are two paths before you and you will end up walking one of them. The first path is to acknowledge that the image of the Creator that you possess is corrupted, decaying, and dying. It is not possible for you to fix it by your own strength. No matter how many "good" things you do, you will still be corrupted. Even if you could live perfectly from today until the day you die, you would still be corrupted. Not only are you corrupted on a genetic level, but each of us has broken God's commandments. The stark reality is that to die in your sins means that you will one day stand before God naked (without a proper covering) and corrupted. There will literally be no place for you in God's presence where you could survive. God's presence is analogous to the sun; we can look at it through a computer screen all we want but if we were to fly close to it we would literally burn up. Recall that Ezekiel saw God with the likeness of Adam and fire and electricity all around. Being in God's presence without the garments of light would prove to be our undoing. However, that is precisely why Jesus came—to restore your image so that you could be with God in His presence in all of His glory. The restoration of your image is free for the asking even though it cost Him His life. However, if you ask Him, He will freely give you that eternal life. If you need to review the mechanics of being born again, please go to Chapter four: "Reborn with the Seed of the Messiah."

The second option is what the transhumanists and Satan want you to believe—that humanity can fix the image, that we can begin to augment our code so that we can become humanity 2.0 by mixing ourselves with animals, machines, and even the demons themselves. However, mixing our image with theirs will simply seal each person's fate, rendering all who go down that path damned because they didn't have on the right covering (Matthew 22:12).

> "But when the king came in to see the guests, he saw a man there who did not have on a wedding garment." So he said to him, "Friend, how did you come in here without a wedding garment?" And he was speechless. "Then the king said to the servants, 'Bind him hand and foot, take him away, and cast [*him*] into outer darkness; there will be weeping and gnashing of teeth'" (Matthew 22:11-13).

The first option is clearly the preferable option: it is free and will last forever. Option two will fail and lead to eternal destruction in the presence of the angels and of Jesus:

> Then a third angel followed them, saying with a loud voice, "If anyone worships the beast **and his image**, and **receives** *his* **mark** on his forehead or on his hand, he himself shall also drink of the wine of the wrath of God, which is poured out full strength into the cup of His indignation. **He shall be tormented with fire and brimstone in the presence of the holy angels and in the presence of the Lamb**" (Revelation 14:9-10).

Jesus made it very clear that we must be a new creation, born from above to inherit the kingdom of God:

> Jesus answered and said to him, "Most assuredly, I say to you, **unless** one is **born again** [from above], he cannot see

the **kingdom of God**." Nicodemus said to Him, "How can a man be born when he is old? Can he enter a second time into his mother's womb and be born?" Jesus answered, "Most assuredly, I say to you, unless one is born of water and the Spirit, he cannot enter the kingdom of God. That which is born of the flesh is flesh, and that which is born of the Spirit is spirit. Do not marvel that I said to you, '**You must be born again**.'"

"For God so loved the world that He gave His only begotten Son, that whoever believes in Him should not perish but have everlasting life. For God did not send His Son into the world to condemn the world, but that the world through Him might be saved. He who believes in Him is not condemned; but he who does not believe is condemned already, because he has not believed in the name of the only begotten Son of God" (John 3:3-7, 16-18).

You see, Jesus (whose name means salvation) told Nicodemus that man is already lost and now we understand that it is because his image is corrupted; the only fix, the only solution is to allow salvation (Jesus) to repair what was lost so that we can have our new bodies in the age to come. Choose life!

APPENDIX ONE

The Triune Nature of God

HOW CAN IT BE that so many, including the leaders of Israel, saw God? There are undeniable passages in the New Testament, spoken by Jesus Himself, that no one has seen God. "No one has seen God at any time" (John 1:18). "And the Father Himself, […] You have neither heard His voice at any time, nor seen His form" (John 5:37). In Exodus 33:20 YHWH said: "you cannot see my face, for man shall not see me and live." How do we explain these clear passages in light of the many times that prophets have seen God including Exodus 24:9 "and they saw the God of Israel"? Do we have contradictions in the Bible?

When Jesus is saying that no one has seen God, He is referring to two things: First, no one had seen the Father but they were obviously able to look upon Jesus, who was the Word made flesh, that is, the second person of the triune God. This is why Jesus responds to Philip by saying: "He who has seen Me has seen the Father; so how can you say, 'Show us the Father'?" (John 14:9).

According to Jesus, if we have seen Jesus we have seen the Father. Second, no one has or can see God in all of His glory. Moses came the closest to it when God hid him in the cleft of the rock and then passed by, allowing Moses to see His "afterwards" (that which came after Him). Thus, it was understood that no one could see God's face, in all of His glory. Therefore when Moses makes the request (in light of his close relationship with God) for God to show him His glory, God says:

> So it shall be, while My glory passes by, that I will put you in the cleft of the rock, and will cover you with My hand while I pass by. Then I will take away My hand, and you shall see My back; but My face shall not be seen (Exodus 33:22-23).

The fact that the prophets did in fact see God's face and live and yet Moses could not is due to the fact that the prophets saw a vision of God, but Moses was in God's very presence. The difference could be likened to a person getting in a spaceship and flying to the sun versus examining the sun through a computer screen or virtual reality. If the person in the spaceship gets too close he will burn up because the heat and energy is too great. However, the sun can be studied in great detail if one uses a camera and projects the image via television or a computer screen. In fact the meaning of television conveys the idea of what was happening for the prophet. The *Online Etymological Dictionary* defines television as: "the action of seeing by means of Hertzian waves or otherwise, what is existing or happening at a place concealed or distant from the observer's eyes."[211] Therefore, God's face was possible to see, causing Isaiah to declare: "Woe is me! **For I am lost**; for I am a man of unclean lips, and I dwell in the midst of a people of unclean lips; for my **eyes have seen the King**, the Lord of hosts!" (Isaiah 6:5). However, to actually *be* in God's presence was just not possible, not even for someone as close to God as Moses. Therefore the prophet's experience was very much like a virtual reality experience where the "seer" sees and can even interact with the things on the screen, but is not bodily there.

CHRISTOPHANIES

When God visits earth in the Old Testament, He comes as a Christophany—that is, Jesus is actually the One being seen and not the Father. Consider just a few examples in which the Angel of the Lord is also called God. These serve to show us that while God the Son has been seen, God the Father has not been. This is consistent with Jesus' words: "Nor does anyone know the Father except the Son, and the one to whom the Son wills to reveal Him" (Matthew 11:27).

> And the **Angel of the LORD** appeared to him in a flame of fire [*b'labat esh* בְּלַבַּת־אֵשׁ] [note: Jesus appeared *in* a flame and not *as* a flame] from the midst of a bush. [...] So when the **LORD** saw that he turned aside to look, **God called to him from the midst of the bush** and said, "Moses, Moses!" And he said, "Here I am." Then He said, "Do not draw near this place. Take your sandals off your feet, for the place where you stand is holy ground." Moreover He said, "I am the God of your father—the God of Abraham, the God of Isaac, and the God of Jacob." And Moses hid his face, for he was afraid to **look upon God** (Exodus 3:2, 4-6).

The Angel of the Lord in the Old Testament is the second person of the Trinity, Jesus. Thus, of the many places where He makes an earthly appearance, the viewer was not seeing God the Father, but God the Son. Let's continue our investigation with Gideon who was visited by the Angel of the Lord:

> And the **Angel of the LORD** [יהוה] appeared to him, and said to him, "The LORD is with you, you mighty man of valor!" [...] And the **LORD** said to him, "Surely I will be with you, [...]" Then he said to Him, "If now I have found favor in Your sight, then show me a sign that it is **You** who talk with me. [...] "Then **the Angel of the LORD** put out the end of the staff that was in His hand, [...] and fire rose out of the rock and consumed the meat and the unleavened bread. [...] Now Gideon perceived that He was the Angel of the LORD. So Gideon said, "Alas, **O Lord GOD! For I have seen the Angel of the LORD face to face.**" Then the **LORD** said to him, "Peace be with you; do not fear, you shall not die" (Judges 6:12-17, 20-23).

Once Gideon realized that he had just seen the Angel of the LORD (YHWH) face to face he became terrified to the point of death. The LORD, the very One that he had just had the encounter with, then calms him, stating that he would not die. Gideon did in fact see God—and in fact even saw the face of the LORD, according to the text. However, the LORD in this instance, just like in Exodus 3 and many other passages, is not God the Father, but is a Christophany—that is an appearance of the pre-incarnate Jesus. Thus, it was possible to see God so long as He was God the Son and not God the Father, so Jesus' declarations are true (as He said in Matthew 11:27).

Paul elaborates on Jesus being the image of God:

> Whose minds the god of this age has blinded, who do not believe, lest the light of the gospel of the glory of Christ, who is **the image of God**, should shine on them (2 Corinthians 4:4).

> He is the **image of the invisible God**, the firstborn over all creation (Colossians 1:15).

From these verses we see that Jesus is the image of the invisible God. God reveals Himself to be three in one. He is the triune God also referred to as a Trinity; God is one but He exists as three distinct persons. Understanding the triune nature of God is challenging for us and various illustrations have been suggested to understand how that can be. Some suggest the three parts of the egg: shell, white, and yolk. Others suggest the three phases of water: ice, water, and steam. While both of those give a minor glimpse, they break down quickly and tend to confuse the nature of God. God does not exist in different phases nor is He dissect-able.

While no illustration is perfect, we might do well to consider the sun as analogous to the triunity of God. We can think of the sun as three in one: The sphere or ball of the sun is likened to the Father, the light rays to the Lord Jesus, and the heat to the Holy Spirit. The sun itself is the source of light and without which no light would emit. However, at the same it is impossible to imagine the sun without light and heat proceeding from it. If it were not for the light the sphere of the sun would be invisible. It is precisely the light which allows us to see the sphere or ball of the sun. In a parallel manner, Paul tells us that Jesus is the image of the invisible God. Without Jesus, we could not see God the Father; but also as the light is generated from the sphere of the sun, so too Jesus is generated from the Father. That is not to make Jesus created, however. To carry our illustration further proves that the sun could not at any point in its

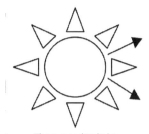

The sun and its light

history could have existed without emitting light and energy. Thus, the light that comes from the sun is co-equal in origin to the sun. Of course, God has no beginning and hence neither does Jesus. The Holy Spirit represented by the heat is analogous to the light; just as the sun emits light, it also emits heat. The heat is dependent on the (ball of the) sun itself but it is impossible to divorce the ball of the sun from the heat that it emits.

THE NICENE CREED

The Nicene Creed codified this concept in an effort to clarify the nature of God:

> We believe in one God, the Father, the Almighty, Maker of heaven and earth, of all that is, seen and unseen. We believe in one Lord, Jesus Christ, the only Son [μονογενη] of God, eternally begotten [γεννηθέν] of the Father, God from God, Light from Light, true God from true God, begotten [γεννηθέντα], not made, of one Being with the Father. Through him all things were made. [...] We believe in the Holy Spirit, the Lord, the giver of life, who proceeds from the Father and the Son. With the Father and the Son he is worshiped and glorified. [...] [212]

The following is the actual Greek text:

ιστεύομεν εις ένα Θεον Πατερα παντοκράτορα, ποιητην ουρανου και γης, ορατων τε πάντων και αορατων. Και εις ένα κύριον Ιησουν Χριστον, τον υιον του θεοθ τον μονογενη, τον ει του πατρος γεννηθέν τα προ πάντων των αιώνων, φως εκ φωτος, θεον αληθινον εκ θεου αληθινου, γεννηθέντα, ου ποιηθέντα, ομοουσιον τωι πατρί· δι' ου τα παντα εγένετο· […] Και εις το Πνευμα, το Άγιον, το κύριον, (και) το ζωοποιόν, το εκ του πατρος εκπορευόμενον [coming out of], το συν πατρι και υιωι συν προσκυνούμενον και συν δοξαζόμενον. [213]

The Greek text demonstrates this understanding by the use of the words "eternally begotten of the Father" [*gennethen ta pro panton ton aionon* γεννηθέν τα προ πάντων των αιώνων]. The root of the word "begotten" has to do with human fathers engendering (generating) children. So just what is meant by that in relation to Jesus? In light of the clear statement that He is "God from God" we can go back to our sun illustration to help us grasp the concept. Jesus is the image of the invisible God. It is only through the light of the sun that we can see the sun. So too with Jesus, only through Him can we see the Father. Jesus then is the eternally generated from the Father. Thus He is dependent on the Father but still without a beginning. He is co-eternal and is the image by which the Father is manifested.[214]

APPENDIX TWO

The Spirit of God in Adam

GENESIS CHAPTER 1 gives us the overview of creation, all the way from the creation of space until the pinnacle of God's creation: Adam. The other creatures—fish, birds, or land animals, the creeping things—all the creatures that God made are lumped together in a few verses. However, the text spends much more time on Adam and in fact, we are told that God said:

> "Let Us make man in Our image, according to Our likeness; let them have dominion over the fish of the sea, over the birds of the air, and over the cattle, over all the earth and over every creeping thing that creeps on the earth." So God created man in His own image; in the image of God He created him; male and female He created them (Genesis 1:27).

Genesis Chapter 2 then focuses solely on the creation of Adam and the privileges and responsibilities that God gave him. Concerning His creation, the text elaborates and states that God formed Adam from the dust of the ground. However, that was not all that God did. The text says:

> And the LORD God formed man of the dust of the ground, and breathed into his nostrils the breath of life; and man became a living soul (Genesis 2:7).

This verse demonstrates that Adam was made (physically, earthly) from the dust (he and we are carbon-based life forms). However, God also breathed into Adam. What we must not miss is that the animals (see Genesis 7:15) also have breath in their lungs but God did not breathe into them. There is something special about the breath that Adam received directly from God. Adam receiving the breath of God is unique and thus he is also spiritual. To put it another way, Adam had a material (physical, earthly) part, that is to say his body, and he also possessed an immaterial (soulish, spiritual, heavenly) side, that is to say his soul or spirit.

MAN'S NON-MATERIAL MAKEUP

Over the centuries scholars of the Bible have debated whether or not man consists of two parts (dichotomous—"cut in two") just body and soul/spirit or in three parts (trichotomous—"cut in three"), body, soul, and spirit. A. H. Strong in his book, *Systematic Theology*, articulates the essence of the essential elements of human nature:

> Man has a **twofold nature**,—on the one hand **material**, on the other hand **immaterial**. He consists of body, and of spirit, or soul. […] Man is as conscious that his immaterial part is a unity, as that his body is a unity. He knows two, and only two, parts of his being—body and soul.

Strong notes that 1 Thessalonians 5:23 ("may your whole spirit and soul and body"), which is the principle passage relied upon as supporting the trichotomous view, may be better explained in that "soul and spirit are not two distinct substances or parts, but that they designate the immaterial principle from different points of view."[215] After all, there are many verses where soul and spirit are used interchangeably. If we are to divide the immaterial makeup of man into soul **and** spirit, then what are we to do with the **heart, mind, and conscience**? They are also immaterial parts of man that Scripture repeatedly makes reference to. Lastly, there are verses that speak of only two parts of a man, as though it constitutes the whole of his being. The following list demonstrates how soul and spirit are used interchangeably.

- his **spirit** was troubled (Genesis 41:8)

- my **soul** is cast down within me (Psalm 42:6)

- now is my **soul** troubled (John 12:27)

- he was troubled in the **spirit** (John 13:21)

- give his life [**soul**—*psuekhen* ψυχὴν] as a ransom for many (Matthew 20:28)

- yielded up his **spirit** (Matthew 27:50)

- And do not fear those who kill the **body** but cannot kill the **soul**. Rather fear him who can destroy both **soul** and **body** in hell (Matthew 10:28 emphasis mine)

- **spirits** of just men made perfect (Hebrews 12:23)

- I saw underneath the altar the **souls** of them that had been slain for the word of God (Revelation 6:9)

THE PLACE OF THE HOLY SPIRIT

What we are observing is that man was created as a three-part being. God created Adam to be a three-part being; the material (body) and immaterial (soul/spirit) were uniquely his and the third part was the "compartment" for the Holy Spirit. At the time of Adam's creation, God, in the person of the Holy Spirit, actually indwelt Adam. However, when Adam disobeyed God through sin, he lost the Spirit of God that had up until that point indwelt him. Thus he truly began to die physically; corruption (data loss) of his genetic code (on a physical level) began, and the spiritual connection that he shared with God was immediately broken. Thus, the Holy Spirit who was to that point dwelling in Adam departed, leaving him spiritually empty and dead; therefore man was left as a two-part being with a "God-shaped hole in his heart" (cf. Pascal). The Holy Spirit is the One who comes and dwells in us when we turn from darkness to light and receive the Lord Jesus as the sacrifice for our sins. Let's go back to our text and understand how that could be possible.

WHEN GOD BREATHED THE FIRST TIME

> And the LORD God formed man of the dust of the ground, and breathed [*vayipakh* וַיִּפַּח] into his nostrils the breath of life [*nishmat khayim* תַמְשֹׁנ סםָיֵח]; and man became a living soul [*l'nephesh khaya* הָיֵח שׁפֶנֶל] (Genesis 2:7).

The obvious feature to note is that God Himself did the breathing. What beautiful imagery: After having created the universe with the stars, sun, moon, animals, vegetation, etc., God bent over Adam's body which He had just formed (like a potter molds the clay), and breathed into Adam's nostrils. Both the Hebrew word *yatzar* (רצי) and the Greek word *plasso* (πλάσσω) carry the idea of forming or fashioning wax or clay.[216] This may have taken God but a moment—however, if we consider the fact that God could have created the world and all therein in less than a microsecond but decided to go slowly and create in six whole days, then when it came to the creation of man He would have given the greatest care! In fact, we could envision the Word of God[217], Jesus the Son, in His preincarnate state[218], carefully taking the dust (carbon atoms and such) of the earth in His hands, pushing, shaping, and molding Adam as a potter would do. Once Adam looked like God, that is to say he resembled the image (shadow) of God, He then gently leaned over this beautiful but still lifeless formation. Opening His mouth, God breathed deep into the nostrils of Adam and then Adam opened his eyes to see the tender but glorious face of the One who had just made him!

This breath of God animated Adam's body in a manner similar to the animals in that they also have breath (*neshama*[219] המשנ) in their nostrils. But it was also so much more, for we know that God did not breathe directly into the animals. Thus the breath that God breathed into Adam must have been so much more than the mere animation of the body (spark of life). It was also the indwelling of the Holy Spirit.[220]

WHEN GOD BREATHED AGAIN

To see evidence of this picture we must fast forward approximately four thousand years to just after the resurrection of Jesus. We find the disciples after the crucifixion behind closed doors for fear of the Jewish leadership. Jesus makes a sudden appearance and walks through a wall in His resurrected body. "And when he had said this, he breathed (literally "inbreathed") [*enephusesen* ενεφυσησεν] on[221] them and said to them, 'Receive the Holy Spirit'" (John 20:22 ESV).

The Greek word *enephusesen* (stem: *emphusao* εμφυσάω) used in the passage above is the same exact word and form of the word that the Greek Septuagint in Genesis 2:7 uses to translate the Hebrew word (*vayipakh* וַיִּפַּח root *naphakh* נפח). This correlation is noted in *Thayers Greek Lexicon*:

> This word used only once by the LXX translators in Gen 2:7 where God breathed on Adam and he became a living soul. Just as the original creation was completed by an act of God, so too the new creation was completed by an act from the Head of the new creation (Thayer's εμφυσάω entry).

The same root (*emphusao* εμφυσάω), though slightly modified, also shows up in Ezekiel 37:9 (37:8 in Greek) and is the same exact Hebrew word as in Genesis 2:7.

> Then he said to me, "Prophesy to the breath [*ruakh* הָרוּחַ]; prophesy, son of man, and say to the breath, Thus says the Lord GOD: Come from the four winds, O breath, and breathe [*naphakh* נפח, Greek εμφυσάω *emphusaw*] on these slain, that they may live" (Ezekiel 37:9).

It would truly seem that when Jesus breathed the Holy Spirit into the disciples, He was in fact doing the same thing that He had done to Adam those many thousands of years ago (the text in Ezekiel 37 will ultimately be fulfilled in the resurrection of the dead—to be discussed in my next book.) Thus, while Adam consisted inherently of two parts, material and immaterial, Jesus Himself breathed not only the life force but also the Holy Spirit; the point at which Adam sinned is when the Spirit departed leaving him all alone. Josephus, the first century Jewish historian, appears to document that as well: "Concerning the formation of man, says thus: […] **God took dust from the ground, and formed man, and inserted in him a spirit and a soul.** This man was called Adam" (Josephus Antiquities, Book 1, Chapter 1:2, emphasis mine). The notes from the NET Bible also give a hint at this:

> The Hebrew word נְשָׁמָה (n'shamah, "breath") is used for God and for **the life imparted to humans, not animals** (see T. C. Mitchell, "The Old Testament Usage of N'shama," VT 11 [1961]: 177-87). Its **usage** in the Bible **conveys more than a breathing living organism** (חַיָּה נֶפֶשׁ, nefesh khayyah). Whatever is given this breath of life becomes animated with the life from God, has spiritual understanding (Job 32:8), and has a functioning conscience (Proverbs 20:27) (NET Bible Notes Genesis 2:7, emphasis mine).

The Targum of Onkelos (Genesis 2:7) also hints at the idea that the Spirit indwelt him: "And the Lord God created Adam from dust of the ground, and breathed upon his face the breath of lives, and it ['the breath of life'] became in Adam a Discoursing Spirit."

John in his gospel makes an interesting observation: "Now this he said about the Spirit, whom those who believed in him were to receive, for as yet the Spirit had not been given, because Jesus was not yet glorified" (John 7:39 ESV). Thus, because Jesus had not yet been crucified and risen from the dead (glorified), no one as of then had received the Holy Spirit. We have seen already that Jesus showed up and inbreathed the Holy Spirit (in) the disciples.

WHEN THE SPIRIT COMES ON AND NOT IN

However, just before Jesus ascends to the Father, He tells them "But you **shall** receive power when the Holy Spirit has come upon (ἐπί) you" (Acts 1:8). We know that the Spirit came upon men of the Old Testament for specific times and purposes. The Spirit came upon Jephthah for a time in order for him to route the Ammonites (Judges 11:29). He came upon Samson (Judges 14:6, 19) to defeat the Philistines but left due to Samson's sinful life (Judges 16:20). The Spirit also came upon David (1 Samuel 16:13) and others. However, the imparting of the Spirit before Jesus' death and resurrection was a temporary and transient experience. The Spirit was not actually **in** the ancient men. He came **upon** them but not in them; the Lord came upon them for a specific job, but not to indwell.[222]

ADAM A SON OF GOD

Remember that Adam was the only person who was created directly as a son of God. John stated that the Holy Spirit had not yet been given, but those who would believe would receive Him. By believing in the name of Jesus one can become a son of God (John 7:39 and 1:12). Thus sons of God today are marked by those who have the Spirit:

- For you are all **sons of God** through faith in Christ Jesus (Galatians 3:26).

- You received the Spirit of adoption by whom we cry out, "Abba, Father." The Spirit Himself bears witness with our spirit that **we are children of God** (Romans 8:15-16).

- Now **we have received**, not the spirit of the world, but the **Spirit who is from God** (1 Corinthians 2:12).

- And **because you are sons,** God has sent forth the **Spirit of His Son into your hearts**, crying out, "Abba, Father!" (Galatians 4:6).

- **Now if anyone does not have the Spirit of Christ, he is not His**. And if Christ is in you, the body is dead because of sin, but the Spirit is life because of righteousness. But **if the Spirit** of Him who raised Jesus from the dead **dwells in you**, He who raised Christ from the dead will also give life to your mortal bodies through His Spirit who dwells in you (Romans 8:11).

Paul says that we have become a new creation in Christ. As new creations we are adopted by God becoming sons of God. The down payment of the Holy Spirit is evidence that we are new creations and are now waiting for the "full package" when we get to heaven. Therefore we conclude that the Holy Spirit must have indwelt Adam prior to his fall because he was classified as a son of God. We are sons of God because we are direct creations of God "Therefore, if anyone is in Christ, he is a new creation" (2 Corinthians 5:17). "For in Christ Jesus neither circumcision nor uncircumcision avails anything, but a new creation" (Galatians 6:15). We share that feature with the angels, whom we shall be like in heaven. However, God did not form them from the earth, nor did He breathe into the angels and so we possess something that sets us apart from them as far as being sons of God is concerned.

The work of the cross was the correction of what had been lost four thousand years before. The Spirit was breathed into Adam, the first (earthly) son of God; he lost it and now the Spirit dwells in the sons of God who we have become by believing in Jesus' name. The Spirit is the guarantee or down payment of what is coming.

APPENDIX THREE

The Image of God and Free Will

WHY DID GOD place the tree of the knowledge of good and evil in the garden when eating from it would result in our first parents experiencing death and separation? Being created in the image of God appears to entail one more aspect: the ability to choose. While God created everything good (that is without any defect whatsoever) and the day that man was created was declared to be "very good," a decision had to be made on Adam's part—would he choose, of his own free will, to follow God or not? In order to accomplish this, God had to give Adam something to choose so that he could exercise his free will. The choice was to obey God or disobey God by eating of the tree of the knowledge of good and evil.

THE CREATION OF EVIL

Isaiah 45:7 states that God is in fact the very One who created evil. However, we will see that the verse really speaks of God's creating of this ability to choose. Notice the parallelism between the forming/making of light/peace and also creating darkness/evil. Thus according to the verse, God is in fact the One who created "evil."

I form the light, and create (בּוֹרֵא) darkness:
I make peace, and create (בּוֹרֵא) evil (ra' רָע):
I the LORD do all these things (Isaiah 45:7 KJV).

To grasp the full impact of this we must go back before God created anything, even before God created the vast black emptiness of space: there was only God, who existed in His own dimension (though we might say *as* His own dimension). In other words, God was not floating around in space for eternity past, which I used to imagine as a boy. There was no space, no dimension, or reality outside of who God intrinsically is. This hurts our heads a bit, but it necessarily must be true since to suggest otherwise would mean that something existed before He created it and Scripture is replete with verses saying that all things have been created by Him.

We need also to consider that God is light (1 John 1:5). Therefore, light, as it pertains to God, is not something that was created (we are not referring to the light of Genesis 1:3, but God's intrinsic light). Because Scripture tells us that God is light, then we understand that the quality of light that emanates from Him is intrinsically and inseparably part of His essence. Therefore, when God decided to create a space/dimension outside of Himself, which was not automatically filled with His light, He then by default created the potential of the absence of light which God called darkness. God then created physical light (photons as waves and/or particles) in order to fill the space.

In the same way, God is good (Exodus 34:6) and no evil or sin or imperfection is in Him. We might say that God has the corner on the market when it comes to good. Good, according to the Bible, is defined as what is in accord with God's will, desire, or plan. Therefore, any deviation from that is by definition not good or therefore "evil." Thus, when God desired to give the angels and man the option to follow Him or to disobey, He must have by default created the potential for them to completely exercise their own will by not choosing the good (that is God's will, desire, or plan). Man cannot choose what does not exist, which is self-evident. Henry Ford once said that people could choose any color Model T they liked so long as it was black. It is also similar to the infamous communist regimes where the people are allowed to vote but there is only one candidate. In reality, having only one candidate (or one color to choose from) is no choice at all. Therefore, God had to create "evil" (the "other candidate" or the "other color") in order for angels and man to have a real choice.

Giving man the choice between two real and viable options, however, is not the same as making us choose the bad option. It is in choosing where we are afforded the opportunity to determine our own path. The two paths are clearly set before us with the consequences of each explained and then it is up to the individual to determine his path. Nevertheless, God created the possibility of letting His creatures choose something that would be contrary to His desires.

THE WORD EVIL (RA רַע)

Some translations render the word (ra רַע) as calamity, which seems to be an option in the context of Isaiah 45:7. Nevertheless, the word is the same that we are first introduced to in Genesis 2:17, where God commands man to not eat of the tree of the knowledge of good and evil (ra רָע).

> And the LORD God commanded the man, saying, "Of every tree of the garden you may freely eat; but of the tree of the knowledge of good and evil (ra רַע) you shall not eat, for in the day that you eat of it you shall surely die" (Genesis 2:16-17).

Why would God place such a tree in the midst of the garden when Adam and Eve just might eat of it? Why not just leave the whole thing out of the garden? How can God declare everything to be very good when he put such a ruinous and abominable tree there? It is like leaving a nuclear bomb in one's living room and telling the kids not to touch the detonator! Do we know for sure that God actually created this tree? We know that God had to be the Creator of that tree for Scripture says it plainly:

> The LORD God planted a garden eastward in Eden, and there He put the man whom He had formed. And out of the ground the LORD God made every tree grow that is pleasant to the sight and good for food. The tree of life was also in the midst of the garden, and the tree of the knowledge of good and evil (Genesis 2:8-9).

The truth is that having the tree in the garden was necessary for man to choose to follow God and therefore good. It was having an option to really choose evil (with all of its consequences) that gave man any choice at all. Let's consider just what evil is in its broadest sense. The Bible states that God is light and in Him is no darkness whatsoever. God is also the essence of all that is good. Following God is to do what is right and good. Thus, if Adam only had all the "good" things that God had made to choose from, then there really was not free choice at all. There had to be a way for Adam to exercise his own will independently, even if it meant it would be contrary to God's. And since everything good was of God, then there needed to be something that would truly allow man to follow his own path and not something that was in accord with God's desire or what God would choose. Thus evil could be defined as any action (choice) that is contrary to God's desire. *Baker's Evangelical Dictionary of Biblical Theology* defines evil in the following manner: "what is right was what was ordained by God, and what is wrong was what was proscribed by him, deviation from this paradigm constitutes what is evil."[223] The *Theological Wordbook of the Old Testament* (TWOT) notes the noun "evil" is defined as "being that condition or action which in his (God's) sight is unacceptable (Jer 52:2; Mal 2:17; cf. Neh 9:28)" (TWOT רָע *ra*).

POTENTIAL EVIL VERSUS KINETIC EVIL

We might think of God creating evil analogous to a large rock on the edge of a cliff. The rock in that position has a tremendous amount of potential energy. It is just waiting for someone to give it a little tap to turn the potential energy into kinetic energy. Just as the rock's potential energy might never be triggered (made kinetic), so too was the evil (a choice contrary to God's) potential and not kinetic. God in a sense told Adam not to push the rock (and the consequences if he did), but Adam of his own free will pushed it and suffered the consequence when the rock's energy became kinetic.

The Serpent, that is Satan, understood the purpose and the potential of the tree and therein was the cunning of his deception. Satan was once in the very presence of God acting as a covering cherub (Ezekiel 28:14) as well as the chief of all the angels (Ezekiel 28:14). At some point Satan became self-deluded, thinking that he could ascend up to the very throne and importance of God (Isaiah 14:13-14). Iniquity was found in his heart (Ezekiel 28:15); he was cast out of God's presence (Ezekiel 28:16) to become the prince of the power of the air (Ephesians 2:2), which he remains until this day. He then set out to trick Adam and Eve, whom God had created in His image and had placed in the garden of Eden.

Satan told Eve the truth about the purpose of the tree (to be like God) but lied about the potential consequence of eating it, "You will not surely die" (Genesis 3:4). God clearly said "the day that you eat of it you shall surely die" (Genesis 2:17). Eve was deceived because of the truth that the Serpent told: "For God knows that in the day you eat of it your eyes will be opened, and you will be like God, knowing good and evil (ra רָע)" (Genesis 3:4-5). We know that his statement concerning the intent of the tree was true because after God pronounced judgment on the three of them, God Himself confirmed it: "And the LORD God said, behold, the man is become as one of us (k'akhad mimenu מִמֶּנּוּ כְּאַחַד), to know good (tov טוֹב) and evil (ra רָע) […]" (Genesis 3:22 KJV).

Certainly, being like God is a good thing; in fact, Scripture is replete with passages that tell us that we shall be in His likeness (Psalm 17:15), "partakers of the divine nature" (2 Peter 1:4), "we shall be like Him" (1 John 3:2), and many others. God also commands us to be like Him:

- You shall therefore consecrate yourselves, and **you shall be holy**; for I *am* holy. […] You shall therefore be holy, **for I** *am* **holy** (Leviticus 11:44-45).

- **You shall be holy**, **for I the LORD your God** *am* **holy** (Leviticus 19:2).

- Consecrate yourselves therefore, and **be holy**, for I *am* the LORD your God (Leviticus 20:7).

- And you shall **be holy to Me**, for **I the LORD** *am* **holy** (Leviticus 20:26).

- Because it is written, "**Be holy, for I am holy**" (1 Peter 1:16).

Therefore, we conclude that the tree of the knowledge of good and evil was good, just as God declared, because it was through that agent that man could exercise his own will—which was something that man had to do in order to be more **fully** like God. However, it must be stressed that man could have (freely) chosen to obey God (and resist the Serpent), and thereby become "like one of us"—**yet without corruption (sin)**! In this way, Jesus had to come as the second Adam (in the form of a servant) and through obedience (even to the point of death cf. Philippians 2:8) He was able to reconcile the sons of Adam with God (Colossians 1:22).

APPENDIX FOUR

Complete Correlation of Nephilim Names

NEPHILIM = ANAKIM

IF WE THINK of the verses giving us the values of an equation, then Genesis 6:4 gives us A=Nephilim (*haNephilim* הַנְּפִילִים). Numbers 13:32-33 give us the second value, B= the sons of Anak (*benei Anak* בְּנֵי עֲנָק).

> The land, through which we have gone to spy it out, is a land that **devours its inhabitants, and all the people that we saw in it are of great height.** There we saw the **giants** [*haNephilim* הַנְּפִילִים] (the descendants of **Anak** [*benei Anak* בְּנֵי עֲנָק] came from the **giants** [*haNephilim* הַנְּפִלִים]) (Numbers 13:32-33).

Anak[224] means long necked or tall; the many verses that speak of the Anakim (the "*im*" being the plural ending in Hebrew) all mention that they were of a great height. This, of course, agrees perfectly with the understanding that we already have of the Nephilim or giants (in the Greek) which were half-man, half-demon hybrids. Thus, if the sons of Anak are of the Nephilim, as the verse says, then that means that they too are half-man, half-demon hybrids as well! As we will see below, many of the peoples of the land were really one and the same but went by different names according to which country was speaking about them.

ANAKIM = REPHAIM = EMIM

- "The people are **greater and taller** than we. The cities are great and fortified up to heaven. And besides, we have seen the sons of the **Anakim** there" (Deuteronomy 1:28 ESV).

- The **Emim** formerly lived there, a people great and many, and **tall** as the **Anakim**. Like the **Anakim** they are also counted as **Rephaim**, but the Moabites call them **Emim** (Deuteronomy 2:10-11 ESV).

REPHAIM = ZAMZUMMIM = ANAKIM

- It is also counted as a land of **Rephaim**. **Rephaim** formerly lived there—but the Ammonites call them **Zamzummim**—a people **great and many**, and **tall** as the **Anakim** (Deuteronomy 2:20-21 ESV).

OG, KING OF BASHAN = REPHAIM = AMORITES

- For Heshbon was the city of **Sihon the king** of the **Amorites**, who had fought against the former king of Moab and had taken all his land out of his hand as far as the Arnon (Numbers 21:26).

- For only **Og the king of Bashan** was left of the remnant of the **Rephaim**. Behold, his bed was a bed of iron. Is it not in Rabbah of the Ammonites? **Nine cubits was its length**, and four cubits its breadth, according to the common cubit (Deuteronomy 3:11 ESV).

- The rest of Gilead, and all **Bashan**, the kingdom of Og, that is, all the region of Argob, I gave to the half-tribe of Manasseh. (All that portion of **Bashan** is called the land of **Rephaim** (Deuteronomy 3:13 ESV).

- And they took possession of his land and the land of **Og**, the king of **Bashan**, the **two kings** of the **Amorites**, who lived to the east beyond the Jordan (Deuteronomy 4:47 ESV).

- Go in to dispossess nations **greater and mightier** than yourselves, cities great and **fortified up to heaven**, a people great and tall, the sons of the **Anakim**, whom you know, and of whom you have heard it said, 'Who can stand before the sons of **Anak**?' (Deuteronomy 9:1-2 ESV).

- What you did to the two kings of the **Amorites** who were on the other side of the Jordan, Sihon and Og, whom you utterly destroyed (Joshua 2:10).

- **Og king of Bashan**, one of the remnant of the **Rephaim**, who lived at Ashtaroth and at Edrei (Joshua 12:4 ESV).

- All the kingdom of **Og in Bashan**, […] (he alone was left of the remnant of the **Rephaim**); these Moses had struck and driven out (Joshua 13:12 ESV).

GOLIATH, LAHMI AND BROTHERS = ANAKIM = REPHAIM

- None of the **Anakim** were left in the land of the children of Israel; they remained only in Gaza, in Gath, and in Ashdod (Joshua 11:22).

- After this there was again war with the Philistines at Gob. Then Sibbecai the Hushathite struck down Saph, who was one of the descendants of the **giants [Rephaim]**. And there was again war with the Philistines at Gob, and Elhanan the son of Jaare-oregim, the Bethlehemite, struck down Goliath the Gittite, the shaft of whose spear was like a weaver's beam. And there was again war at Gath, where there was a man of **great stature**, who had **six fingers on each hand**, and **six toes on each foot, twenty-four in number**, and he also was descended from the **giants [Rephaim, LXX reads: from the giants, γιγαντων]**. And when he taunted Israel, Jonathan the son of Shimei, David's brother, struck him down. These four were descended from the **giants in Gath**, and they fell by the hand of David and by the hand of his servants (2 Samuel 21:18-22 ESV)

- And after this there arose war with the Philistines at Gezer. Then Sibbecai the Hushathite struck down Sippai, who was one of the **descendants of the giants**, and the Philistines were subdued. And there was again war with the Philistines, and Elhanan the son of Jair struck down **Lahmi the brother of Goliath the Gittite** [Gath], the shaft of whose spear was like a weaver's beam. And there was again war at Gath, where there was a **man of great stature, who had six fingers on each hand and six toes on each foot, twenty-four in number,** and he also was **descended from the giants [Rephaim,** LXX reads: giants, γιγαντες]. And when he taunted Israel, Jonathan the son of Shimea, David's brother, struck him down. These were descended from the **giants** in Gath, and they fell by the hand of David and by the hand of his servants (1 Chronicles 20:4-8 ESV).

A parallel passage to 1 Chronicles 20:8 is 2 Samuel 21:22, which adds this important information:

"These four were born to the **giant** in Gath [Septuagint reads: 'the giants in Geth, the family of Rapha' *ton giganton en geth to* *rapha* των γιγαντων εν γεθ τω ραφα], and fell by the hand of David and by the hand of his servants" (2 Samuel 21:22).

APPENDIX FIVE

From Where the Beast Rises

Why WILL SATAN will give the Beast (Antichrist) all of his power and authority and why will the world follow this person as their savior, worship him, and take his mark? While we cannot know him by name, we can draw a composite with the biblical elements of what this person will be like just like the witness to a crime can, with the help of an artist, reconstruct the face of the defendant. He will come geographically from the former Roman Empire (Daniel 9:26), which surrounded the entire Mediterranean Sea (Daniel 7:2; Revelation 13:1); he (and/or his empire) will possess the qualities (and perhaps geographic locations) of the former beasts (Revelation 13:2); he will rise up to be among the ten horns of the last beast (empire); he will have all the power and authority of Satan (2 Thessalonians 2:9; Revelation 13:2, 4); he will sit in the temple, show his powers as god, and erect an image (Daniel 8:11, 9:27, 11:31, 12:12; Matthew 24:15; 2 Thessalonians 2:4; Revelation 13:15); he will be the genetic son of Satan (Genesis 3:15; 2 Thessalonians 2:3; Daniel 2:43). Now let's consider in detail all of these qualities.

FROM THE FORMER ROMAN EMPIRE

The former Roman Empire was an area that stretched from West North Africa to parts of the Middle East. He may be European

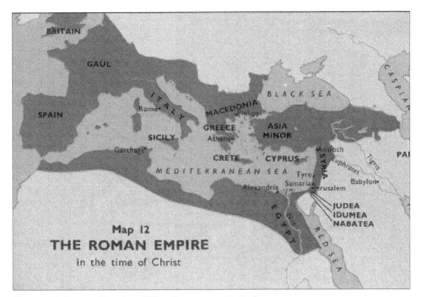

Figure 18 Roman Empire of New Testament Period

but he could also be from North Africa, Turkey, or from the Middle East. He could be from a Muslim country or from a historically Christian country, though he himself will not truly be a believer in either (Daniel 1:37). Nevertheless, he will most likely be nominally religious for appearances.

RISES UP OUT OF THE GREAT SEA

The Great Sea (Daniel 7:2; Revelation 13:1), as spoken of by Daniel, is simply the Hebrew way of saying the Mediterranean Sea. Therefore, the general area that the Beast will come out of is the countries surrounding the Mediterranean, confirmation that he will rise out of the previous Roman Empire.

POSSIBLE CANDIDATES

There are a number of groups such as the Theosophists, Yale's Skull and Bones Society, Illuminati, and the Masons that fit extremely well the description of the coming Antichrist (see the table below). There are many similarities between these groups and very generally speaking they are working toward the same goals. However, for simplicity, we will focus on the Masons since they comprehensively cover the beliefs and practices of the secret societies in general. As a note, the goal is not to give a complete exposé of the Masons as that would require several

COMPARISON OF THE ANTICHRIST WITH THE BELIEFS AND PLANS OF THE MASONS	
BIBLE (ANTICHRIST)	MASONS (AND OTHERS) beliefs, plans, doctrines
Serves Lucifer (Satan)	Serves Lucifer (Satan)
Opposed to God	Beleive Adonai (God) is bad
Focused on the temple	Temple of Solomon of central importance
Rebuild temple (in order to be able to sit in it)	Awaiting right man with vision to rebuild
Will rule over the entire earth	Will establish the New World Order
Understands sinister schemes	Uses deception and symbols to keep secrets even from lower level initiates

tomes[225] but to see why one of their own best fits the description of the coming Antichrist. What we see is that the keys points of the coming Antichrist are in fact the key beliefs of the Masons (and others).

SERVES LUCIFER

Only at the highest levels of his craft does the Mason discover who is the "Great Architect of the Universe" that he so often refers to. Whereas many lower level Masons are led to believe that he must be the Judeo-Christian God, the truth is that they are worshipping Lucifer. Albert Pike, one of the great Masonic historians, reveals that the name of the being that the Masons are worshipping is in fact Lucifer. He says:

Lucifer, the Light Bearer! Strange and mysterious name to give to the Spirit of Darkness! Lucifer, the Son of the Morning! Is it he who bears the Light and with its splendors intolerable blinds feeble, sensual or selfish Souls?[226]

However, perhaps the most revealing as to what Pike truly believed he stated on July 14, 1889, in *Instructions to the 23 Supreme Councils of the World*:

The **masonic religion** should be, by all of us initiates of the high degrees, maintained in the purity of the **Luciferian doctrine** […] Yes, **Lucifer is God**, and unfortunately Adonay also is God […] and the true and philosophical religion is the belief in Lucifer, the equal of Adonay; but Lucifer, God of light and God of good, is struggling against Adonay, the God of darkness and evil.[227]

Pike was not alone in his understanding that the Masons (and other esoteric societies) were worshipping Lucifer. Manly P. Hall, eulogized by the Scottish Rite Journal after his death in 1990 as the "greatest of all Masonic philosophers," divulged one of Masonry's darkest secrets:

When the Mason learns that the key to the warrior on the block is the proper application of **the dynamo of living power**, he has learned the mystery of his Craft. The **seething energies of Lucifer** are in his hands and before he may step onward and upward, he must prove his ability to properly handle energy (emphasis mine). [228]

It is the "seething energies of Lucifer" that the man who would be the Antichrist will endeavor to have—that "dynamo of living power." Even though this person has presumably everything that a person could potentially desire (power, money, etc.), it is the lust for ever greater power that will cause the person to combine himself with the dark lord that he serves.

HE WILL REBUILD THE TEMPLE

Many people have assumed that the Antichrist will necessarily be Jewish because of his intense drive to rebuild the temple. While it is true that there are many Jews that desire the rebuilding of the temple, the Masons (and other esoteric societies) are perhaps just as passionate about seeing the temple of Solomon rebuilt. In fact, the temple is of central importance and without the focus on the temple they would cease to exist. John Wesley Kelchner writes in the foreword to *The Holy Bible: The Great Light In Masonry, King James Version, Temple Illustrated Edition*: "The Temple of Solomon is the spiritual home of every Mason."[229] He also declares the following:

> The traditions and romance of **King Solomon's Temple** [...] are of **transcendent importance to Masons**. The Temple is the outstanding symbol in Masonry, and the legendary story of the building of the **Temple is the fundamental basis of the Masonic rule** and guide for conduct in life (emphasis mine).[230]

In the *Encyclopaedia of Freemasonry*, Albert Mackey, MD, 33rd and Charles T. McClenachan, 33rd affirm that the temple is the most important object of Masonry:

> Of all the objects which constitute the Masonic science of symbolism, the most important, the most cherished, by the Mason, and by far the **most significant, is the Temple of Jerusalem**. The spiritualizing of the Temple is the first, the most prominent and the most pervading, of all symbols of Freemasonry [...] Take from Freemasonry its dependence on the Temple; leave out of its ritual all references to that **sacred edifice**, and to the legends and traditions connected with it, and the system itself would **at once decay and die** (emphasis mine).[231]

THE MAN TO REBUILD

Not only is the temple of central importance but there is also a need to "build up" the temple for truth:

> The great body of the Masonic Craft, looking only to this first Temple erected by the wisdom of King Solomon, make it the symbol of life; and **as the great object of Masonry is the search**

after truth, they are directed to build up this temple as a fitting receptacle for truth.[232]

John Wesley Kelchner in the *Temple Illustrated Version* (KJV) takes the "building up" a step further by indicating that there are so many minute details associated with the temple that all that is needed is for someone with vision to come along and rebuild the temple.

> It is known to every reader of the Bible and student of Solomon's days, that an amazingly detailed description of the Temple and its associated structures has been carried down from the mists of antiquity by the Scriptures. Lineal measurements, materials employed, and ornamental detail are so graphically presented that **restoration of the Temple,** at any time within a score of centuries past, **awaited only the coming of a man with the vision to recognize its historic value,** and the **imagination to undertake the task.**[233]

Edward Waite, writing in *A New Encyclopedia of Freemasonry and of Cognate Instituted Mysteries: The Rites, Literature and History,* declares: "in the **High Grades [of Masonry]** we hear of a **secret intention** to **build yet another temple at Jerusalem.**"[234] We therefore see that there are plans to rebuild the temple and they are waiting for a man with vision to undertake the task.

THE BALFOUR DECLARATION NOVEMBER 2, 1917

Of course, no one could even consider the reconstruction of the temple if the people of the temple are not actually in the land. Hence, it was necessary that the Jewish people be back in the land. One of the foundational movements toward that reality was the Balfour Declaration ,which was a letter sent by Arthur James Lord Balfour to Lord Rothschild. The letter "represents the first political recognition of Zionist aims by a Great Power."[235]

What is significant about this correspondence is that according to researcher Dr. Stanley Monteith, Balfour was a high-ranking Mason (we note, however, that God often allows and uses the wicked to bring about His own purposes, i.e. He used the Assyrians to punish the northern kingdom of Israel in 722 BC; see also 2 Kings 21:14). In fact, we will see that the Masons were centrally responsible for Israel's reestablishment. Dr. Monteith has summarized what Freemason Cecil Rhodes wrote in his "Confession of Faith": "Lord Milner was a 33rd degree Mason, William T. Stead was a spiritualist and a Theosophist, and Arthur Balfour was a spiritualist, a Mason, and a member of the Society for

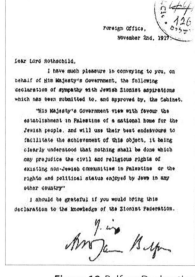

Figure 19 Balfour Declaration

Psychical Research." Dr. Monteith rightly notes: "What most researchers have missed is the fact that most of the men who joined Cecil Rhodes' secret society were involved in the occult."[236] Dr. Monteith again quotes from Cecil Rhodes "Confessions of Faith" wherein he states that he has become a Mason and then states the goal of bringing the world under British control.

> In the present day I become a member of the **Masonic Order**. [...] Why should we not form a secret society with but one object, the furtherance of the British Empire, for the bringing of the whole uncivilized world under British rule, for the recovery of the United States, for the making the Anglo-Saxon race but one Empire (emphasis mine).

Professor Quigley notes that there were "two power blocs that controlled Great Britain during the early decades of the twentieth century. One was led by Lord Cecil, the other by Lord Milner." Quigley writes:

> One of the enduring creations of the Cecil Bloc is the **Society for Psychical Research**, which holds a position in the history of the Cecil Bloc similar to that held by the Royal Institute of

International Affairs in the Milner Group. **The Society was founded in 1882 by the Balfour family** and their in-laws (emphasis mine).[237]

Israeli author and reporter Barry Chamish states the Masonic administration over the establishment of Israel in no uncertain terms:

> **Without British Freemasonry there would be no modern state of Israel**. In the 1860s, the British-Israelite movement was initiated from within Freemasonry. Its goal was to establish a Jewish-Masonic state in the Turkish province of Palestine. Of course, that would mean dealing with the Turks at some point down the line, but first the country would have to be repopulated with Jews. And the idea wasn't to bring in more of the same religious Jews who already were the majority in Jerusalem and elsewhere, but the kind of Jews who would eventually accept the Masonic view of history.
>
> Initially, British Jewish Masonic families like the Rothschilds and Montefiores provided the capital to build the infrastructure for the anticipated wave of immigration. However, luring the Jews to Israel was proving difficult. They, simply, liked European life too much to abandon it. So Europe was to be turned into a nightmare for the Jews. This led to the rise of pogroms and Zionism. […] Then things began moving quickly. **British Masons like Arthur Balfour** and Herbert Samuel led the campaign for official British recognition of a Jewish homeland during World War One. **At the same time, a million British troops, badly needed in the trenches of Europe, were sent marching to Palestine to oust the Ottomans.**
>
> When the war ended, the campaign for a Jewish state went into full speed at Versailles. In 1919, The Royal Institute of International Affairs was founded in London and two years later, the Council On Foreign Relations began its nefarious activities in New York. Their agendas called for a world governmental takeover and a **global religion based in Jerusalem** (emphasis mine).[238]

The above evidence strongly affirms that the Masons were behind the establishment of the modern state of Israel.[239] Given their intense interest in the temple and their desire to rebuild it, such testimony becomes strong circumstantial evidence that the Masons were behind the reestablishment of Israel because they desire to rebuild the temple which is central to their entire dogma. We can only guess they desire the temple rebuilt because their dark lord, Lucifer desires to have his savior for the world, the Antichrist, go in and declare himself to be god.

SINISTER SCHEMES

To tie it all together, we need to ask what the connection is that the Masons have with the demons posing as "aliens"? We recall that the (demon) "aliens" have been telling contactees and abductees that some terrible things will come upon the earth but they will raise up a leader to help us. David Lewis, in his book, *UFO: End Time Delusion*, discusses the "aliens'" plan to set up a human and give him superhuman powers.

> Aliens […] are preparing to intervene again in world history, to lead mankind to a higher level of consciousness. **They will select a human person and endow him with superhuman powers and knowledge. This man will lead us to world government and world peace** (emphasis mine).[240]

This leader will come from regular "human stock" apparently and then be endowed with super powers; he will become the counterfeit Christ. New England Director of the House of Theosophy, Bill Lambert, made an important statement concerning the relationship between the "aliens" and the New World Order, which is primarily controlled by the high level Masons. Mr. Lambert states:

> *UFO's and Aliens are part of the New World Order.* They are benevolent beings which will aid mankind in attaining the goal of becoming one humanity. They will appear at the proper time to enable mankind to make that Quantum Leap of Collective Consciousness—when the Anti-Christ appears (emphasis mine). [241]

The writer from the Cutting Edge website[242] noted that Bill Lambert ended with this revelation linking the coming of the great leader of the Masons (called the "Christ" or "Matreiya").

> Finally, a *sound* will be heard world-wide which will **herald the coming of Maitreya the Christ**. Prompted by this sound, people will be aware of his coming on three distinct levels: Spiritual, physical, and emotional. [243]

The similarities between the last trump that is mentioned in 1 Thessalonians 4, the classic passage which describes in detail the event of the rapture and the description of the coming of the Maitreya, are uncanny. It would appear that what is suggested here is that the sound of the trumpet will indeed be something that the entire world will hear and in an attempt to distort its meaning it will be ascribed to the coming of the false Christ rather than the rapture of the true believers.

The Masonic secrets we have learned are purposefully hidden from the lower levels until they are deemed worthy to receive the truth as stated by Sovereign Grand Commander Albert Pike in his massive book of over nine hundred pages, *Morals and Dogma*.

> Masonry, like all the Religions, all the Mysteries, Hermeticism and Alchemy, **conceals its secrets** from all except the Adepts and Sages, or the Elect, and uses **false explanations** and **misinterpretations** of its symbols to **mislead** those who deserve only to be misled; **to conceal the Truth, which it calls Light**, from them, and to draw them away from it. Truth is not for those who are unworthy or unable to receive it, or would pervert it [...] The truth must be kept secret, and the masses need a teaching proportioned to their imperfect reason.[244]

The deliberate false explanations and plethora of hidden symbols appears to be a confirmation of what was revealed to the Prophet Daniel when the angel interpreted the vision by saying that the little horn will understand **sinister schemes**. The Hebrew word *khidot* (חִידוֹת) means "riddle, difficult question, parable, enigmatic saying or question, perplexing saying or question;"[245]

that is a very good description of what they themselves have revealed—the secrets must be kept from all but the Adepts and Sages. Albert Pike even advocated the creation of a secret society within a secret society—certainly an organization of sinister schemes and enigmatic sayings!

> We must **create a super rite**, which will **remain unknown**, to which we will call those Masons of high degree of whom we shall select. With regard to our brothers in Masonry, these men must be pledges to the strictest secrecy. Through this **supreme rite**, we **will govern all Freemasonry** which will become the one international center, the more powerful because its direction will be unknown.[246]

What emerges from all that we have seen is a picture of a man who will have risen up through the ranks of an organization that at its core is committed to serving Lucifer, is taking grand steps to rebuilding the temple, has a sinister scheme to establish a New World Order, which it acknowledges is related to the "alien" agenda. By connecting the dots we see a picture emerge that all of the efforts of the Masons in the reestablishment of Israel have been to rebuild the temple so that their leader, who will be "raised up" by the "aliens," may go into the temple and declare himself to be god. He will declare himself to be god because he will be mingled with Satan. He will be the seed of the Serpent who God spoke of in the garden those many years ago.[247]

APPENDIX SIX

The Fig Tree Has Budded

Evidence from Matthew 24 that the Lord will return
in the span of a generation from Israel's birth

INTRODUCTION

As a boy I remember feeling the rush of the wind strike my face, the sky grow dark as ominous clouds rolled in and covered the sun. Then the sounds of the thunder could be heard in the distance and the sky flashed. It was a time of great anticipation and excitement. Even though the storm was several miles away, it was clear to all that it was coming. The end times can be likened a great deal to a coming storm. We can see the storm coming and feel its effect even though it has not yet arrived fully. So it is with the Lord's return—the signs are evident even though the event itself has not yet arrived.

Concerning the time of the Lord's return, Jesus' disciples asked Him: "What will be the sign of your coming and of the end of the age?" (Matthew 24:3). Jesus then began to describe the many things that would precede His second coming—many of which are being fulfilled before our eyes. Jesus said "For many will come in My name, saying, 'I am the Christ,' and will deceive many" (Matthew 24:5). Since 1900 there have been dozens who have either claimed to be Jesus or the Christ in one form or another. Some of the most notable are Sun Myung Moon, founder of the Unification Church, David Koresh of the Branch Davidian religious sect, Ariffin Mohamed from Malaysia, and Sergei Torop from Russia.

He then spoke of wars, rumors of war, and nation against nation.

> And you will hear of wars and rumors of wars. See that you are not troubled; for all these things must come to pass, but the end is not yet. For nation will rise against nation, and kingdom against kingdom. And there will be famines, pestilences, and earthquakes in various places. All these are the beginning of sorrows (Matthew 24:6-8).

Only in the twentieth century have we seen the entire world at war not just once but twice. The projected death toll for the Second World War alone is upwards of 50 million people—a number unheard of before in human history. The past century could easily be classified as wars, rumors of wars, nation against nation, and kingdom against kingdom.

There are many signs of the Lord's second coming just as there were for His first coming, and the Lord rebuked the leaders of His day for not picking up on the revealed signs that were evident of His first coming.

> When you see a cloud rising in the west, you say at once, "A shower is coming." And so it happens. And when you see the south wind blowing, you say, "There will be scorching heat," and it happens. You hypocrites! **You know how to interpret the appearance of earth and sky, but why do you not know how to interpret the present time?** (Luke 12:54-56).

Just as the signs of the coming storm were obvious to me as a boy, so should those leaders have known that their Messiah was coming. Jesus noted that they could easily and successfully forecast the weather by simply looking at the sky, yet they failed to see (or at least to accept) the Messiah in front of them. We too see the last days' signs that Jesus spoke about are either happening or about to happen in our day.

KNOWING THE TIMES AND SEASONS

Paul, in his letter to the Thessalonians, wrote that believers could and should know the times and seasons of the Lord's (second) coming since they were not in the darkness like others.

> Now concerning the times and the seasons, brothers, you have no need to have anything written to you. For you yourselves are fully aware that the day of the Lord will come like a thief in the night. While people are saying, "There is peace and security," then sudden destruction will come upon them as labor pains come upon a pregnant woman, and they will not escape. **But you are <u>not in darkness</u>, brothers, for that day to surprise you like a thief.** For you are all children of light, children of the day. We are not of the night or of the darkness (1 Thessalonians 5:1-5).

BIRTH CONTRACTIONS

Jesus likened all of the events mentioned above to birth pains by saying: "All these are but the beginning of the birth pains," (Matthew 24:8). Just like for a woman in labor, the contractions will get closer and closer until finally the child is born, so it is if we were to consider today's events in terms of giving birth, we might say that prophetically all that is left is to push the baby out. All that the Lord had said so far (discussed above) was a response to the disciples' question "What will be the sign of Your coming and of the end of the age?"

THE FIG TREE IS THE SIGN OF HIS COMING

Jesus then gave an important sign to look for concerning His coming: the fig tree. The sign of His coming and the end of the age is the fig tree:

Now learn this parable from the **fig tree**: When its branch has already become tender and puts forth leaves, you know that summer is near. So you also, **when you see all these things**, know that it is near—at the doors! Assuredly, I say to you, this **generation** will by no means pass away till all these things take place (Matthew 24:32-34).

THE FIG TREE IS ISRAEL

There are two obvious questions concerning this parable: who or what is the fig tree and how long is a generation? The answer to the first question is unmistakably Israel. God clearly compares Israel with a fig tree. The following verses are given in chronological order.

> I found **Israel** like grapes in the wilderness; I saw your **fathers** as the firstfruits on the **fig tree** in its first season (Hosea 9:10).

Here God compares Israel to grapes and the fathers to fruits of the fig tree. Then in Joel He speaks of "My land" as being comparable to "my fig tree," again showing that Israel (both ethnically/nationally and geographically) is symbolized as a fig tree.

> For a nation has come up against **My land**, strong, and without number; his teeth are the teeth of a lion, and he has the fangs of a fierce lion. He has laid waste My vine, and ruined **My fig tree**; he has stripped it bare and thrown it away; its branches are made white (Joel 1:6-7).

Next God shows Jeremiah a vision of baskets of good figs and bad figs. Note that both the good and the bad are representative of Israel (Judah). The "good" are taken out of the land, that is, out of danger, and the "bad" are left to be judged.[248]

> One basket had very good **figs**, like the **figs** that are first ripe; and the other basket had very bad **figs** which could not be eaten, they were so bad. Then the LORD said to me, "What do you see, Jeremiah?" And I said, "**Figs**, the good **figs**, very good; and the bad, very bad, which cannot be eaten, they are

so bad." "Thus says the LORD, the God of Israel: 'Like these good **figs**, so will I acknowledge those who are carried away captive from **Judah**, whom **I have sent out of this place for their own good**, into the land of the Chaldeans. And as the **bad** figs which cannot be eaten, they are so bad'—surely thus says the LORD—"so will I give up **Zedekiah** the king of **Judah**, his princes, the residue of **Jerusalem** who remain in this land, and those who dwell in the land of Egypt'" (Jeremiah 24:2-3, 5, 8).

Jesus continues the correlation of Israel with a fig tree during the final stage of His ministry. Keep in mind that Jesus had been ministering in Israel for about three years when He gave this parable. Just like the illustration of God seeking good fruit from His vineyard and finding none in Isaiah 5:1-7, so too Jesus had come in person expecting to find some good fruit and found little or none.

He also spoke this parable: "A certain man had a fig tree planted in his vineyard, and he came seeking fruit on it and found none. Then he said to the keeper of his vineyard, 'Look, for **three years I have come seeking fruit on this fig tree and find none**. Cut it down; why does it use up the ground?' But he answered and said to him, 'Sir, let it alone this year also, until I dig around it and fertilize it. And if it bears fruit, well. But if not, after that you can cut it down' "(Luke 13:6-9).

That Jesus had Israel in mind is confirmed at the end of the chapter when He laments over Jerusalem because of their unwillingness to receive their Messiah and declares that their house is left desolate. Furthermore, the Jewish leaders of Jerusalem could in no way say "blessed is He …" so long as they were not living in the land of Israel (during the time of their exile).

O Jerusalem, Jerusalem, the one who kills the prophets and stones those who are sent to her! How often I wanted to gather your children together, as a hen gathers her brood under her wings, but you were not willing! See! Your house is left to you desolate; and assuredly, I say to you, you shall not see Me until the time comes when you say, "Blessed is He who comes in the name of the LORD!" (Luke 13:34-35).

THE CURSED TREE

Jewish men were to present themselves before the Lord three times a year. Jesus came up to Jerusalem via Jericho on a number of occasions during the three plus years of His ministry in order to celebrate the feasts. There was a fig tree by the road (Matthew 21:19) that He invariably must have seen on a number of occasions as He went up to Jerusalem. The day of the triumphal entry, as He came up from Jericho on His way to Jerusalem, Jesus must have seen the tree and noted that there was not any fruit on it—just as the land owner in the parable found none. Coming into Jerusalem, He was hailed as the Messiah by the masses. He then drove out the money changers from the temple, foreshadowing His coming pronouncement that Israel, like the fig tree, was barren. In the evening He set out for Bethany to spend the night with His friends Mary, Martha, and Lazarus (Bethany was on the same road which came up from Jericho). Returning to Jerusalem in the morning, Jesus passed by the fig tree, noted that there was no fruit on it when there should have been at least some early fruit. Seeing that the tree was unfruitful, He then cursed it.

> And seeing a fig tree by the road, He came to it and found nothing on it but leaves, and said to it, "Let no fruit grow on you ever again." Immediately the fig tree withered away (Matthew 21:19).

Thus, just like His parable of the fig tree, He had come looking for fruit from the Jewish leadership for over three years and found none. They were like the barren fig tree with no fruit to be found and so He then pronounced judgment on the worthless tree, causing it to die immediately, which symbolized the nation. With all of that as our backdrop, we then come to the time markers that He gave us during the Olivet Discourse, this time reading Luke's account:

> Then He spoke to them a parable: "Look at the fig tree, and all the trees. When they are already budding, you see and know for yourselves that summer is now near" (Luke 21:29-30).

When Jesus commanded them to learn a parable from the fig tree, they must have had swirling in their minds the recent events of the parable and the cursed fig tree. The Hebrew Bible (OT) background makes it clear that Jesus is likening Israel to the fig tree and just as the fig tree withered, so too would Israel soon be destroyed by the Romans.

Israel was destroyed by the Romans in 70 AD and then again in 135 AD. After the second Jewish revolt they were warned not to return to Jerusalem upon pain of death. They were then dispersed to the four corners of the earth—without a homeland for nearly 1900 years. Furthermore, the curse appears to apply to the land itself as well. Rabbi Menachem Kohen of Brooklyn discovered that the land of Israel "suffered an unprecedented, severe and inexplicable (by anything other than supernatural explanations) drought that lasted from the first century until the 20th—a period of 1,800 years coinciding with the forced dispersion of the Jews." [249] Journalist Joseph Farah, prompted by the research of Rabbi Kohen, later discovered that only after the Jews returned did the rain begin to come:

> For 1,800 years, it hardly ever rained in Israel. This was the barren land discovered by Mark Twain. So-called "Palestine" was a wasteland—nobody lived there. There was no indigenous Arab population to speak of. It only came *after* the Jews came back. Beginning in AD 70 and lasting until the early 1900s— about 660,000 days—no rain.

> I decided to check this out as best I could and examined the rainfall data for 150 years in Israel beginning in the early 1800s and leading up to the 1960s. What I found was astonishing— increasing rainfall almost every single year—with the heaviest rainfall coming in and around 1948 and 1967.[250]

Then after those many years and just as Isaiah had foretold, Israel was born in one day:

Who has heard such a thing? Who has seen such things? Shall the earth[251] be made to give birth in one day? Or shall a nation be born at once? For as soon as Zion was in labor, She gave birth to her children (Isaiah 66:8).

On May 14, 1948, Israel (the fig tree) declared independence and then was ratified as a nation by edict of the United Nations and literally was born in one day. The Year 1948[252] becomes the standard by which a generation can be measured against.

EARLY CHRISTIAN COMMENTARY CONFIRMS ISRAEL IS THE FIG TREE

Getting a second opinion is always advisable when there is a lot riding on a decision or when contemplating a new perspective. Thus investigating what early Christians thought about the fig tree parable would seem prudent. An early Christian writing, the *Apocalypse of Peter,* clearly identifies the fig tree as Israel and the time of its budding as the time of the end.[253] While we do **not** consider extra-biblical sources to be Scripture, they can occasionally serve as a type of **commentary** from early Christians. Scholars generally accept a date of composition[254] around AD 135. This is a significant date because the early Christians had seen Israel destroyed once in AD 70 under Titus who destroyed the temple, killed upwards of a million Jews, and took the rest as slaves. However, not all of the Jews were taken away and those that remained made a comeback.

Caesar Hadrian visited the city in AD 130 and had intimated that he might rebuild the city as a gift to the Jews. When he changed his mind and also outlawed circumcision, the Jews found themselves once again in a deadly conflict with the Romans a mere sixty two years after the destruction of the temple. The Jews rallied behind a man named Simon Bar Koseba. Rabbi Akiva would later declare him to be the Messiah, at which point the Christians who had been helping in the battle left the non-believing Jews to fight for themselves. Hadrian squashed the rebellion in AD 135. He was so angry that he changed the name of the land from Judea to Syria Palestina and salted the land so that nothing would grow. Jerusalem was renamed Aelia Capitolina and a temple to Zeus would eventually be built on the ruins of the temple mount. Hadrian also banished all Jews from the city on pain of death. With this in mind, to find a text that declares that Israel, which had been utterly decimated, would one day flourish again is truly incredible.

This text, which again, we are treating like a commentary on the Scripture (and not equal to Scripture), clearly states that when the fig tree has budded, the end of the world would come. The text has interpreted Jesus' parable of the fig tree to be speaking of Israel. When Israel comes back as a nation, then the last days would come:

> (Learn a parable) from **the fig-tree: so soon as the shoot thereof is come forth and the twigs grown, the end of the world shall come.** [...] **Hast thou not understood that the fig-tree is the house of Israel?** [...] **when the twigs thereof have sprouted forth in the last days**, then shall feigned Christs come and awake expectation saying: I am the Christ, that am now come into the world. [...] But this deceiver is not the Christ. And when they [Israel] reject him [the deceiver] he shall slay with the sword, and there shall be many martyrs. Then **shall the twigs of the fig-tree, that is, the house of Israel, shoot forth:** [...] Enoch and Elias shall be sent to teach them that this is the deceiver which must come into the world and do signs and wonders to deceive.[255]

The correlation of the fig tree being Israel in the text is unequivocal. According to this text, Israel, likened to a fig tree, was cut down (twice in fact) and exiled (in agreement with the parable of the land owner in Luke 13:6-9). Thus the author clearly saw Israel removed from her land and the people no more. But the author firmly believed that they would come back as a nation: "when the twigs thereof have sprouted forth in the last days" and then the end will come in the days of their sprouting. Notice also that the two witnesses (Enoch and Elias) will come back in the days of their shooting forth and be killed by the false Christ (Antichrist). This text certainly proves that some in the ancient church interpreted the end times in a very literal fashion. However, it also demonstrates that Israel was considered to be the fig tree and that the shooting forth of its branches would happen in the time of the end and more specifically, at the time of the Lord's coming. Thus we have ancient testimony that Jesus' mention of the fig tree was a reference to Israel. Her putting forth branches and becoming tender was a reference to her rebirth in the last days, which would also be the time of the two witnesses and the Antichrist.

ALL THE TREES

We have seen that the fig tree represents Israel in the parable that Jesus told His disciples. No less than three prophets clearly used the fig tree as a representation of Israel. Jesus also did so in the parable of the land owner and the fig tree. He then cursed a fig tree and told the parable of the fig tree concerning the last days. However, when we read in Luke's gospel that Jesus also mentioned "all the trees"—just what are we to make of this? Jesus said to learn the parable of the fig tree and all the trees. We learned what the scriptural meaning of the fig tree is, but what do "all the trees" represent? Sometimes when Jesus would tell a parable He would then give its interpretation. For example in Matthew 13:18, Jesus interpreted the meaning of the parable of the sower in which each ground represented a type of person and their particular spiritual condition. So it is with our parable, and for the answer, we need to go to God's Word.

Since the fig tree represents Israel as a nation, then we should expect that "all the trees" would represent nations as well. Looking in the pages of God's Word we find this to indeed be the case. In fact, we find that trees are often used to represent people and especially nations in at least eight passages of the Old Testament alone. We first encounter a parable of trees in Judges 9:7-16 where Jotham, a son of Gideon, addresses the men

THE FIG TREE HAS BUDDED

of Shechem who had just killed seventy of his brothers in order to follow his other brother Abimelech.

> The trees once went forth to anoint a king over them. And they said to the olive tree, 'Reign over us!' But the olive tree said to them, 'Should I cease giving my oil, with which they honor God and men, and go to sway over trees?' Then the trees said to the fig tree, 'You come [and] reign over us!' But the fig tree said to them, 'Should I cease my sweetness and my good fruit, and go to sway over trees?' Then the trees said to the vine, 'You come [and] reign over us!' But the vine said to them, 'Should I cease my new wine, which cheers [both] God and men, and go to sway over trees?' Then all the trees said to the bramble, 'You come [and] reign over us!' And the bramble said to the trees, 'If in truth you anoint me as king over you, [Then] come [and] take shelter in my shade; but if not, let fire come out of the bramble and devour the cedars of Lebanon!' Now therefore, if you have acted in truth and sincerity in making Abimelech king, and if you have dealt well with Jerubbaal and his house, and have done to him as he deserves (Judges 9:8-16).

In Isaiah 10:33 God refers to chopping off "the tops of trees" as to those who are arrogant and will be "hewn down." Similar imagery is used in the book of Ezekiel. In Ezekiel 15:2-6 God likens the wood of the vine to the inhabitants of Jerusalem, which will be burned in the fire because they are useless (that is idolatrous). God uses the tree motif to speak of Judah being taken into captivity in chapter 17 as well. "Thus says the Lord GOD: 'A great eagle with large wings and long pinions, full of feathers of various colors, came to Lebanon and took from the cedar the highest branch. He cropped off its topmost young twig and carried it to a land of trade; He set it in a city of merchants'" (Ezekiel 17:3-4). In 606/5 BC Nebuchadnezzar took some of the leadership of Judah into captivity—thus Judah is likened to the cedar of Lebanon and the highest branch represents the leadership, which probably included Daniel. We know this to be the case because God gives the interpretation: "Say now to the rebellious house: 'Do you not know what these *things mean?*' Tell *them,* 'Indeed the king of Babylon went to Jerusalem and took its king and princes, and led them with him to Babylon'" (Ezekiel 17:12).

God later in the chapter tells what He is going to do with the highest branches in contrast to what King Nebuchadnezzar had done. Whereas King Nebuchadnezzar made it a "spreading vine of low stature" (Ezekiel 17:6) God would set up a king and a kingdom that would be great among the nations. "On the mountain height of Israel I will plant it; and it will bring forth boughs, and bear fruit, and be a majestic cedar. Under it will dwell birds of every sort; in the shadow of its branches they will dwell" (Ezekiel 17:23). God then makes reference to all the trees of the field, which represent the nations. Whether all the trees represent all the nations of the world or just the nations of the area is not clear. "and all the trees of the field shall know that I, the LORD, have brought down the high tree and exalted the low tree, dried up the green tree and made the dry tree flourish; I, the LORD, have spoken and have done *it*" (Ezekiel 17:24).

Ezekiel 20:46-48 contains another example of nations represented as trees. However, perhaps the most telling of all is Ezekiel 31:3-15. There Assyria is likened to a cedar of Lebanon that was greater than all the other trees (which is to say nations). "Therefore its height was exalted above **all the trees of the field** [...] and in its shadow **all great nations** made their home" (Ezekiel 31:5-6). God describes how Assyria, the cedar of Lebanon, was greater than other kinds of trees though God would send another to cut it down.

> 'The cedars in the garden of God could not hide it; the fir trees were not like its boughs, and the chestnut trees were not like its branches; no tree in the garden of God was like it in beauty. I made it beautiful with a multitude of branches, so that all the trees of Eden envied it, that *were* in the garden of God'. Therefore thus says the Lord GOD: 'Because you have increased in height, and it set its top among the thick boughs,

and its heart was lifted up in its height, therefore I will deliver it into the hand of the mighty one of the nations, and he shall surely deal with it; I have driven it out for its wickedness' (Ezekiel 31:8-11).

Daniel 4:10-11 and Zechariah 11:2 also offer more examples of rulers and nations represented as trees. With the background of the Old Testament, we can now turn back to the New Testament and find Jesus' use of seed (Matthew 13:6, 40), vine branches (John 15:6), and trees (Luke 3:9, 21:29) to represent people or nations—not surprising but very much in keeping with the Scriptures. Therefore, let's look again at Luke 21:29: "Then He spoke to them a parable: 'Look at the fig tree, and all the trees.'" The fig tree is Israel and therefore all the trees are other nations. The question then becomes which nations was He referring to?

The answer comes from the comparison with the fig tree; it was dried and then sprouted again. Israel was dried for many years and then came back to be a nation. It would appear therefore that Jesus was referring to other nations close to Israel which would also be reborn. What is astounding to discover is that all of the countries that border Israel came back to be independent nation states around the same time as Israel. The CIA World Factbook discusses how Lebanon, Jordan, Syria, and Egypt gained their independence all between the years 1943 and 1952—all within five years of the birth of Israel.

LEBANON

Following World War I, France acquired a mandate over the northern portion of the former Ottoman Empire province of Syria. The French separated out the region of Lebanon in 1920, and granted **this area independence in 1943**.

JORDAN

Following World War I and the dissolution of the Ottoman Empire, the UK received a mandate to govern much of the

Middle East. Britain separated out a semi-autonomous region of Transjordan from Palestine in the early 1920s, and **the area gained its independence in 1946**; it adopted the name of Jordan in 1950.

SYRIA

Following World War I, France acquired a mandate over the northern portion of the former Ottoman Empire province of Syria. **The French administered the area as Syria until granting it independence in 1946**.

EGYPT

Following the completion of the Suez Canal in 1869, Egypt became an important world transportation hub, but also fell heavily into debt. Ostensibly to protect its investments, Britain seized control of Egypt's government in 1882, but nominal allegiance to the Ottoman Empire continued until 1914. Partially independent from the UK in 1922, **Egypt acquired full sovereignty with the overthrow of the British-backed monarchy in 1952**(CIA World Factbook, emphasis mine).

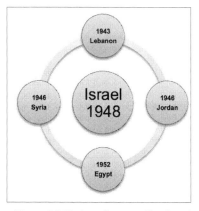

Figure 20 Nations Surrounding Israel

These countries, like Israel, did not exist as independent countries until 1943 and after. They were simply parts of the Ottoman Empire and then parts of the British Empire or a colony of the French. Their birth around the birth of Israel strengthens the significance of 1948.

WHAT IS A GENERATION?

We have determined what the fig tree represents and now we must determine what a generation is. "Assuredly, I say to you, this generation [*genea* γενεα] will by no means pass away till all these things take place" (Matthew 24:34). When considering this question we might do well to remember that Jesus was not speaking Greek to His disciples but Hebrew, which is documented in my book *Discovering the Language of Jesus.* Not only was Jesus speaking Hebrew to the Jews of His day, which most certainly included His disciples, but according to what are known as the fragments of Papias, the book of Matthew was first written in Hebrew and then later translated to Greek.

> Papias was one of the early Church fathers who lived from 70 to 155 AD. The early church historian Eusebius notes that he "had the privilege of association with Polycarp, in the friendship of St. John himself, and of 'others who had seen the Lord.'" (Eusebius 3.39.15) […] He says about Matthew (fragment VI) "Matthew put together the oracles [of the Lord] in the Hebrew language, and each one interpreted them as best he could" (Eusebius, III, 39, 1) (Hamp, 2005 *Discovering the Language of Jesus*).

Given that Jesus was speaking Hebrew, the word that we ought to be truly considering is the Hebrew word *dor* (דוֹר), which underlies the Greek word *genea* (γενεα) (the Greek Septuagint translates *dor* as *genea*). *Dor* is defined by Gesenius' Hebrew Lexicon as "(1) *an age, generation* of men, as if *the period* and *circuit* of the years of life." Brown Driver Briggs defines it primarily as "1. *period, age, generation*, mostly poet.: a. of duration in the past, *former age(s)*" and also as "2. of men living at a particular time (period, age)." Based on my own research where I examined the seventy nine times that word is used in the Hebrew Bible, the word should be defined as the period of a person's life. In other words, generation is defined **both** as *period of time* and a *group of people* which cannot be separated. *The Theological Wordbook of the Old Testament* (TWOT) explains the meaning of generation as it relates to the entirety of a person's life:

> Occasionally there is a Hebrew word wherein etymology, as a route to discovery of ancient thought patterns, is all-important in discovering the true life-situation in which the word must be

understood. Such is the case here. Authorities all agree that dor, the noun, is derived from dur, the verb. The simple primitive sense, not expressly found in any biblical text, is to move in a circle, surround. [...] In this manner an original meaning of "go in a circle" [...] provide[s] the basis for a word of important theological meaning. [...] By a thoroughly understandable figure, a man's lifetime beginning with the womb of earth and returning thereto (Gen 3:19) is a dor (TWOT *Dor*).

While it is true that a new generation begins with the birth of one's offspring, that still does not negate the fact that the length of a particular generation is the total life span. In reality, the Hebrew, or Greek word is not that different from their English equivalent. If we talk about my parents' generation it is the people group born around the similar time as them. I am not in my parents' generation—I am the second generation. In fact, I was born some thirty years into my parents' life. However, we should not define the length of a generation as the interval between the two but rather as the lifetime of a given person. After all, my mother is still alive and many people in her generation are too. Some people in her generation, like my father, have already passed on. However, there will be some that will live into their eighties and even a few into their nineties.

Let's consider the following verses that show that the *people group* of a certain *period of time* all died: "And **Joseph** died, all **his brothers**, and **all that generation**" (Exodus 1:6 emphasis mine). The verse clearly was not talking about people in Abraham's day or people in Moses' day. It was the people group of a particular time that died—that is a generation. The psalmist demonstrates a similar usage wherein he is exhorting those living at his time to not be like the generation (time of) their fathers: "And may not be like their fathers, a stubborn and rebellious generation, a generation *that* did not set its heart aright, and whose spirit was not faithful to God" (Psalm 78:8). Notice that generation is being used as both a people group (fathers) and also a time period (since fathers necessarily come before their progeny). Therefore, when the psalmist says "a generation that did not set its heart aright," he is talking about a specific group of people who lived at a specific time.

This is reinforced by Deuteronomy 2:14 where Moses discusses the time that was spent in the desert as punishment against the generation that rebelled against the Lord. "and the time we took to come from Kadesh Barnea until we crossed over the Valley of the Zered *was* thirty-eight years, until all the generation of the men of war was consumed from the midst of the camp, just as the LORD had sworn to them" (Deuteronomy 2:14). The generation was the lifetime (forty years plus twenty) of a group of men as derived from the book of Numbers in which God gives the minimum time of a generation [Hebrew: *dor* רוד Greek: *genea* γενεα] as sixty years (twenty and above plus wandering forty years):

> Surely none of the men who came up from Egypt, from **twenty** years old and above, shall see the land of which I swore to Abraham, Isaac, and Jacob, because they have not wholly followed Me … So the LORD's anger was aroused against Israel, and He made them wander in the wilderness **forty** years, until all the **generation** [LXX reads: *genea* γενεα] that had done evil in the sight of the LORD was gone (Numbers 32:11, 13).

Thus the minimum age of a generation is sixty years (forty years is never a generation in Scripture contrary to what many have claimed). However, there is another verse that provides a more average life span of a human being which is also the key to see approximately when the Lord will return the second time (a fact pointed out to me by Dr. Kenton Beshore, Sr.).

> The days of our lives are seventy years; and if by reason of strength they are eighty years, yet their boast is only labor and sorrow; for it is soon cut off, and we fly away (Psalm 90:10).

The fullness of a generation being seventy or eighty years is striking when one considers that Moses, the author of this Psalm, lived to be 120 years old. Bible commentator Thomas Constable points out:

> It is interesting that he said the normal human life span was 70 years. He lived to be 120, Aaron was 123 when he died, and Joshua died at 110. Their long lives testify to God's faithfulness in providing long lives to the godly as He promised under the Mosaic Covenant (Constable, Psalm 90).

It would seem that the Holy Spirit guided Moses to write of what a typical lifetime is, versus his (and other ancients') lifetime.[257] We find further biblical evidence that a generation is a lifetime which is equivalent to seventy (or eighty) years in Isaiah 23:15 which correlates: "seventy years like the days of one king."

MODERN RESEARCH CONFIRMS PSALM 90:10

According to the CIA Worldfact Book[258] the longest average life expectancy (by country) for 2009 was 84.36 years in the country of Macau. The Swiss had the 10th longest life expectancy of 80.85. Israelis ranked 12th in the world and on average lived to be 80.73 years old, Americans ranked 49th with an expectancy of 78.11 years, and Guatemalans ranked 143rd with an expectancy of 70.29. People in only 38 countries (out of 224) live less than 60 years on average.

Psalm 90:10 therefore provides a very realistic picture of how long a generation is. The vast majority of people (by nationality) on the planet live until they are sixty (185/224 or 82.5 percent). Fewer, though a majority still, live into their seventies (144/224 or 64.2 percent). However, only a fraction live on average into their eighties (22/224 or 9.8 percent).

Matthew provides our last clue in the beginning of his gospel when discussing the number of generations from Abraham until Christ, thereby demonstrating that generation (*genea* γενεά— the same word used in Matthew 24:34) signifies the lifetime of a person:

So all the **generations** [*genea* γενεα] from Abraham to David are fourteen **generations** [*genea* γενεα], from David until the captivity in Babylon are fourteen **generations** [*genea* γενεα], and from the captivity in Babylon until the Christ are fourteen **generations** [*genea* γενεα] (Matthew 1:17).

Here we see that a generation was the lifetime of a person and not the specific amount of years though we have learned that the duration of a generation is anywhere from sixty years to eighty. We need to understand that generations overlap one another. When a father and mother have children a new generation is born, but so long as all the people born around their birthdates

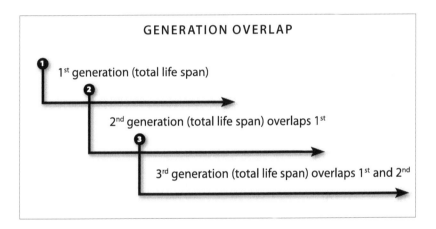

GENERATION OVERLAP

❶ 1ˢᵗ generation (total life span)

❷ 2ⁿᵈ generation (total life span) overlaps 1ˢᵗ

❸ 3ʳᵈ generation (total life span) overlaps 1ˢᵗ and 2ⁿᵈ

are living, their generation has not passed away. Think of it this way: the Baby Boomer generation (born between 1946 and 1964) has not yet passed away. In fact, the oldest members would just now be reaching their mid-sixties. Certainly some of its members have passed away already, but the majority can expect to make it well into their seventies and some into their eighties. In the same way, the generation spoken of by Jesus will not pass away until all the things He mentioned take place. The preceding diagram depicts how generations overlap one another. The 1ˢᵗ generation could be likened to the Baby Boomer generation. Generation X (2ⁿᵈ Generation) was born toward the beginning of a Baby Boomers life (generation) but they are not of the Baby Boomer generation. Considering all the evidence we explored, I'd like to propose that the Baby Boomer generation is the generation that will not pass away until the Lord comes back.

WHICH GENERATION?

> So you also, when you see all these things, know that it is near—at the doors! Assuredly, I say to you, this **generation** will by no means pass away till all these things take place (Matthew 24:33-34).

The generation spoken of here must be the generation that would see all of the things that Jesus spoke of when the disciples questioned Him and specifically it would be the generation that would see the "fig tree budding." Since we have seen that the fig tree was Israel in both the prophets and according to Jesus, then "this generation" must be the one that began at the commencement of the new state of Israel.[259]

THE FIG TREE HAS BUDDED

Thus we see Israel was a dried tree for about 1900 years and then miraculously the branch put forth leaves in one day on May 14, 1948. Jesus told us that when this happens His return is at the doors! He said that the generation that saw this would by no means pass away. A generation is the lifetime of a person and that is on average between seventy or eighty years. Thus, according to the above considerations we could write out our equation in the following manner:

$$1948 + 70 \approx 2018$$
OR if by reason of strength
$$1948 + 80 \approx 2028$$

The parable of the fig tree was the answer to the disciples' original question at the beginning of the chapter:

> As he sat on the Mount of Olives, the disciples came to him privately, saying, "Tell us, when will these things be, and what

will be the sign of your coming and of the end of the age?" (Matthew 24:3 ESV).

The observant student of the Word has noted that this reference to when the end of the age will be is in seeming contradiction to Jesus' own words in Acts 1:6-8.

Figure 21 *Palestine Post*, Israel is Born

Therefore, when they had come together, they asked Him, saying, 'Lord, will You at this time restore the kingdom to Israel?' And He said to them, 'It is not for you to know times or seasons which the Father has put in His own authority. But you shall receive power when the Holy Spirit has come upon you; and you shall be witnesses to Me in Jerusalem, and in all Judea and Samaria, and to the end of the earth' (Acts 1:6-8).

This apparent contradiction is resolved, however, when we consider just who Jesus was talking to—the disciples that He was speaking to in Acts were the same men who, only some forty days earlier, He had told what to look for at the end of the age. And the sign that He told them would definitively mark the beginning of the generation that would see the end was nothing less than the fig tree putting forth its branch and becoming tender. **Thus, the solution is the fig tree.** They asked a question which He had already answered for them—look for the revival of the fig tree (which Jesus had pronounced cursed). In other words, there was no point in looking for the end of the age so long as Israel was a dried tree! There was no point in looking for the second coming so long as the fig tree remained cursed (that is: not a nation). Only when it would become tender could the restoration of the kingdom occur. That is why Jesus told the disciples of what they would receive in the meantime ("but you shall receive power") and what their task was to be ("and you shall be witnesses to Me") until the revival of the fig tree and ultimately His coming.

Therefore, until the fig tree (Israel) was revived, there would be no restoration of the kingdom to Israel—which is of course only logical: Israel cannot have the kingdom if they do not exist as a national entity (a dried tree). But within a generation (lifetime of a person) of the revival of the fig tree (Israel) the kingdom will be restored in the millennial/messianic era.

OCCUPY UNTIL HE COMES

We have seen that the biblical interpretation of the fig tree is clearly Israel. We have also seen that a generation is the lifetime of a person which, according to Psalm 90:10, is generally seventy or eighty years. Whether or not the Lord is required to return within eighty years exactly we obviously cannot be dogmatic. Nevertheless, in light of the incredible accuracy of His first coming, we ought to be persuaded that the years previously mentioned are both reasonable and likely. The Lord's second coming, therefore, **appears** to be between 2018—2028.[260] The beginning of the great tribulation (subtract seven years) then would **most likely** commence between 2011—2021.[261] Remember, we are to know the times and the seasons, yet Jesus said very literally that the **day** and the **hour** no one can know. The Lord's second coming between 2018 and 2028 is seemingly the time and the season but is **not** predictive of the day or the hour. In light of the events that are happening in numerous categories (economics, natural disasters, etc.) on a global scale, the Lord's return within the eighty years from the reestablishment of Israel in 1948 appears almost certain. Nevertheless, no matter when the Lord returns, occupy until He does and tell others the good news of the gospel. Heed Jesus' warning:

"Constantly be on your guard so that your hearts may not be loaded down with self-indulgence, drunkenness, and the worries of this life, or that day will take you by surprise like a trap. For it will come on all who live on the face of the earth. So be alert at all times, praying that you may have strength to escape all these things that are going to take place and to take your stand in the presence of the Son of Man" (Luke 21:34-36 ISV).

The Battle in the Spiritual Realm

This list of verses speaks of the current and future battle that is raging in the spiritual dimension.

THE WICKED ONE

- But with righteousness He shall judge the poor, and decide with equity for the meek of the earth; He shall strike the earth with the rod of His mouth, and with the breath of His lips He shall slay **the wicked** ["the wicked one" *rasha* רָשָׁע] (Isaiah 11:4).

- The LORD has made all for Himself, Yes, even **the wicked** ["the wicked one" *rasha* רָשָׁע] for the day of doom (Proverbs 16:4).

THE DEFEAT OF THE HOST/PRINCIPALITIES

- For the indignation of the LORD [is] against all nations, and [His] fury against all their armies; He has utterly destroyed them, He has given them over to the slaughter.

Also their slain shall be thrown out; their stench shall rise from their corpses, and the mountains shall be melted with their blood. All the **host of heaven shall be dissolved**, and the heavens shall be rolled up like a scroll; **all their host shall fall down** as the leaf falls from the vine, And as [*fruit*] falling from a fig tree. "**For My sword shall be bathed in heaven**; indeed it shall come down on Edom, and on the people of My curse, for judgment "(Isaiah 34:2-5).

- But the LORD [*is*] the true God; He [*is*] the living God and the everlasting King. At His wrath the earth will tremble, and the nations will not be able to endure His indignation. Thus you shall say to them: "The **gods that have not made the heavens and the earth shall perish from the earth and from under these heavens**" (Jeremiah 10:10-11).

- Then the **kingdom and dominion, and the greatness of the kingdoms under the whole** heaven, shall be given to the people, the saints of the Most High. His kingdom [*is*] an everlasting kingdom, and all dominions shall serve and obey Him (Daniel 7:27).

- The LORD [*will be*] awesome to them, for He will **reduce to nothing all the gods of the earth** (Zephaniah 2:11).

- Then [*comes*] the end, when He delivers the kingdom to God the Father, when He puts an end to all **rule and all authority and power**. For He must reign till He has put all enemies under His feet. The last enemy [*that*] will be destroyed [*is*] death (1 Corinthians 15:24-26).

- For such [*are*] false apostles, deceitful workers, transforming themselves into apostles of Christ. And no wonder! For Satan himself transforms himself into an angel of light (2 Corinthians 11:13-14).

- Far above all **principality and power and might and dominion**, and every name that is named, not only in this age but also in that which is to come (Ephesians 1:21).

- aAnd to make all see what [*is*] the fellowship of the mystery, which from the beginning of the ages has been hidden in God who created all things through Jesus Christ; to the intent that now the manifold wisdom of God might be made known by the church to the **principalities and powers in the heavenly** [*places*] (Ephesians 3:9-10).

- For by Him all things were created that are in heaven and that are on earth, visible and invisible, whether **thrones or dominions or principalities or powers**. All things were created through Him and for Him (Colossians 1:16).

- Having disarmed **principalities and powers**, He made a public spectacle of them, triumphing over them in it (Colossians 2:15).

- Who has gone into heaven and is at the right hand of God, **angels and authorities and powers having been made subject to Him** (1 Peter 3:22).

- And I saw **three unclean spirits like frogs** [*coming*] out of the mouth of the dragon, out of the **mouth of the beast, and out of the mouth of the false prophet**. For they are **spirits of demons**, performing signs, [*which*] go out to the kings of the earth and of the whole world, to gather them to the battle of that great day of God Almighty (Revelation 16:13-14).

- The ten horns which you saw are ten kings who have received no kingdom as yet, but they receive authority for one hour as kings with the beast. These are of one mind, and they will give their power and authority to the beast. **These will make war with the Lamb**, and the Lamb will overcome them, for He is Lord of lords and King of kings; and those [*who are*] with Him [*are*] called, chosen, and faithful (Revelation 17:12-14).

THE PRINCIPALITIES AND THE HOST ON HIGH CAST INTO THE PIT

* He laid hold of the dragon, that Serpent of old, who is [*the*] Devil and Satan, and bound him for a thousand years; and he cast him into the **bottomless pit**, and **shut him up**, and set a seal on him, so that he should deceive the nations no more till the thousand years were finished. But after these things he must be released for a little while (Revelation 20:2-3).

* It shall come to pass in that day [*That*] the LORD will **punish on high the host of exalted ones**, and on the earth the kings of the earth. **They will be gathered together, [*As*] prisoners are gathered in the pit,** and will be shut up in the prison; after many days they will be punished (Isaiah 24:21-22).

ABOUT THE AUTHOR

Douglas Hamp, author of *Discovering the Language of Jesus,
The First Six Days,* and *Corrupting the Image,* earned his MA in
the Hebrew Bible and the Ancient Near East from the Hebrew
University of Jerusalem, Israel. During his three years in Israel,
he studied both modern and biblical Hebrew, biblical Aramaic,
Koine Greek, and other ancient languages as well as ancient
texts and the archeology of the Bible. He has served as an
assistant pastor at Calvary Chapel Costa Mesa, where he has
taught at the School of Ministry, Spanish School of Ministry, and
Calvary Chapel Bible College Graduate School for eight years.
Douglas has given numerous lectures on prophecy, creationism,
and biblical languages in the United States and internationally.
Douglas is a committed follower of Jesus (Yeshua). He lives with
his wife and three children in Southern California. He can be
reached at *www.douglashamp.com.*

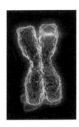

NOTES AND WORKS CITED

1   The Expository Notes of Dr. Thomas L. Constable, 2009, retrieved from theWord Bible Software, theword.net.

2   Important sources to consider when addressing the issue of how ancient interpreters understood the Bible are the Targumim. Targumim (*Targum* is singular) are the Aramaic translations of the Old Testament Scriptures. They were for the most part written both in and outside of Israel a few centuries after the time of Jesus. Those Jews were no longer comfortable reading the Scriptures solely in Hebrew, but needed the help of a translation as they read along in the original Hebrew. However, the Targumim were much more than merely word for word translations and because they were in Aramaic and not Hebrew, there was no risk that the commentaries might be mistaken for the actual words of the Bible itself. For a detailed explanation of the language of Israel in the first century, see Hamp (2005) *Discovering the Language of Jesus*, Calvary Chapel Publishing, Santa Ana, CA.

3   Apparently Eve believed that Cain was the fulfillment of this promise because upon his birth she declares that she has gotten (obtained) a son with the Lord. The Hebrew is clear that she (not Adam) is the one talking when she says (וַתֹּאמֶר) "I obtained" (קָנִיתִי), the same root as Cain's name (קַיִן). The fact that she says "with the Lord" (*et YHWH* אֶת־יְהוָה) proves that she had expected her son to be a product of herself and the Lord which is a foreshadow of Mary conceiving with the Holy Spirit.

4   Iranaeus, Against Heresies, Book 3 Ch. 21:7 (Ante-Nicene Fathers, Volume 1).

5   Ibid Book 4 Ch. 39.

6   Richard Seed, *TechnoCalyps - Part II - Preparing for the Singularity* November 14, 2008.

7   God's image is a topic that must be approached with care, and so let's state clearly what we are not saying. Founder of the Mormon Cult, Joseph Smith, said in the King Follet Sermon, "God himself was once as we are now, and is an exalted man, and sits enthroned in yonder heavens! That is the great secret." Retrieved March 17, 2010, from: http://www.utlm.org/onlineresources/sermons_talks_interviews/ kingfolletsermon.htm. Later, fifth LDS President Lorenzo Snow in June of 1840 declared, "As man is, God once was; as God is, man may become." According to LDS theology (which we consider heretical), eternal life is synonymous with godhood. In the words of LDS Apostle Bruce McConkie, "Thus those who gain eternal life receive exaltation ... They are gods" (Mormon Doctrine, pg. 237). Retrieved March 17, 2010 from: http://www.mrm.org/lorenzo-snow-couplet. **We completely renounce such talk as utter heresy** because they believe that God had parents who also had parents (etc.) and that through God's (Elohim's) good living He became a god and we can do the same. **This thinking is a complete perversion of who God is and what Scripture has to say about Him.**

8   See http://www.douglashamp.com/books/the-first-six-days.

9   The English Standard Version translates the word as "shadow" in Psalm 39:6: "Surely a man goes about as a shadow!" and "phantoms" in Psalm 73:20: "Like a dream when one awakes, [...] you despise them as phantoms."

10   Gesenius Hebrew and Chaldee Lexicon (1846) defines image as follows: "צֶלֶם m. with suff. צַלְמוֹ—(1) *a shadow*, Psalm 39:7; metaph. used of anything vain, Psalm. 73:20. Hence— (2) *an image, likeness* (so called from its shadowing forth; compare σκία, σκίασμα, σκιαγραφέω), Genesis 1:27; 5:3; 9:6; an image, idol, 2 Kings 11:18; Am. 5:26."

11   In Deuteronomy we find the same idea: "They sacrificed to **demons**, not to God, to gods they did not know, to new gods, new arrivals that your fathers did not fear. They have provoked Me to jealousy by what is not God; they have moved Me to anger by their foolish **idols**" (Deuteronomy 32:17, 21).

12   Consider also the following verses: "Therefore you shall make **images** of your tumors and **images** of your rats that ravage the land, and you shall give glory to the God of Israel; perhaps He will lighten His hand from you, from your **gods**, and from your land" (1 Samuel 6:5). "The **images** of their tumors" (1 Samuel 6:11). "And all the people of the land went to the temple of Baal, and tore it down. They thoroughly broke in pieces its altars and **images**" (2 Kings 11:18; see also 2 Chronicles 23:17). "You also carried Sikkuth your king and Chiun, your idols, the star of your gods, which you made for yourselves," (Amos 5:26).

13   The Hebrew word esh אֵשׁ (fire) is almost identical to the Hebrew word *ish* אִישׁ (man).

14   The church Father Tertullian (AD 145-220) commented on the kind of spiritual body we will obtain in his work on the resurrection based on Paul's writings: **"This corruptible must put on incorruption, and this mortal must put on immortality,"** **(1 Corinthians 15:51-53) this will assuredly be that house from heaven,** with which we so earnestly desire to be clothed upon, whilst groaning in this our present body, - meaning, of course, over this flesh in which we shall be surprised at last; because he says that we are burdened whilst in this tabernacle, which we do not wish indeed to be stripped of, but rather to be in it clothed over, in such a way that mortality may be swallowed up of life, that is, by putting on over us whilst we are **transformed that vesture** which is from heaven. [...] **the change that is to come over it, will assume the condition of angels.** [...] in other words, that the **flesh (be covered) with the heavenly and eternal raiment** (Tertullian chapter 47, emphasis mine).

15   The mountain must have been Hermon because Caesarea Philippi (Matthew 16:13) is at the base of Mount Hermon and Mount Hermon is the highest mountain in the entire region.

16   The Doctrine of Revelation: *The State of Saints in Glory*, Arthur Pink. Retrieved from the Word Bible Software, theword.net.

17   Soncino Zohar of Bereshith, Section 1, Page 36b. Retrieved March 13, 2010, from http://www.yashanet.com/studies/judaism101/sidebars/ohr.htm.

18   Soncino Zohar, Shemoth, Section 2, Page 229b.

19   Pseudepigrapha Lost Books of Eden, The First Book of the Life of Adam and Eve, chapter. LI., pages 2, 5, 6-7, emphasis mine.

20   Arnobius, Against Heathens, Book 7, Ante-Nicene Fathers Volume 6: Covered with garments, note 59, book iii, emphasis mine.

21   Methodius, Ten Virgins, Part 3 Ante-Nicene Fathers Volume 6 Chapter. V.

22   Revelation of Peter (6-9, 17), first published by the Abbe Sylvain Grebaut in Revue de l'Orient Chretien, 1910: a fresh translation from his Ethiopic text by H. Duensing appeared in Zeitschr. f. ntl. Wiss., 1913.

23   Ibid.

24   The words are not exactly the same, however, for the singular of *arummim* (עֲרוּמִּים), which has a dagesh in the mem is *arom* (עָרֹם) and the plural of arum (עָרום) does not have a dagesh in the mem (*arumim* עֲרוּמִים).

25   See also: Genesis 3:1, Job 5:12, Job 15:5, Proverbs 12:16, Proverbs 12:23, Proverbs 13:16, Proverbs 14:8, Proverbs 14:15, Proverbs 14:18, Proverbs 22:3, Proverbs 27:12.

26 Targum of Onkelos and Jonathan Ben Uzziel, On the Pentateuch with the Fragments of the Jerusalem Targum, From the Chaldee By J. W. Etheridge, M.A., First Published 1862.

27 See Genesis 3:7, Genesis 3:10, Genesis 3:11, Deuteronomy 28:48, Ezekiel 16:7, Ezekiel 16:22, Ezekiel 16:39, Ezekiel 18:7, Ezekiel 18:16, Ezekiel 23:29.

28 *naked*, Job 1:21. But naked is also used for—*(a) ragged, badly clad*, Job 22:6; 24:7, 10; Isa. 58:7; comp. Gr. γυμνός, James 2:15; and as to the Lat. nudus Seneca, De Benef., 5:13; Arabic stripped, **ill-clad.**—(b) used of one who, having taken off his mantle, **goes only clad in his tunic,** כְּתֹנֶת) 1 Sam. 19:24; Isa. 20:2. Compare John 21:7 (Gesenius Hebrew Lexicon עָרֹם, emphasis mine).

29 Thayer's Greek Lexicon lexical entry: γυμνός [*Gumnos*]. Definition: 1. properly: a. unclad, without clothing, the naked body; b. ill clad; c. clad in undergarments only (the outer garments or cloak being laid aside); d. of the soul, whose garment is the body, stripped of the body, without a body.

30 Fritz-Albert Popp Institut retrieved February 9, 2011, from: http://www.biophotonik.de/biophotonik_geschichte.php.

31 Colli L, Facchini U, Guidotti G, Dugnani-Lonati R, Orsenigo M (1955). Further Measurements on the Bioluminescence of the Seedlings. Experientia (Basel) 11: 479–481.

32 Fritz-Albert Popp Institut retrieved February 9, 2011, from: http://www.biophotonik.de/biophotonik_geschichte.php.

33 Ibid.

34 Ibid.

35 T. Amano 1, M. Kobayashi 2, B. Devaraj 2, M. Usa 2 and H. Inaba 2, 3 (1) Department of Urology, School of Medicine, Kanazawa University, 920 Kanazawa, Japan. Retrieved March 3, 2010, from: http://nourishedmagazine.com.au/blog/articles/the-secrets-of-light-cancer-and-the-sun.

36 Fels, D (2009) Cellular Communication through Light. Retrieved September 15, 2010, from http://www.plosone.org/article/info:doi/10.1371/journal.pone.0005086.

37 Retrieved June 17, 2010, from: http://www.wisegeek.com/how-do-things-glow-in-the-dark.htm.

38 Electricity is a fair translation; we read from the *Treasury of Scripture Knowledge:* "Amber is a hard, inflammable, bituminous substance, of a beautiful yellow colour, very transparent, and susceptible of an exquisite polish. When rubbed it is highly

endowed with electricity; a name which the moderns have formed from its Greek name [elektron.] But, as amber becomes dim as soon as it feels the fire, and is speedily consumed, it is probable that the original {chashmal,} which Bochart derives from the Chaldee {nechash,} copper, and {melala,} gold, was a mixed metal, similar to that which the Greeks called [elektron,] electrum, as the LXX and Vulgate render, from its resemblance to amber in colour" (*Treasury of Scripture Knowledge*, Ezekiel 8:2).

39   This line proves that Jesus has all the rights of the throne through His adoptive father Joseph. However, in no way can we say that Jesus was connected by blood to Joseph. If that were the case then the very idea of a virgin birth would be disqualified. If we look carefully at the Matthean genealogy, we see that it includes the cursed line of Coniah. In fact, if Jesus were connected by Joseph then He would be disqualified from being the rightful heir since God cursed that branch of the Davidic line in Jeremiah 22:28-30. "Is this man Coniah [Jechoniah] a despised, broken idol—a vessel in which is no pleasure?" [...] Thus says the LORD: "Write this man down as childless, a man who shall not prosper in his days; for none of his descendants shall prosper, sitting on the throne of David, and ruling anymore in Judah." What might have seemed like God shooting Himself in the foot was really just another example of Him being in control of the future.

40   Henry Morris, Creation and the Virgin Birth, Retrieved June 6, 2010, from: http://www.icr.org/article/76/.

41   Gamete "sexual protoplasmic body," 1886, name introduced in Modern Latin by Austrian biologist Gregor Mendel (1822-1884), from Gk. *gamete* "a wife," *gametes* "a husband," from *gamein*,"to take to wife, to marry," from PIE base*gem(e)-*"to marry" [...] This also is the source of the suffix in *monogamy*, etc." Retrieved March 16, 2010, from: http://www.etymonline.com/index.php?search=Gametes+&searchmode=none.

42   During sexual reproduction, approximately 250 million sperm are released into the woman's body where they begin to make an arduous journey in search of the ovum. Most never reach the egg and even those that do will fail because only one is permitted to enter.

43   Dr. Werner Gitt, *In the Beginning Was Information*. 90 Bielefeld, Germany: Christliche Literatur-Verbreitung e. V., 1997, English Edition 2000.

44   Ibid.

45   John Sanford, *Genetic Entropy and the Mystery of the Genome*, October 2005, pg. 83.

46   Dr. Werner Gitt, *In the Beginning Was Information* Theorem 24: (pg. 85).

47   Ibid, pg. 45.

48   Ibid, pg. 49.

49   Retreived September 24, 2010, http://www.answers.com/library/Genetics%20
     Encyclopedia-cid-50766.

50   Retrieved September 24, 2010, http://www.answers.com/library/
     Britannica+Concise+Encyclopedia-cid-50766.

51   Underhill, Peter A. "Y Chromosome." Genetics, 2003. Retrieved September
     29, 2010, from Encyclopedia.com: http://www.encyclopedia.com/
     doc/1G2-3406500290.html.

52   Retrieved September 24, 2010, from http://www.learner.org/courses/biology/
     textbook/gender/gender_3.html.

53   Neil Bradman and Mark Thomas, *Why Y? The Y Chromosome in the Study of Human
     Evolution, Migration and Prehistory*. See also http://www.ramsdale.org/dna13.htm.

54   Retrieved September 30, 2010 from: http://www.ucl.ac.uk/tcga/ScienceSpectra-
     pages/SciSpect-14-98.html Science Spectra Magazine Number 14, 1998.

55   Ibid.

56   Young's literal translation of the Bible seems preferable at this junction in that the
     phrase appears to be a predicate genitive—that is, no verb is actually present in
     the Greek. επειδη γαρ δι ανθρωπου ο θανατος και δι ανθρωπου αναστασις νεκρων,
     (1 Corinthians 15:21). My suggested translation is: "For (*the*) death (*is*) through
     (*a*) man, and the resurrection of the dead through (*a*) man." A. T. Robertson in
     Grammar of the Greek New Testament in the Light of Historical Research, page 395,
     states: "this copula is not always considered necessary. It can be readily dispensed
     with when both subject and the real predicate are present."

57   The terms are simply meant to explain the process and in no way detract from who
     Jesus is as the eternal God.

58   Peter's text uses a variant word for seed (*sporas* σπορας) though the meaning is the
     same, cf. Thayer's Greek definitions.

59   The righteous before Jesus (e.g. Abraham) died and went to a place called paradise
     as mere sons of Adam. Since they were not born again, technically speaking, they
     could not enter into God's presence. However, when Jesus descended He took
     those that were captive up to heaven with Him. Ephesians 4:8, "Therefore it says,
     'When he ascended on high he led a host of captives, and he gave gifts to men'"
     (Ephesians 4:8 ESV).

60   "You are the children of the LORD your God; [banim atem laYHWH eloheikhem
     בָּנִים אַתֶּם לַיהוָה אֱלֹהֵיכֶם]," (Deuteronomy 14:1 NKJV). The Targumim render it in
     the following manner, which confirm that they were not considered "sons of God":
     "Children are you before the Lord your God" (Targum Onkelos Deuteronomy 14:1).
     "As beloved children before the Lord your God, [...] [JERUSALEM. You are beloved
     children before the Lord your God...]" (Targum Jonathan Deuteronomy 14:1). "υιοι
     εστε κυριου του θεου υμων" (Septuagint Deuteronomy 14:1). They are not "sons of
     God" but are sons for God—implying a purpose (perhaps future and perhaps just
     positionally).

61   Tom Pickett Population of the PreFlood World retrieved October 22, 2010, from
     http://www.ldolphin.org/pickett.html.

62   The Aramaic Targum (translation) of Job likewise translates "sons of God" as sons of
     the angels (benei malachia בני מאלכיא).

63   For a detailed explanation of Satan's origin and fall visit www.douglashamp.com/
     satans-origin-and-fall/.

64   Cast them down to hell (tartarōsas). First aorist active participle of tartaroō,
     late word (from tartaros, old word in Homer, Pindar, LXX Job 40:15; 41:23, Philo,
     inscriptions, the dark and doleful abode of the wicked dead like the Gehenna of
     the Jews), found here alone save in a scholion on Homer. Tartaros occurs in Enoch
     20:2 as the place of punishment of the fallen angels, while Gehenna is for apostate
     Jews, (Robertson's Word Pictures, Archibald Thomas Robertson, 1923).

65   David Bivin definitively shows that such talk indicated that from the demons'
     perspective, Jesus was messing with their turf. 2006 Workshop: Exploring the
     Jewish and Hebraic Background to Twenty-five Difficult Sayings of Jesus. See also
     www.jerusalemperspective.com.

66   The demons are apparently referring to their coming incarceration mentioned in
     Isaiah 24: "They will be gathered together, as prisoners are gathered in the pit, and
     will be shut up in the prison; after many days they will be punished," (Isaiah 24:22).
     This incarceration takes place before the final judgment of the lake of fire which
     will be "after many days."

67   μί-ασμα, ατος, τό, (μιαίνω) stain, defilement, esp. by murder or other crime, taint
     of guilt [...] that which defiles, pollution, of persons.

68   New American Bible, footnotes p. 1370, referring to verse 7. See also: http://www.
     newworldencyclopedia.org/entry/Nephilim.

69   The notes of the NET Bible in Jude verse 6 states: "'Angels' is not in the Greek text; but
     the masculine demonstrative pronoun most likely refers back to the angels of v. 6."

70   Origin being the possible exception though that is questionable; he writes: "In my opinion, however, it is certain **wicked demons**, and, so to speak, of **the race of Titans or Giants, who have been guilty of impiety towards the true God**, and towards the angels in heaven, and who have fallen from it, […] secretly enter the bodies of the more rapacious and savage and wicked of animals" (Origen, Against Celsus Book IV, Chap. XCII, emphasis mine).

71   ANF Volume 2 Athenagoras Chapter 24, emphasis mine.

72   Ibid chapter 25, emphasis mine.

73   Commodianus III, emphasis mine.

74   The Extant Writings of Julius Africanus, I, The Epistle to Aristides II. 44, emphasis mine.

75   Faulk and Scott: Genesis Apocryphon: 1Q20Tales of the Patriarchs 1 Qap Gen=1Q20 Paraphrase and comments by Lesley Faulk and Amanda Scott Introduction The "Tales of the Patriarchs," which deals with the descendants of Adam, is sometimes referred to as the "Genesis Apocryphon."

76   See 1 Kings 14:24 concerning the role of a sodomite (kadesh) which is of the same root as holy.

77   *The Dead Sea scrolls translated: the Qumran texts in English* By Florentino García Martínez, W. G. E. Watson Brill, 1996.

78   An Aramaic text reads "Watchers" here (J. T. Milik, Aramaic Fragments of Qumran Cave 4 [Oxford: Clarendon Press, 1976], p. 167).

79   "Then their leader Samyaza said to them; I fear that you may perhaps be indisposed to the performance of this enterprise; 4 and that I alone shall suffer for so grievous a crime. 5 But they answered him and said; We all swear; 6 and bind ourselves by mutual execrations, that we will not change our intention, but execute our projected undertaking."

80   Upon Ardis. Or, "in the days of Jared" (R. H. Charles, ed. and trans., The Book of Enoch [Oxford: Clarendon Press, 1893], p. 63).

81   Mt. Armon, or Mt. Harmon, derives its name from the Hebrew word *herem*, a curse (Charles, p. 63).

82   The Aramaic texts preserve an earlier list of names of these Watchers: Semihazah; Artqoph; Ramtel; Kokabel; Ramel; Danieal; Zeqiel; Baraqel; Asael; Hermoni; Matarel; Ananel; Stawel; Samsiel; Sahriel; Tummiel; Turiel; Yomiel; Yhaddiel (Milik, p. 151).

83 The Greek texts vary considerably from the Ethiopic text here. One Greek manuscript adds to this section, "And they [the women] bore to them [the Watchers] three races—first, the great giants. The giants brought forth [some say "slew"] the Nephilim, and the Nephilim brought forth [or "slew"] the Elioud. And they existed, increasing in power according to their greatness." See the account in the Book of Jubilees.

84 "Their flesh one after another." Or, "one another's flesh." R. H. Charles notes that this phrase may refer to the destruction of one class of giants by another (Charles, p. 65).

85 Philo, *On the Giants*, II, 6.

86 Philo, *Questions and Answers on Genesis* part 4, note 92.

87 *The Works Of Philo Judaeus*, Complete And Unabridged New Updated Edition Translated By Charles Duke Yonge, London, H. G. Bohn, 1854-1890.

88 Josephus, *Antiquities of the Jews* Book 1, chapter 3.

89 Ibid.

90 Josephus, *Antiquities of the Jews* chapter 3 footnote 11.

91 Secrets Of Enoch 18:3.

92 Aquinas sufficiently summarizes Augustine's words though they differ slightly from the original reproduced here: "Giants therefore might well be born, even before the sons of God, who are also called angels of God, formed a connection with the daughters of men, or of those living according to men, that is to say, before the sons of Seth formed a connection with the daughters of Cain." (Augustine St. Augustine's *City of God and Christian Doctrine*) Retrieved November 21, 2010, from http://www.ccel.org/ccel/schaff/npnf102.iv.XV.23.html.

93 Aquinas *Summa Theologica* Question 51 Of The Angels in Comparison with Bodies (Three Articles) Reply to Objection 6.

94 Calvin *Commentary Genesis* 6:1.

95 Ibid.

96 Ibid.

97 Hawkers *Poor Man's Commentary* Genesis 6:2.

98 The two other (out of seven) passages that speak of Seth merely mention his name: "Adam, Seth, Enosh," (1 Chr 1:1); "The son of Enosh, the son of Seth, the son of Adam, the son of God," (Luke 3:38).

CORRUPTING THE IMAGE

99   Brown Driver Briggs (BDB) Hebrew English Lexicon provides the following definition. The most common definition is "1. to **profane, defile, pollute, desecrate, begin.**" BDB then goes on to give the various forms of how the root is used in each of the binyanim (verbal paradigms). In the a. (Niphal) it means to: 1. to profane oneself, defile oneself, pollute oneself; b. ritually; c. sexually; 1. to be polluted, be defiled; d. (Piel): 1. to profane, make common, defile, pollute; 2. to violate the honour of, dishonour; 3. to violate (a covenant); 4. to treat as common; e. (Pual) to profane (name of God); f. (Hiphil): 1. **to let be profaned; 2. to begin; g. (Hophal) to be begun**" (emphasis mine). The Hophal is simply the passive of the Hiphil—therefore, if the Hiphil occasionally means to let be profaned then the one occurrence of the Hophal might also be translated as profaned rather than begin.

100 Liddell, Scott and Jones Classical Greek Lexicon defines the word: "Γῑγάντ-ειος, α, ον, gigantic, [...]: Γῑγαντικός, ή, όν, of or for the Giants, τὰ -κά Plu. 2.360f; monstrous."

101 He cites the following from Homer, Iliad 2.547-48; Herodotos 8.55. Retrieved September 30, 2010 from: http://books.google.com/books?id= GgzPPOepK2YC&lpg=PA53&ots=HakJzgTHru&dq=gegenes%20earth%20 born&pg=PA53#v=onepage&q=gegenes%20earth%20born&f=false.

102 Retrieved October 1, 2010, from: http://www.theoi.com/Gigante/Gigantes.html.

103 Retrieved October 1, 2010, from: http://www.theoi.com/greek-mythology/giants. html.

104 Retrieved October 1, 2010, from: http://www.theoi.com/Heros/Kekrops.html.

105 Behemoth is the plural of the feminine noun "behema," which simply means "beast." It is curious to note here that behemoth, though plural, takes a singular and masculine verb (in Hebrew the number and gender of nouns and verbs must agree) thereby signifying not beasts, but a specific type of creature. Thus, the word behemoth here is not just a plural form, but a completely different creature or beast (Douglas Hamp, *The First Six Days*, Yoel Press, 2007).

106 Retrieved September 10, 2010, from http://www.buzzle.com/articles/cedar-tree-identification.html.

107 Douglas Hamp, *The First Six Days*, Yoel Press, (2007).

108 Retrieved March 21, 2010 from: http://www.thebigzoo.com/animals/Diplodocus.asp.

109 Retrieved September 10, 2010, http://www.worldwideflood.com/ark/noahs_cubit/ cubit_references.htm.

110 "The basic, or *Root* royal Egyptian cubit, is 12/7 English feet, or 1.7142857ft; this is the English cubit of 1.57 ft. plus one seventh. Many examples of the use of this value are recognized with close precision. One of the three ritualistic standard cubit rods of the Egyptian Museum of Turin (Fig. 1) is given as 20.587 inches, and 12/7 English feet are 20.5714 inches. John Perring, when he surveyed the pyramid of Amenemhet III at Dashur, found the base side to measure 342.5 ft., and 200 royal cubits of 12/7 ft. are 342.8571 ft. The cubit of construction in the step pyramid of Zoser is given as 20.55 inches. Therefore is possible to state in absolute terms, this length, among others, as a standard expression of the *royal cubit*. "It is by the addition of the 440th part to this *Root* cubit that it becomes the Standard royal cubit of 1.71818 ft. This is the precise length of the cubit of the Giza complex, as established by Petrie's survey of 1882. Both of these, Root and Standard royal Egyptian cubits, develop into the other recognised variants by the addition or subtraction of their 175th part." Retrieved April 10, 2010, from: http://freepages.history.rootsweb.ancestry.com/~rgrosser/amarna/neywetaten/measures.htm

111 The size of the cubit is also confirmed by William Whiston, the translator of Josephus' *Antiquities of the Jews*. In Book 1, chapter 3, where Josephus is making reference to the size of Noah's ark, Whiston notes that the "cubit is about 21 English inches."

112 Retrieved September 11, 2010, http://home.fuse.net/clymer/bmi/thanks to Norm Robinson for pointing this out to me.

113 Retrieved September 11, 2010, http://www.dietitian.com/calories.html#14.

114 Retrieved September 11, 2010, http://home.fuse.net/clymer/bmi/for a 150-pound person.

115 Where each cheeseburger is 359 calories including condiments, retrieved September 11, 2010, from http://caloriecount.about.com/calories-cheeseburger-regular-single-patty-i21091

116 An adult lamb weighs about 125 pounds. Approximately 50 percent is non-edible (wool, bones, etc.), then there are approximately 1,000 ounces of edible meat. We know that a four ounce lamb chop has about 200 calories. Therefore the amount of portions would be 250 and multiplied by 200 calories equals 50,000 calories in an average lamb.

117 Josephus, *Antiquities of the Jews*, Book 5:2:3.

118 Book of Jubilees 29:1-12; cf. Genesis 31.

119 Tertullian Volume Three Chap. XLII.

120 This book was scanned and is available for download at http://www.archive.org/ details/tracesofelderfai00wood.

121 Retrieved July 3, 2010, Wood-Martin, *Traces of the Elder Faiths of Ireland: A Folklore Sketch*, Volume 1, (1901), pg. 57.

122 Retrieved July 3, 2010, http://en.wikipedia.org/wiki/Hundredweight.

123 That is not to say that if a person has six fingers or toes he is necessarily of the Nephilim, but it is certainly one of the characteristics of them.

124 Retrieved July 3, 2010, from: http://chillicothe.newspaperarchive.com/PdfViewer.as px?img=114247083&firstvisit=true&src=search&currentResult=0&currentPage=0.

125 Retrieved July 3, 2010, from: http://chroniclingamerica.loc.gov/lccn/ sn83030214/1909-02-02/ed-1/seq-1/;words=giants+GIANT+prehistoric+skeleton+ Mexico+giant+PREHISTORIC+Skeleton.

126 Retrieved September 11, 2010, http://chroniclingamerica.loc.gov/lccn/ sn94056415/1895-03-08/ed-1/seq-3/;words=Prehistoric+recently+Montpellier+ce metery+France+uncovered+prehistoric. The McCook Tribune (McCook, Neb.) 1886-1936, March 08, 1895, Image 3.

127 Retrieved July 13, 2010, from: http://s8int.com/phile/giants27.html.

128 With the exception of Adam, no human was a direct creation of God before Jesus paid for our sins.

129 Paul Joüon, T. Muraoka suggest that "in Aramaic, the form *hitpaal* is probably a secondarily passivised reflexive form; cf. Joüon 1920: 354ff." The idea then would be "they will be mixed together with something." This would suggest that "they" are not the agents, but merely the passive recipients of the verb. This interpretation is captured in the Douay-Rheims Bible "they shall be mingled **indeed together with the seed of man**" A Grammar of Biblical Hebrew: 2 Volume Set. Vol. 1, Part 1. Orthography And Phonetics; Part 2. Morphology. Vol. 2, Part 3 Syntax (Subsidia Biblica, 14/1-14/2), pg. 146.

130 Dr. Chuck Missler suggested that this might be referring to the fallen angels: http:// www.khouse.org/articles/1997/22/.

131 This glorious one is an angel and not the Lord Jesus due to the fact that he was withstood by the Prince of Persia and only when the archangel Michael came could he proceed.

132 For a discussion of the ten horns in relation to Satan visit: http://www. douglashamp.com/satans-origin-and-fall.

133 Thanks to my friend Bob Rico for pointing out this insight to me.

134 Walter Martin, Jill Martin Rische, Kurt Van Gorden, *The Kingdom of The Occult*, Thomas Nelson Publishing, Nashville, TN, 2008, pages 371-372.

135 Ibid. pg. 373.

136 David Hunt, *The Cult Explosion* (tract), n.p. 1981.

137 Ankerberg and Weldon, *Facts on UFOs and Other Supernatural Phenomena*. Eugene, OR: Harvest House 1992. p. 44.

138 Goetz, William R. *UFOs Friend, Foe, or Fantasy*, Camp Hill, Pennsylvania. Horizon Books. 1997, pg.142.

139 Dr. Pierre Guerin, FSR Vol. 25, No. 1.

140 Retrieved September 11, 2010 , http://www.cuttingedgeministries.net/NEWS/n1912.cfm.

141 William Frederick, *The Coming Epiphany* (2009). Book downloaded from: www.thecomingepiphany.com.

142 Retrieved April 25, 2010, http://www.timesonline.co.uk/tol/news/science/space/article7107207.ece.

143 Retrieved December 2, 2010, from: http://www.suite101.com/content/fallen-returns-to-abc-family-a25424.

144 http://abcnews.go.com/Primetime/story?id=8330290 August17, 2009.

145 The following quotes were compiled from the following websites: http://ufos.my100megs.com/ufoquotes.htm.

146 For example, some people have asserted that the Lord Jesus did not even exist as a historical person. However, regardless of what someone concludes about Him being God, the fact that He lived and walked on this earth is incontrovertible. The Talmud, which was written and compiled by Jews that did not receive Jesus as their Messiah, confirmed that Jesus existed. Furthermore, they stated that He was crucified on the eve of Passover and that He was a doer of magic. Thus, they admit three crucial things about a Man that they in fact wanted to forget: 1) He existed, 2) He was crucified, and 3) He performed supernatural acts. Thus, the very ones that tried to ignore Him gave us three foundational facts concerning Him. Considering that they didn't have any vested interest in Him, we can rest assured that their testimony is certain.

147 Retrieved July 16, 2010, from: http://www.religioustolerance.org/worldrel.htm.

148 Chuck Missler, Mark Eastman, *Alien Encounters*, Koinonia House (1997).

149 Retrieved July 16, 2010, http://thecomingepiphany.com/BookArticles/alien.htm#_ftn4.

150 Barbara Marciniak, *Bringers of the Dawn: Teachings from the Pleiadians,* Bear and Co., 1992.

151 Ibid.

152 Tuella, *Project World Evacuation,* Inner Light Publications, 1993 edition.

153 Ibid.

154 Ibid.

155 Ibid.

156 Ibid.

157 Ibid.

158 Retrieved December 2, 2010, *http://gator.naples.net/~nfn02191/10.28.96ch.htm.*

159 Johanna Michaelson, *Like Lambs to the Slaughter: Your Child and the Occult,* Harvest House, Eugene, OR, 1989.

160 Retrieved December 2, 2010, from http://www.his-forever.com/the_rapture_according_to_new_age.htm.

161 Ibid.

162 Dr. Jacques Vallée, *The Invisible College: What a Group of Scientists Has Discovered About UFO Influences on the Human Race*, pg. 233, Dutton; 1st edition 1975.

163 Dr. Jacques Vallée, *Dimensions: A Casebook of Alien Contact,* Ballantine Books, USA, 1988, pgs. 143-144.

164 Dr. Jacques Vallée, *Confrontations,* Ballantine Books; reprint edition, 1991, pg. 13.

165 Dr. Jacques Vallée citing the extensive research of Bertrand Meheust [Science-Fiction et Soucoupes Volantes (Paris, 1978); Soucoupes Volantes et Folklore (Paris, 1985)], in *Confrontations* pgs. 146, 159-161.

166 Retrieved July 14, 2010, http://www.johnemackinstitute.org/center/bio.asp?id=1.

167 All quotations from Dr. John Mack were retrieved July 14, 2010, from: http://www.pbs.org/wgbh/nova/aliens/johnmack.html (all emphasis mine).

168 Ibid.

169 Retrieved July 14, 2010, http://web.archive.org/web/20080330221339/ aliensandchildren.org/InterviewwithProf.htm.

170 All citations from Dr. David Jacobs were retrieved August 13, 2010, from: http:// web.archive.org/web/20080330221339/aliensandchildren.org/InterviewwithProf. htm (all emphasis mine).

171 Chamish also reports that Arabs have reported encounters with demons. "On October 14, Dr. Harav Ibn Bari, a physician at Hasharon Hospital in Petach Tikveh, was returning from Beersheva by car with his cousin Dudi Muhmad at the wheel". He relates, "After passing the bridge to Tel Aviv at 3:30 AM, I saw a strange figure on the opposite side of the road. We did a U-turn and stopped the car. **The figure came out of the shadows and into the light. He was small and his body colour, light. He lifted his right leg and approached us at terrific speed. He had huge, bulging, round black eyes. They contrasted with the white colour around them**. It was as if he was reading my thoughts and I couldn't take my eyes off his for six seconds. He lifted his right hand and Muhmad pressed on the gas and took off" (emphasis mine). "If one can generalize, Israeli Jewish close encounters since 1993 have mostly been with giant entities and UFO activity has always accompanied the incidents, while Arabs of the region are mostly encountering grotesque monsters, with less direct-UFO activity involved. Both the giants and the monsters are capable of disappearing into thin air."

172 David Ruffino and Joe Jordan, *Unholy Communion: The Alien Abduction Phenomenon, Where It Originates—And How It Stops*, Defender, (2010).

173 Alien Abductions Stopped By the Name of Jesus Christ by Stephen Yulish PhD March 29, 2007, retrieved from: http://www.ufodigest.com/news/0109/abductions-stopped.html.

174 Ibid.

175 Retrieved March 9, 2008 from: http://www.scienceray.com/Biology/Zoology/ Hybrid-Spider-Goats.519813.

176 Story from BBC NEWS: http://news.bbc.co.uk/go/pr/fr/-/2/hi/asia-pacific/4605202. stm Published: 2006/01/12 11:04:37 GMT.

177 National Geographic News, January 25, 2005, Maryann Mott http://news. nationalgeographic.com/news/pf/62295276.html.

178 Retrieved July 2008, http://www.onenewsnow.com/Culture/Default. aspx?id=170410.

179 Ibid.

180 Ibid.

181 Retrieved July 6, 2010, from: http://arstechnica.com/science/news/2009/02/we-are-becoming-a-new-species-we-are-becoming-homo-evolutis.ars.

182 Retrieved July 6, 2010, *The Singularity Is Near: When Humans Transcend Biology,* Ray Kurzweil http://brittgillette.com/WordPress/?p=54.

183 Retrieved May 25, 2010, from: http://en.wikiquote.org/wiki/Richard_Seed.

184 Retrieved July 6, 2010, from: http://www.time.com/time/magazine/article/0,9171,987685-2,00.html#ixzz0swSIYWCh.

185 Richard Seed, *TechnoCalyps - Part II - Preparing for the Singularity,* November 14, 2008.

186 Retrieved July 6, 2010, from: http://www.defendproclaimthefaith.org/DaysNoah.htm.

187 Retrieved July 6, 2010, http://www.dailymail.co.uk/sciencetech/article-1223617/No-men-OR-women-needed-artificial-sperm-eggs-created-time.html.

188 Retrieved July 6, 2010, Genetic Armageddon (Transhuman: As The Days of Noah Were) By John P. McTernan, Ph.D. Retreived from: http://www.defendproclaimthefaith.org/DaysNoah.htm.

189 Ibid.

190 "Could Modern Science Play A Role In The Coming Of Apollo?" By Thomas Horn August 29, 2009. Retrieved from: http://www.newswithviews.com/Horn/thomas121.htm.

191 Retrieved October 25, 2010, from: http://www.lifenews.com/bio2823.html.

192 See also, http://www.singularity-universe.com/technologicalsingularity.

193 Retrieved October 25, 2010, from: http://www.nickbostrom.com/ethics/values.html—special thanks to Tom Horn for his initial research into the subject cf. his August 29, 2009, article: "Could Modern Science Play a Role in the Coming of Apollo?"

194 Retrieved October 25, 2010, from: http://www.nickbostrom.com/ethics/values.html.

195 Retrieved October 25, 2010, from: http://www.aei.org/book/295 c.f. http://www.newswithviews.com/Horn/thomas121.htm. Thanks to Tom Horn for bringing this

to my attention.

196 Constable Daniel 8.

197 Only Daniel chapters 2-7 are in Aramaic, the rest of the book is in Hebrew.

198 The Hebrew text employs the hiphil form (stem, binyan), which is causative, signifying that someone makes him great.

199 Retrieved October 24, 2010, (Horn) http://www.newswithviews.com/Horn/thomas114.htm.

200 I wanted to double check the linguistic association that Horn is making and after searching several lexicons and commentaries and not finding anything definitive, I decided to call to my Greek friend Costas (in Greece) to inquire if *apoleia* can be thought of as identical to *Apollyon/Apollo*. He replied that it is plausibly true though not an absolutely necessary relationship.

201 "The LORD works [*pa'al* פָּעַל] everything for its own ends—even the wicked [*rasha* עָשָׁע] for the day of disaster" (Proverbs 16:4 NET). This verse is commonly interpreted in a Calvinistic sense which is to say that God has predestined even the evil people for destruction (hell). We need to note that the word for "wicked" here is not in the plural (though that does appear in the Bible frequently) but is singular. This could also be translated "wicked one," that is, the Antichrist. The same word is also used in Isaiah 11:4 in reference to whom the Lord will slay with the breath of His lips (just like 2 Thessalonians 2:8)—thus the verse is not speaking of God predestining some to eternal damnation but to how even the Antichrist (the Wicked One, the Lawless One) the Lord will use according to His own ends. The day of disaster is presumably the great tribulation.

202 Liddell-Scott-Jones *Lexicon of Classical Greek* θηρίον.

203 Retrieved October 25, 2010, http://www.pantheon.org/articles/s/satyrs.html.

204 Retrieved October 27, 2010, from: http://www.answers.com/library/Biology+Q%26A-cid-67690.

205 Recombinant DNA. (2008, April 2). *New World Encyclopedia*. Retrieved October 23, 2010, from http://www.newworldencyclopedia.org/entry/Recombinant_DNA?oldid=682672. Berg et al. 2007.

206 Plasmids, small extra-chromosomal circles of bacterial DNA, can be used to carry DNA into bacterial cells. Each plasmid contains about five genes, and doesn't mind carrying around one more. Once the bacteria has a copy of the foreign gene, it treats it as one of its own and replicates it every time it replicates the plasmid (this

is called DNA cloning). Over the course of a day or two, billions of bacteria will be churning out the protein coded by the gene inserted. Restriction Enzymes are produced by bacteria in response to bacteriophage (viral) infection. The enzymes chop the invading DNA up into pieces by recognizing specific DNA sequences (called restriction sites)—usually palindromic. When these enzymes cut DNA, they often leave overhangs on the ends of the DNA called "sticky ends."

207 Horn's research has served as a catalyst for some of the ideas in this book.

208 Retrieved October 25, 2010, from: http://www.newswithviews.com/Horn/thomas123.htm.

209 Retrieved October 25, 2010, from: http://newswithviews.com/Horn/thomas160.htm.

210 David Lewis, *UFO: End-Time Delusion*, p. 46.

211 Retrieved October 28, 2010, http://www.etymonline.com/index.php?search=television&searchmode=none.

212 International Consultation on English Texts translation as printed in: *The Lutheran Book of Worship, The Book of Common Prayer* (Episcopal).

213 The Greek Church Greek text from the *Acts of the First Council of Constantinople* and in *The Acts of the Council of Chalcedon*. Retrieved March 13, 2010, from: http://www.creeds.net/ancient/nicene.htm.

214 Therefore when God the Father declares concerning the Son: "You [are] My Son, Today I have begotten You" (Psalm 2:7), we can understand that God is in the eternal now and hence He is eternally begetting the Son.

215 Augustus Hopkins Strong, *Systematic Theology*, 1893, 243.

216 πλάσσω *Thayer's Greek Lexicon of the New Testament*.

217 According to the Targumim, one called the Memra [word], was in the beginning with God creating with Him. According to the Jerusalem Targum the Word created man. "And the Word [Memra] of the Lord created man in His likeness, in the likeness of the presence of the Lord He created him, the male and his yoke-fellow He created them" (Targum Jerusalem, Genesis 1:27).

218 "For the divine writing itself teaches us that Adam said that he had heard the voice. But what else is this voice but the Word of God, who is also His Son?" (Theophilus, To Autolycus. Book 2, ch 13-30 Ante-Nicene Fathers, Volume 2).

219 "Human life is described here as consisting of a body (made from soil from the

ground) and breath (given by God). Both animals and humans are called 'a living being' (נֶפֶשׁ חַיָּה) but humankind became that in a different and more significant way. The Hebrew term נֶפֶשׁ (nefesh, 'being') is often translated 'soul,' but the word usually refers to the whole person. The phrase נֶפֶשׁ חַיָּה (nefesh khayyah, 'living being') is used of both animals and human beings (see 1:20, 24, 30; 2:19)" (NET Bible Notes Genesis 2:7).

220 See also: "In Him was life, and the life was the light of men" (John 1:4); "For as the Father raises the dead and gives life to them, even so the Son gives life to whom He will" (John 5:21); "For as the Father has life in Himself, so He has granted the Son to have life in Himself" (John 5:26); "And so it is written, 'The first man Adam became a living being.' The last Adam became a life-giving spirit" (1 Corinthians 15:45); "He who has the Son has life; he who does not have the Son of God does not have life" (1 John 5:12).

221 In the Greek text *enephusesen* (ενεφυσησεν) is followed by the dative which is complementary to the word en εν which follows the Hebrew in Genesis 2:7 extremely well.

222 Then the LORD came down in the cloud, and spoke to him, and took of the Spirit that was upon him, and placed the same upon the seventy elders; and it happened, when **the Spirit rested upon them, that they** prophesied, although they never did so again (Numbers 11:25, emphasis mine). But the Spirit of the LORD came **upon** Gideon (Judges 6:34 emphasis mine). Then the Spirit of the LORD **came upon** Jephthah (Judges 11:29 emphasis mine). And the **Spirit of the LORD came mightily upon** him, and he tore the lion apart (Judges 14:6 emphasis mine). Then the **Spirit of the LORD came upon** him mightily, (Judges 14:19 emphasis mine).

Then Samuel took the horn of oil and anointed […] and the **Spirit of the LORD came upon** David (1 Samuel 16:13 emphasis mine). See also: Judges 3:10, 15:14; 2 Chronicles 20:14, 24:20.

223 Baker's *Evangelical Dictionary of Biblical Theology* (1996): Evil.

224 (2) i.q. Arab. length of neck and stature (compare long-necked); […] The Anakim (prop. men with long necks, of high stature), pr. n. of a Canaanite nation, famous on account of their height, […]. Gesenius Hebrew and Chaldee Lexicon (1846).

225 The reader is encouraged to visit douglashamp.com where resources are recommended for further study.

226 Albert Pike, *Morals and Dogma of the Ancient and Accepted Scottish Rite of Freemasonry*, p. 321, 19th Degree of Grand Pontiff. See also: http://www.cuttingedge.org/free11.html.

227 From "Instructions to the 23 Supreme Councils of the World" on July 14, 1889—Albert Pike.

228 Manly P. Hall, *The Lost Keys of Freemasonry*, p. 124.

229 *Masonic Holy Bible, Temple Illustrated Edition*, A. J. Holman Co., 1968, p. 11-14.

230 *The Holy Bible: The Great Light In Masonry*, King James Version, Temple Illustrated Edition, A. J. Holman Company, 1968, Foreword entitled, "The Bible and King Solomon's Temple in Masonry," by John Wesley Kelchner.

231 *Encyclopaedia of Freemasonry*, by Albert Mackey, MD, 33rd and Charles T. McClenachan, 33rd Revised Edition, by Edward L. Hawkins, 30th and William J. Hughan, 32nd, Volume II, M-Z, published by The Masonic History Company, Chicago, New York, London, 1873, A.G. Mackey, 1927, by the Masonic History Company.

232 Ibid. p. 774.

233 Foreword, *The Bible and King Solomon's Temple in Masonry,*" by John Wesley Kelchner, 1968, A. J. Holman Company.

234 Edward Waite, p. 486-7, *"A New Encyclopedia of Freemasonry and of Cognate Instituted Mysteries: The Rites, Literature and History,"* Volume II, reprinted in 1970 by Weathervane Books.

235 Retrieved December 13, 2010, http://www.mfa.gov.il/MFA/Peace+Process/Guide+to+the+Peace+Process/The+Balfour+Declaration.htm.

236 Retrieved December 13, http://www.modernhistoryproject.org/mhp/ArticleDisplay.php?Article=BrotherDark03.

237 Carroll Quigley, *The Anglo-American Establishment*, Books in Focus, 1981, pp. 31-32.

238 Retrieved December 13, 2010, from: http://www.rense.com/general28/brit.htm.

239 A point of clarification is necessary here: while nefarious forces are indeed at work to bring about the one-world government, God is nevertheless on His throne. Satan and his forces are acting in the world for their own selfish desires, and yet God has a plan that He will accomplish— oftentimes through the ill intent of His enemies. Just as He allowed various nations to discipline His people in the past, it would appear that He is now allowing the Masons (and other secret societies) to work toward the fulfillment of their evil plans but all the while God's greater plan is sovereignly over them.

240 David Lewis, *UFO: End-Time Delusion*, p. 46.

241 Retrieved December 13, 2010. http://www.cuttingedge.org/news/n1052.html.

242 Ibid.

243 Ibid.

244 Albert Pike, *Morals and Dogma of the Ancient and Accepted Scottish Rite of Freemasonry*, p. 321, 19th Degree of Grand Pontiff. See also: http://www.cuttingedge.org/free11.html.

245 According to BDB.

246 Retrieved November 8, 2010, from: http://www.michaeljournal.org/nwo1.htm.

247 The above considerations are not exhaustive but serve as a stepping-stone into further research. The reader is greatly encouraged to consult the following resources to gain a deeper understanding of how the Masons and similar groups are indeed planning a Bible-apocalypse-type of takeover of the world: *Apollyon Rising* by Tom Horn; *Secret Mysteries of America's Beginnings*, Volume I, II, III Produced by Antiquities Research Films, Written & Directed by Chris Pinto; *Save Israel* and *Shabathai Tzvi, Labor Zionism and the Holocaust* by Barry Chamish.

248 This is analogous to the rapture in that the "good" are taken out of the land and the "bad" are left to be judged.

249 Retrieved October 4, 2010, from: http://www.wnd.com/index.php?fa=PAGE.printable&pageId=65288. Thanks to my friend Bob Rico for bringing this to my attention.

250 Ibid.

251 Could the earth be a representation of the UN?

252 An interesting circumstantial confirmation of the 1948 date is found concerning the birth of Abraham. According to biblical chronology (reading from the Masoretic text) he was born 1,948 years after creation (anno mundi). While that calculation is based on the year of creation and not the Gregorian calendar, the same number is striking. Furthermore, the date of Abraham receiving the covenant in Genesis 15 was given 2,018 years anno mundi. Given that the birth of Abraham, the father of the nation, and the rebirth of the nation both occurred in the same year (on their respective calendars), is it possible that AD 2,018 (on the Gregorian calendar) will also be significant?

253 My study of the Scriptures was **not** influenced by the *Apocalypse of Peter*—I in fact found it after I had written most of the chapter.

254 Retrieved July 15, 2010, from: http://www.ntcanon.org/Apocalypse_of_Peter.shtml. The authorship of the work is uncertain though some suggest that it was Clement, Peter's disciple, since he is mentioned in the work itself.

255 First published by the Abbe Sylvain Grebaut in Revue de l'Orient Chretien, 1910: a fresh translation from his Ethiopic text by H. Duensing appeared in Zeitschr. f. ntl. Wiss., 1913.

256 Retrieved July 30, 2010, https://www.cia.gov/library/publications/the-world-factbook/geos/xx.html.

257 If we understand from Genesis 15 that Abraham's descendants will be afflicted for four hundred years and that they would come back in the fourth generation, then the maximum life span would appear to be onehundred years—which again demonstrates that generation is the life span of an individual.

258 Retrieved May 3, 2010, from: https://www.cia.gov/library/publications/the-world-factbook/rankorder/2102rank.html.

259 A speech given by Benjamin Netanyahu May 16, 2010, at Ammunition Hill in honor of Jerusalem Day confirms that he is of the generation that saw the rebirth of Jerusalem. Netanyahu was born in 1949, which makes him just one year younger than the nation itself. "We are the generation which was lucky enough to see our holy sites liberated and returned to our hands, and it is upon us to transfer this right to our children." Retrieved May 20, 2010, from: http://www.jpost.com/Israel/Article.aspx?id=175392.

260 Thanks to my friend Dr. Beshore for his valuable insights into these dates via personal communication.

261 These dates seem to be confirmed extra-biblically by virtue of several discoveries: a massive Coronal Mass Ejection from the sun is expected between 2012-2014; there will be a series of four total lunar eclipses (tetrad) between 2014-2015, all of which fall on biblical feast days (as discovered by Mark Biltz) which potentially spells trouble for Israel; the all-seeing eye on the back of the dollar bill (as discovered by Tom Horn) point to the coming of the Antichrist between 2012 and 2016; both the Mayan and Aztec calendars have ending dates of 2012.

Personal Notes

Made in the USA
Columbia, SC
04 April 2021